The resurrection and Ascen: arguably the most important events in human history. After His death on the cross, the resurrected Son of God spent weeks on earth revealing His glory to His followers! This wonder deserves to be studied, pondered, and marveled at. Yet most Western Christians, perhaps because of the hurried pace of our lives, have condensed these pivotal moments in the ministry of Jesus into a blip on the screen. I am so grateful for my friend Mark Pearson for helping to fill in the blanks. *Fifty Days of Glory* should be studied by all Christians—especially by those who want to walk in the true resurrection power of Christ.

—J. Lee Grady, author of
The Holy Spirit Is Not for Sale
and *Fearless Daughters of the Bible*

Mark Pearson's new book is a spot-on analysis of a historical event that has perplexed mankind for two thousand years: the resurrection of Jesus Christ. Mark does an amazing job at interweaving scripture with contemporary life, while making practical application to challenging and at times obscure biblical passages. With a breadth of historical knowledge wed to solid scholarship, Mark creates a mosaic of Jesus' life reaching down through the centuries and capturing the hearts of his readers with encouragement for their journey in Christ. A wonderful study. I highly recommend it!

—Pastor Scott Kelso, author of
Let's See What Sticks and Chairman of the
Charismatic Leaders Fellowship

If you rate the quality of a study book by the quality of the questions asked, then this book comes out on top. The thought-provoking questions at the end of each chapter really do open the way for honest sharing and in-depth discussion.

—Dr. Paul Worthley, senior physician, Burrswood Hospital and Christian Healing Center, Groombridge, Tunbridge Wells, Kent, England

This is a very interesting and readable work, suitable for both clergy and laity. Not only does Canon Pearson examine the historical events of the fifty days of Easter, he addresses issues raised by these events. Thus does the reader consider what the post-Resurrection appearances of Jesus mean for him personally in his own Christian life.

—The Most Reverend David R. Simpson, Bishop of Florida, the Charismatic Episcopal Church

In *Fifty Days of Glory*, Mark Pearson offers not only a valuable resource for both churches and individual readers but a powerful revelation about our Lord. On the cross He said, "It is finished," and His resurrection is the climax of history, but through this book we learn that Jesus still had *much* to teach His followers in the fifty days following Easter. Pearson reminds us of how Jesus demonstrates His love for us—using those precious last days on Earth to heal broken hearts and

bring transformation to the fledgling church to prepare it for the days, years, and centuries to come!

—FAITH J. H. MCDONNELL, DIRECTOR, RELIGIOUS
LIBERTY PROGRAM AND CHURCH ALLIANCE FOR A NEW
SUDAN, THE INSTITUTE ON RELIGION AND DEMOCRACY,
WASHINGTON, DC

In *Fifty Days of Glory*, readers will find both pastoral
wisdom and helpful historical and literary contexts
to aid them in understanding this crucial part of the
gospel narrative. Canon Pearson gives judicious commentary on these passages, applying helpful cultural
and social dimensions and incorporating intriguing
insights from a variety of traditional and contemporary sources.

—DR. EDITH M. HUMPHREY, WILLIAM F. ORR PROFESSOR
OF NEW TESTAMENT, PITTSBURGH THEOLOGICAL
SEMINARY

Canon Pearson invites us to encounter Jesus as Lord,
now risen and ascended. A fine sequel for the Christian who invests a lot in Lent and Holy Week but feels
a void after Easter Day.

—THE RT. REV. DANIEL W. HERZOG, THE EIGHTH BISHOP
OF ALBANY, THE EPISCOPAL CHURCH, RETIRED

This is wonderful material! It not only presents a thorough apologetic for the truth of the Resurrection and
its importance to us as believers but at the same time

leads us to know Jesus better. Read properly, it can lead the reader to a deeper intimacy with our Lord.

—Loren Sandford, pastor of New Song Church and Ministries, Denver, Colorado; internationally known conference speaker; and author of *Purifying the Prophetic*, *Understanding Prophetic People*, *The Prophetic Church*, *Renewal for the Wounded Warrior* and most recently, *Visions of the Coming Days*

Canon Mark Pearson has created an intelligent, moving, and well-researched examination of a neglected time period in our Lord's life. As a physician lay leader in the healing ministry for many years, I discovered in reading these chapters many rich implications and insights for our own lives. Walk with Christ today.

—John A. Harler, MD, CCHP, medical director, Henrico Sheriff's Office, Virginia

For several years I have known and worked with Mark Pearson, a gifted communicator, teacher, minister of whole-person healing. I am pleased to endorse this insightful book, predicting a positive impact and blessing for all readers.

—Dr. James K. Wagner, United Methodist minister, pastor, author, former director of The Upper Room Prayer and Healing Ministries, Nashville, Tennessee

In *Fifty Days of Glory* Canon Mark Pearson draws upon his extensive experience as a pastor, preacher, conference leader, and a leader in Charismatic Renewal to offer a wide-ranging and engaging discussion of the Scriptural accounts of what took place between Jesus' resurrection and the Day of Pentecost. Drawing upon a variety of resources both ancient and modern, and providing a mixture of homiletical and scholarly details, reflections, and insights, Canon Mark traces out some of the possible implications found in the encounters with the risen Christ recorded in the four gospels. As he tours these accounts he makes both intellectual and spiritual connections that at times offer comfort and at other times challenge. May the Spirit use these reflections in many lives!

—THE REV. DR. RODNEY A. WHITACRE, PROFESSOR OF
BIBLICAL STUDIES, TRINITY SCHOOL FOR MINISTRY,
AMBRIDGE, PENNSYLVANIA

Quintessential Pearson. Scholarly, in depth and relatively uncharted water. As one who has labored twenty-two years for the church "streams" to come together, I highly recommend this book. Canon Mark dredges new channels with the post-Resurrection appearances of Christ to allow the revelation of Scripture to heal church perceptions and help us see the value in our diversity.

—KEN BOSSE, SENIOR PASTOR, NEW LIFE ASSEMBLY
OF GOD CHURCH, RAYMOND, NEW HAMPSHIRE, AND
PRESIDENT OF COACH FORWARD

Jesus rose! But just saying it doesn't mean that we've risen ourselves to live in the full impact of resurrection life. Mark Pearson changes that, as he brings to life the significance of our Lord's resurrection through a fascinating exploration of the gospel's stories about Easter and the days following.

—REV. KEITH HILL, PASTOR, ST. GILES PRESBYTERIAN CHURCH, RICHMOND, VIRGINIA

Mark Pearson has done us all a great service by opening up the Resurrection appearances' stories for us in such a profound and helpful way. His meticulous scholarly research unearths meanings in these biblical passages we have never considered before. Through his application of these stories to our lives and current contexts we are confronted as never before with their ongoing relevance for us. Read this book and encounter the risen Christ anew and afresh.

—DR. STEPHEN A. SEAMANDS, PROFESSOR OF CHRISTIAN DOCTRINE, ASBURY THEOLOGICAL SEMINARY, WILMORE, KENTUCKY

This is a long overdue book. We need to be reminded that Jesus is out of the box, not confined to heaven but moving amongst us to change our world and us with it.

—REV. DR. RUSS PARKER, DIRECTOR OF THE ACORN CHRISTIAN HEALING FOUNDATION, UK, AND PREACHER-AT-LARGE FOR THE DIOCESE OF GUILDFORD, UK

I so enjoyed reading the manuscript. Canon Mark is a gifted writer with the ability to give thought-provoking information and inspiration. He is able to expound on scripture verses in a new and refreshing way that has caused my heart to worship the risen Lord! His writing reminds us of the frailty of humanity while revealing the compassion of Christ for us all. I highly recommend this book to readers who are hungry to fall in love with Jesus again and experience a fresh touch of God that will ignite a greater passion to know and love Him more and to share His love with others.

—MARLENE J. YEO, FOUNDER AND DIRECTOR OF SOMEBODY CARES NEW ENGLAND; FOUNDER AND LEAD PASTOR OF COMMUNITY CHRISTIAN FELLOWSHIP, HAVERHILL, MASSACHUSETTS; AND AUTHOR OF *WHERE IS GOD ON TUESDAY?*

Mark Pearson is a well-established and highly respected author, speaker, and pastor. Everything he writes flows from prayer, a careful study of Scripture, and years of ministry experience.

Fifty Days of Glory is one of the most refreshing and insightful books I have read on the time from the Resurrection to Pentecost. This work is at once biblical, accessible and rich in insights, with many golden nuggets for sermons and Bible teaching. Anyone who wants to know the Lord Jesus Christ more intimately will be blessed by reading this refreshing book.

—DR. LYLE W. DORSETT, BILLY GRAHAM PROFESSOR OF EVANGELISM, BEESON DIVINITY SCHOOL, SAMFORD UNIVERSITY, BIRMINGHAM, ALABAMA

How is it that some authors can take portions of the Bible and find something that we had never quite seen before, though we know those passages well? Canon Pearson has that gift. Each of the post-Resurrection appearances of Jesus has something to teach the church about her character and mission after His Ascension—and on into the present day. I sensed my anticipation build the deeper I read into the narrative. I am better for it. You can read this book in a matter of hours, but the impact could well remain with you throughout your continuing walk with God.

—Dr. Robert G. Tuttle Jr.,
Professor emeritus of World Christianity,
Asbury Theological Seminary, and cofounder of
United Methodist Renewal Services Fellowship,
now Aldersgate Renewal Ministries

Canon Mark Pearson's books have always proved extremely helpful to clergy and laity alike. They are always of excellent scholarship. His writings are read all over the world. I am convinced that his new work will be of the same caliber and I intend on purchasing a copy for all my clergy.

—The Most Rev. Craig W. Bates, Patriarch,
International Communion of the Charismatic
Episcopal Church

Mark Pearson writes with a wealth of knowledge enhanced by a rich personal experience both of the Lord and in ministry to others. He takes that and communicates it with both depth of thought and clarity of expression.

—HARRY C. GRIFFITH,
FOUNDER, BIBLE READING FELLOWSHIP, US

Mark Pearson's *Fifty Days of Glory* is a welcome addition to the devotional literature on the period from Easter to Pentecost. It will be very helpful to laymen as well as clergy for both preaching and daily inspirational reading. I plan to use it every year from now on.

—VINSON SYNAN, DEAN EMERITUS, REGENT UNIVERSITY
SCHOOL OF DIVINITY, VIRGINIA BEACH, VIRGINIA

FIFTY
DAYS *of*
GLORY

FROM EASTER MORNING TO THE **EVE OF PENTECOST**

FIFTY DAYS of GLORY

FROM **EASTER MORNING** TO THE **EVE OF PENTECOST**

MARK PEARSON

CREATION
HOUSE

FIFTY DAYS OF GLORY by Mark Pearson
Published by Creation House
A Charisma Media Company
600 Rinehart Road
Lake Mary, Florida 32746
www.charismamedia.com

Design Director: Bill Johnson
Cover design by Terry Clifton
Author photo by Cathy Bates

Visit the author's website: www.newcreationhc.org.

Library of Congress Cataloging-in-Publication Data: 5710901

International Standard Book Number: 978-1-62136-710-9
E-book International Standard Book Number: 978-1-62136-711-6

While the author has made every effort to provide accurate telephone
numbers and Internet addresses at the time of publication, neither
the publisher nor the author assumes any responsibility for errors or
for changes that occur after publication.

First edition

14 15 16 17 — 9 8 7 6 5 4 3 2 1
Printed in Canada

DEDICATION

We should expect that in the life of a person who has
lived six and a half decades and has served in ordained
ministry for forty of those, many people to have been of
good influence. As I look back over my shoulder there
have been five people for whom I especially wish to thank
God for my spiritual and ministerial development.

Grace Marion Jewett (1891–1983). Miss Jewett was both the
principal of my elementary school and a Sunday school
teacher at the church I attended the first sixteen years
of my life, Pilgrim Congregational Church, Leominster,
Massachusetts. She modeled for me a warm and personal
love of Jesus as Lord and Savior. When she asked me, at
about age twelve, what I wanted to do with my life, I told her
I was called to ordained ministry. Her response was, "I was
hoping you'd say that." It was the encouragement I needed.

The Rev. James C. Logan (1932–2009). While pursuing his doctorate from Boston University, United Methodist pastor Jim was director of Christian education at Pilgrim Church. I was called into the ministry at a young age and needed positive clergy role models. He demonstrated to me that a person could be a minister, a scholar, and a fun guy. Dr. Logan was later professor of systematic theology (1966–1990) and the first E. Stanley Jones professor of evangelism (1990–2001) at Wesley Theological Seminary, Washington, DC.

Donald G. Wilcox (1910–1968). Mr. Wilcox was organist-choirmaster of Christ Church, Fitchburg, Massachusetts (1945–1967). He was my first organ teacher and led the men and boys choir in which numerous male relatives and I had sung for four generations going back to the nineteenth century. His quiet faith was often gently expressed as he taught classical church music, reinforcing for me the essential link between deep faith and rich culture.

The Rt. Rev. Alexander D. Stewart (1926–1999). Alex Stewart was the bishop of the Episcopal Diocese of Western Massachusetts (1970–1984) who ordained me a deacon on September 15, 1974. He always encouraged me, a very young and immature seminarian and clergyman, sometimes in his gruff Scottish way, but always lovingly, as I sought to be and do better for the Lord.

The Rev. Ross Whetstone (1919–2012). Ross was a United Methodist pastor and one of the early pioneers in the Charismatic Renewal in the mainline church. He was cofounder and first executive director of the United Methodist Renewal Services Fellowship, now called Aldersgate Renewal Ministries. As I accompanied him and other United Methodist Renewal leaders in teaching at regional conferences around the United States, I was lovingly, patiently mentored by Ross both in personal discipleship and in ministering.

CONTENTS

⚜Acknowledgments⚜

THIS BOOK CAME about in response to frustration—mine and that of others—in trying to find good materials to aid the preparation of sermons on the events of those fifty days between Easter morning and the eve of Pentecost. There was and is ample material on Christ's resurrection and on the events of Pentecost. There was not and is not that much helpful material on the intervening seven weeks, despite this period being the focus of several chapters of the New Testament. Over the years I have asked numerous preachers what they used to help them prepare their sermons, and their answers were usually variations of the statement, "I really haven't found that much."

The events of the seven weeks are touched on in commentaries, but only briefly. There are a few rather technical tomes on the Ascension. But as for help to guide the preacher or Bible teacher in explaining the events of these fifty days and in applying their lessons to the listeners' personal spirituality and ministry service, there was and is just not that much. As I continued to ask others about what resources they used, I was increasingly encouraged to write something helpful myself.

Numerous people have assisted this project as it has developed over the past several years. Thank you especially to the congregation of Trinity Church, Kingston, New Hampshire, whom I have been privileged to serve since 1994. Year after year you heard this material as it took shape and responded with many practical suggestions. Thank you to the clergy of the Diocese of Canterbury, England, as I presented this material during a continuing education day, and to the clergy of the Diocese of Fort Worth, Texas, as I presented it at a clergy conference. I much appreciate your many helpful suggestions. Thank you to preachers, lay and ordained, of many denominations, onto whom I bounced sections of this book to make sure it was relevant to your needs. Thank you to numerous theologians and Greek scholars for answering technical questions. Thank you to my non-technical readers who made sure that, without my dumbing down the content, I would communicate clearly to a wide audience. Thank you to Harry Camp, a Christian attorney from Tennessee, a leading figure in Aldersgate Renewal Ministries, a ministry working for Holy Spirit Renewal in the United Methodist Church. Harry wrote the study questions which appear at the end of many of the book's chapters.

Finally, thank you to ever so many people who upheld this project in prayer over the years.

There were numerous people who made helpful additions to this book. Rather than cite them here I will mention them when their contributions appear in the text.

☙INTRODUCTION❧

I F THE STORY had ended with the Crucifixion, it would be a biography of a great man who taught many truths but who ultimately failed in his mission and was proven wrong on one of his main assertions.

America's third president, Thomas Jefferson, wrote such a biography, which he titled *The Life and Morals of Jesus of Nazareth*. Jefferson took various verses from the four Gospels and arranged them in what he believed was the correct chronological order, omitting anything supernatural—in particular, the virginal conception of Jesus, His divinity, and His bodily resurrection. Jefferson's Bible ends this way: "Now in the place where He was crucified there was a garden; and in the garden a new sepulchre, wherein was never man yet laid. There laid they Jesus: and rolled a great stone to the door of the sepulchre, and departed."[1] For Jefferson, Jesus was a good moral teacher, nothing more.

Had this been true, as Merrill C. Tenney observes, "…the main narrative would have been closed with a sense of frustration. His claims would have been negated, his aspirations would have been unrealized, and his teachings would have seemed too lofty to be true."[2] Bonnell Spencer adds, "Had this been the end of the story, it would have indicated that God's final effort to save man had failed. God Himself could not overcome such impenitence and hardness of heart. Man had had and had lost his last chance. The Christian message would have been one of despair. For the past century, some scholars have asserted, in one form or another, that it was not Jesus who was changed but the disciples. Jesus did not rise, but, somehow, the apostles so came to revere their dead friend that they made up fanciful stories about Him.[3] Bruce Birdsey speaks about the "banal reductionism of [some] contemporary investigators. Their account seems so flat, so uninspiring. Who could get very interested in the private epiphanies of a dead man's friends?"[4] Who would die for a story they knew they had made up? Yet, except for John (and, of course, Judas), each of the apostles died a martyr's death for what he knew to be fact.

In response to such facile criticism of Jesus' bodily resurrection, John Updike wrote:

> Make no mistake: if He rose at all
> it was as His body...
> Let us not mock God with metaphor,
> analogy, sidestepping, transcendence;
> making of the event a parable, a sign painted in the
> faded credulity of earlier ages:
> let us walk through the door.[5]

Ask a number of orthodox Christians why they believe Jesus Christ rose from the dead and a good percentage of them will respond, "Because an empty tomb was found." While this is true—an empty tomb was found—that by itself is not sufficient. All an empty tomb proves, even if it is the tomb in which the body of the crucified Christ had been placed, is that no one is there. It does not prove the body of Christ was raised from the dead. It is the various appearances of the risen Christ during the forty-day Easter season that proves the Resurrection. The crucified Christ, as Luke begins his second book, "presented himself alive to them after suffering by many proofs" (Acts 1:3).

In the Old Testament Elijah had raised the son of the widow of Zarephath (1 Kings 17:8–24) and Elisha had raised the son of the Shunammite woman (2 Kings 4:18–37). Jesus had raised Lazarus (John 11:1–44), the son of the widow in Nain (Luke 7:11–17), and maybe Jairus's daughter (depending on whether we are to take literally Jesus' statement, "she is not dead but sleeping" [Luke 8:40–42, 49–56]), but that was about it. And, in every case, these were resuscitations to the state they had been in previously, not resurrections to something different.

But the Gospels assert that something quite different had happened: Jesus had risen from the dead, literally and bodily, and with that event everything changes. Notes Robert Tuttle, Jesus rose with a "glorified body. This counters those who think we are speaking merely of a resuscitation."[6] Christ's resurrection means death—physical death—has been conquered.

It is why the poet and Church of England priest John Donne (1572–1631) could write:

> Death be not proud, though some have called thee
> Mighty and dreadfull, for, thou art not so...[7]

N. T. Wright notes, "The resurrection isn't just a surprise happy ending for one person; it is instead the turning point for everything else. It is the point at which all the old promises come true at last: the promises of David's unshakable kingdom; the promises of Israel's return from the greatest exile of them all; and behind that again, quite explicit in Matthew, Luke, and John, the promise that all nations will now be blessed through the seed of Abraham."[8] In raising Christ's physical body from the grave, God the Father again give His approval to physical creation and with it our concern for both this world and the next.

Many Christians, particularly those in non-liturgical churches, will, of course, acknowledge that there was a forty day post-Resurrection period before Jesus ascended back to the Father. After all, the Bible does mention it (Acts 1:3), and portions of the Gospels (particularly Luke 24 and John 20 and 21) unfold some of the events that took place during it.

But the corporate worship life of their churches generally does not reference the events of this crucial period. In non-liturgical churches Easter means Easter morning. There are no "Sundays of Easter" with appointed collects (prayers thematic to particular Sundays) or assigned Scripture readings about Jesus' post-Resurrection appearances. There is no special Paschal (Easter) candle burning as a visual and symbolic reminder. Ascension Thursday is never observed. And when did the church members last hear anything in depth about the ten-day period when the disciples were waiting in Jerusalem for the coming of the Spirit? After the last Easter morning service is over, clergy and lay leaders in non-liturgical churches start thinking about and planning for the next big events in their church calendar, usually Mother's Day and Children's Sunday.

Contemporary Christian music does not help. Rick Founds's otherwise masterful hymn "Lord, I Lift Your Name on High" leaves out the forty-day Easter period altogether! He traces Jesus' journey from heaven to earth, to the cross, to the grave and then to the sky. But it was *not* from the grave to the sky. It was from the grave *to the earth* for forty days, "present[ing] himself alive after his passion by many proofs" (Acts 1:3, RSV) and then to the sky.

By contrast, hymnody in the more historic, liturgical denominations better references the events of the forgotten fifty-day period of Easter morning to the eve of Pentecost. "O Filii et Filiae" ("O Songs and Daughters, Let Us Sing!"), a fifteenth-century French carol translated into English in the nineteenth century by John Mason Neale, references both the apostles meeting in fear that first Easter night and Thomas' doubt and subsequent faith. The recent hymn "Come, Risen Lord, and Deign to Be Our Guest" by George W. Briggs speaks of the experience of the Emmaus travelers, ending with a request that God will be known to us "in the breaking of the bread."[10]

Having said that, though, far too few of the members of congregations in those historic, liturgical denominations think much about the importance of these special Sundays in the Easter season, understand and appreciate the meaning of that Pascal candle, or attend church on Ascension Thursday.

We need to focus, individually and corporately, as Christians and as church congregations, on the forty-day Easter season with the various accounts of Jesus' appearances, on Jesus' Ascension, and on the ten days leading up to Pentecost. These events are in the Bible for good reasons, even if we don't yet know what the reasons are.

But if the *fact* of Jesus' post-Resurrection appearances is important in its proving His resurrection, the *manner* in which Jesus appeared is also important. When the resurrected Christ appeared to His followers He was not immediately recognized for who He was. While it is true He was now in His resurrection body, and while it is true that they were not expecting Him to appear—despite His constant teaching that He would be raised from the dead—the reason they did not recognize Him was because God the Father prevented them from initially recognizing Him. Why? So the *manner* in which He was revealed would be understood to be important.

The various ways Christ was revealed illustrate important focal points for the life of the church, both at the church's beginning and for today. The Lord was simply a gardener to Mary Magdalene until He called her by name (John 20:16). Our individual and corporate Christian life has many aspects to it, and one of those is a personal relationship with Jesus. This is an emphasis in evangelical Protestant churches, and rightly so.

The Lord was simply a fascinating stranger to the two who

walked the road to Emmaus until He broke bread (an early church term for Holy Communion; Luke 24:30–35). Our individual and corporate Christian life has many aspects to it, and one of those is a regular and fervent participation in this sacrament. This is an emphasis in sacramental, liturgical churches, and rightly so.

The Lord was simply some guy on a beach until He correctly told them where fish were to be found (John 21:4–8). Since it is doubtful that anyone at daybreak, a hundred yards away, could see fish in (not on top of) the water in a way those directly on the scene could not, we must assume something supernatural was at work. Our individual and corporate Christian life has many aspects to it, and one of those is a participation in the supernatural workings of the Holy Spirit. This is an emphasis in charismatic and Pentecostal churches, and rightly so.

One thesis of this book is that God wants His church to participate in *all* of these ways of "doing church"—the evangelical, the sacramental/liturgical, and the charismatic/Pentecostal. Many church historians note that this is what the church was like in her early centuries. People with way too narrow a denominational focus attempt to assert that the primitive church was like just one of these ways (the one they're a part of), but such an assertion leads to both impoverishment and imbalance. One of the movements of God over the last half century is what some have called the Convergence Movement—the bringing back together of various aspects of the Christian faith that never should have been separated from each other. Right here in this forty-day period we find the evangelical, the sacramental/liturgical, and the charismatic/Pentecostal aspects of the faith.

Then, after the forty days were complete, Jesus ascended back to the Father. If the forty-day Easter season is neglected in many churches, the celebration of the Ascension is even more neglected. When was the last time you heard a sermon on Jesus' Ascension? How many churches have a service on Ascension Thursday (the fortieth day after Easter)? And even in those churches that have such a celebration, how widely is it attended? Yet the Ascension of Jesus is vital for our Christian discipleship. In this book we will look at this most important event in the life of Jesus and note its importance to our walk with and our work for Christ today.

And even more neglected yet is the ten-day period when the leading disciples waited in Jerusalem. Most keen Christians want to get on with the work God has given us, and, no doubt, these keen Christians, excited by their unexpected and precious fellowship with the risen Christ, also wanted to get busy making "disciples of all nations" (Matt. 28:19). But they were told to wait for the outpouring of the Holy Spirit (Acts 1:4–5). This was, however, no idle hanging out. There were several things that needed to happen during this week and a half so that when the Spirit fell they would be ready for ministry and ready to do it right.

These things are the very things that need to happen to us individually and corporately if our Spirit-empowered zeal for the Lord will bring Him glory and not shame. In this book we will examine these things as well.

May the risen, ascended, and future-returning Christ richly bless you as you walk with me through these fifty days of glory, from Easter morning to the eve of Pentecost.

CHAPTER 1

JESUS CALLED TO HER BY NAME

Matthew 28:1–10; Mark 16:1–10;
Luke 24:1–11; and John 20:1–18

JESUS HAD PREDICTED He would rise from the dead. Each of the four Gospels records some women going to the tomb on Sunday, the first Easter morning. It's one of the relatively few stories recorded in each of the four Gospels (Matt. 28:1–10; Mark 16:1–10; Luke 24:1–11; and John 20:1–18).

First, note the commonalities in these stories. In all four Gospels the time was around dawn on the first day of the week. Mary Magdalene was present and discovered the stone had been removed. There was an appearance of one or more angels who spoke. And, most importantly, the corpse of Jesus was not there.

Second, we notice particular details noted by one or more, but not all, of the evangelists. Matthew tells us it was an earthquake that had removed the stone. Mark tells us Salome was present, and Luke adds Joanna. None of the evangelists gives a complete account.

As we read the accounts, however, we notice that there are some seeming discrepancies in the details from one Gospel to

1

the next. For example, John tells us that Mary Magdalene saw the stone had been taken away. She ran and told Peter and John, who then went to the tomb and "believed" (John 20:1–9). Luke, by contrast, has her entering the tomb and then being told to go tell the eleven, who dismissed her account as "an idle tale" (Luke 24:1–11).

What conclusion can we draw from these apparent contradictions? Over the centuries some have concluded this is sufficient reason to dismiss belief in the resurrection, the accuracy of Scripture, and, indeed, in the whole Christian message. I believe, on the contrary, such seeming discrepancies prove rather than disprove the truth of the major assertion of these passages, that Jesus is bodily raised from the dead.

These four Gospel narratives are raw accounts, told and retold from the very first, then written down quite soon after the event and finally enfolded into the four evangelists' written telling of the Christ story. It is like a news story covered by several reporters. They all observe the same event but each notes particular details. Each brings out different aspects of the story deemed to be of importance to the reporter's particular audience. N. T. Wright asserts, "Surface discrepancies do not mean that nothing happened. Indeed, they are a reasonable indication that something remarkable happened, so remarkable that the first witnesses were bewildered into telling different stories about it."[1] Several lawyers have told me that there is always variation in the stories of the witnesses who have seen an event happen. If the witnesses are identical, then you expect collusion.

There was no committee that met to harmonize the details of Jesus' first appearance and agree on a story that would become the official version. There was no conspiracy of church leaders. What we have are raw, first person observations.[2]

Frederick Buechner notes the simplicity of the story:

> It is really not much of a story when you come down to
> it, and that of course is the power of it. It doesn't have
> the ring of great drama. It has the ring of truth. If the
> Gospel writers had wanted to tell it in a way to convince
> the world that Jesus indeed rose from the dead, they pre-
> sumably would have done it with all the skill and fan-
> fare they could muster. Here there is no skill, no fanfare.
> They seem to be telling it the way it was. The narrative
> is as fragmented, shadowy and incomplete as life itself.[3]

Another reason why we can trust the biblical record is how
realistically it portrays the heroes of our faith. Mary Magdalene,
and later Peter and John, are featured in this account. None of
them grasped the significance of the empty tomb, despite Jesus'
frequent teaching that He would rise from the dead. (See, for
example, Luke 18:33.) Scripture is believable, among many reasons, because it does not gloss over the imperfections—even blatant sins—of its principal characters.

One further reason why we can trust the account of this initial resurrection appearance of Jesus is that the story centers on
women. First-century Jewish women were not given credibility in
a court of law. It is significant, then, that the four Gospel writers
report that *women* were the first to discover the empty tomb.
Why, "even though it hurts their case in the view of their audience?" asks Lee Strobel. His answer is, "I believe it's because they
[the Gospel writers] were trying to accurately record what actually took place."[4] Zambian Baptist scholar Joe M. Kapolyo agrees:

> Matthew would not have made up this detail, because
> men would not have accepted it. The story is told this
> way because it is the historical truth.[5]

Had the resurrection of Jesus been invented by Jesus' inner
circle, we would have expected a concocted story more acceptable to their audience. Jo Kadlecek asks, "Why put the most

3

important message…in the hands of very minor characters?" She answers her own question, "Because it was *not* fiction."[6]

In addition to this post-Resurrection appearance being to women, our Lord's subsequent appearance on the road to Emmaus was to two relatively minor characters, one of whom is not even named. Paul later observed that in the Corinthian church there were not many who were wise according to worldly standards, nor were there many who were powerful, nor were there many who were of noble birth (1 Cor. 1:26).

There is no attempt to explain the details of how the Resurrection happened any more than Genesis attempts to explain the physics of the Creation. Instead, in both cases, we're simply given the results. We might ask, Had we been given the scientific details, could we possibly understand them?

Jesus had been crucified just a few hours before the Sabbath began on Friday night. The proper preparation of His body would now have to wait until the Sabbath was over. Jews reckoned days from sundown to sundown, so the Sabbath would be over once the sun had set on Saturday night. It was before dawn early Sunday morning when some women came to the tomb. They did not come expecting the tomb to be empty. They came to place the spices, something Joseph of Arimathea had previously not had time to do. To their horror, the stone was rolled away and the body was gone! Joseph Fitzmyer notes that tombs in the area have been found from the first century AD fitted with huge circular stone discs set in traverse channels hollowed out of stone, along which the discs would be rolled. These stones were not boulders.[7]

David Kletzing reported that he asked his congregation one Easter morning, "Why do you think the angel rolled the stone away from the tomb entrance?" He anticipated at least one person would say, "To let Jesus out." The correct answer, he notes, is, "To let people in."[8] The problem is not with Jesus coming to us. He makes every effort to do so. The problem is, will we let Him truly come to us? Several preachers of various denominations have told me their challenge to their people was to remove the rocks from the tombs of your lives. That is to say, take away those things which keep people trapped from truly knowing Jesus as the risen Lord and Savior of their lives.

The women's immediate assumption would have been that grave robbers had broken in. Such a crime happened all too often. But what items of value had been placed in the tomb of Jesus? Lutheran pastor Paul M. Youngdahl notes that before British General Allenby captured Jerusalem at the end of World War I the Turks looted Jerusalem of its treasures. But they could not take Christ's tomb. He writes:

> The treasures of that tomb were not the gold and silver and precious stones with which it had been adorned. The real treasure neither the Turks nor anyone else could steal. The real treasure is the empty tomb. The real treasure is that Jesus Christ has triumphed and that He has risen from the dead.[9]

The Jewish leaders had not feared grave robbers looking for treasure but Christian disciples who would steal the body so they could later say Christ had risen. For this reason they asked for Roman guards to be placed to guard Christ's tomb (Matt. 27:62–66; 28:4, 11–15). Joe Kapolyo points out how difficult it should be to believe "that a unit of professional guards would possibly sleep through a grave robbery, and not hear a sound."[10]

Who went to the tomb? John said it was Mary Magdalene. Mark adds two women, Mary the mother of James and Salome, and Luke adds Joanna and the other women. Though Peter and John saw the empty tomb (John 20:1–10), Jesus appeared first to Mary Magdalene (John 20:11–18).

But why were the women so honored? Why was Mary Magdalene the first one to witness the resurrection? She, with other women, accompanied Jesus on a preaching tour and helped support Him out of their resources. Also, it was the women who refused to be driven away and who refused to abandon Him at the Cross while all the apostles except John, had fled (Matt. 27:55–56; John 20:10–11). And, in addition, notes Jo Kadlecek, "During his post-death time on earth, he was merely doing what he'd always done: pursuing those he loved."[11] "Those he loved" included the rich and the poor, the famous and the obscure, those He had called to be apostles and those not in leadership—in short, what the *Book of Common Prayer* calls "all sorts and conditions of men" and women.[12]

Mary Magdalene came to the tomb while it was dark (John 20:1). Rebecca Hall reminded me that we usually think of Easter and its joy as being during daylight, with warm spring weather, with flowers and colors. But Mary's first Easter was dark. We might add, Hall suggests, that this is symbolic of Mary's own darkness.[13] Just as Jesus came to Mary where she was emotionally and spiritually, Jesus comes to us where we are. He does not ask us to become more morally pure or more spiritually committed before He reaches out to us. In fact, without His reaching out to us we can never become those things.

What sins had she committed prior to her coming to Christ? Luke 8:2 simply states that "from [her] seven demons had gone out." It is but an assumption that she was the same person as the repentant prostitute of Luke 7:37. While this identification was made later in church history—and it may well be true—it is not a biblical teaching. There is no automatic connection between one's sin and one's being demon possessed. Whatever specific sins she had committed, Mary Magdalene, like us all, came to Christ with a background.

John tells us Mary Magdalene was "weeping outside the tomb" (John 20:11). The word for "weeping" is the same one used for the mourners at Lazarus' funeral (John 11:31, 33) and at the seeming death of Jairus's daughter (Luke 8:52). It is a loud and uncontrollable wailing, and Mary was doing so because Jesus had died and because someone had stolen His body.

"Where is He?" she wondered. We sometimes wonder when tragedy strikes, Where is God? Elie Wiesel, incarcerated in a Nazi concentration camp, tells of watching a boy his own age (ten) being hanged. As he died some people asked aloud, "Where is God?" In his book *Night,* Wiesel records a fellow prisoner as saying, "God is there, hanging on the gallows."[14] Indeed, sometimes God blesses us by taking the problem away, sometimes by turning a loss into a gain, other times by giving us grace to persevere in tough times, and sometimes by taking a believer home to Him, even at a relatively young age.

Mary feels that she is alone, "like other sorrowful disciples since."[15] Yet, "she actually has angels in front of her and the Lord behind her."[16] God and His angels are with us, no matter what we may perceive. It is like the story preachers often tell of the street person thinking himself impoverished. All the while, lawyers were seeking him, the man who had just inherited millions.

We might wonder about the depth of Mary's faith because she was weeping. Had she not believed Jesus when He said He would rise from the dead? Yet, the other disciples had not believed either.

We tend to patronize the ancients, thinking they are gullible. Because we so conclude, we then dismiss what they say when they speak about miracles. At the same time we are hard on them because they do not believe. The fact is, faith and doubt, and extremes of credulity and skepticism, exist throughout history. N. T. Wright notes, "[It] isn't a matter of ancient people being credulous and modern people being skeptical. There is a great deal of credulity in our present world, and there was a great deal of skepticism in the ancient world."[17] The followers of Jesus were not naïve in believing in the Resurrection. It took a great struggle for them to come to this conclusion. Even James, the brother of Jesus, was not a believer until he saw the resurrected

Jesus for himself. Doesn't this make their testimony all the more believable?

Even if Mary had believed, tears would not have been inappropriate. Though Christians are not to grieve as people without hope (1 Thess. 4:13) we can and should feel sorrow. Not to feel this sorrow is denial of the hard realities of this life, not superior faith. It is not ungodly to weep for believers who die, even though we know we will see Christian believers in the afterlife. No matter how much we know there is an afterlife in heaven for Christians, we are still sad and feel deprived. Christians are indeed citizens of heaven, but for now we live right here. Even "Jesus wept" (John 11:35). Jesus knew that He would raise Lazarus from the dead. But, because this world is fallen and therefore subject to death, Lazarus would eventually die again.

When Mary Magdalene entered the tomb, two figures spoke to her. They were angels looking like men but in "dazzling apparel" (Luke 24:4). J. Lee Grady wonders if the angels, poised head and foot at Jesus' grave, are like "the cherubim that decorated the cover of the ark of the covenant—the golden box that housed the very presence of God in the tabernacle of Moses."[18] The ark was hidden in the temple, off-limits to all but the high priest, and to him but once a year. But now, because Jesus had paid the penalty price for our sins, we can enter the holy of holies by the blood of the Lamb. Grady continues, "The two angels appeared on top of His grave to show us that the glory of the God was now accessible to us."[19]

The angels challenged the women, even gently rebuked them. The angels did not bring the women comfort (Luke 24:6-7). Why? Norval Geldenhuys points out that it was because Jesus had told them more than once He would be crucified and rise from the dead so they should have known (Luke 9:22; 18:31-3).[20] The angels had told the women that "the Son of Man must be delivered into the hands of sinful men and be crucified and on the third day rise" (Luke 24:7). The operative word here is *must*.

The Crucifixion is not the tragic end of the promising career of a young Bible teacher. It is God's plan.

According to Mark, the angel told the women to tell the disciples and Peter that Jesus would be going to Galilee and "there you will see him" (Mark 16:7). In our walk with the Lord there is always something present right now and also something that draws us to the next thing. *It is both.* We are not to enjoy the present moment with the Lord in such a way that we fail to hear His call onward. Yet, our eyes are not to be focused on the horizon in such a way that we miss the present moment where God also is. Again, *it is both.*

Notice how Peter is specially mentioned. While Jesus will appear to Peter later that evening (Luke 24:36–43; John 20:19–25), one week later (John 20:26–29), and, Paul tells us, on one other occasion one on one (1 Cor. 15:5), there will eventually be a special time of reconciliation and recommitment just for Peter (John 21:15–23). Peter truly had a bad Holy Week, but Jesus' way is to reconcile with everyone who would welcome such reconciliation. Would you welcome this?

While the angels were speaking, Jesus appeared (John 20:14). St. John Chrysostom (c. 347–407) suggests, "While she was speaking, Christ suddenly appeared behind her, striking the angels with awe."[21] Mary Magdalene turned around and saw Jesus, although she did not know it was Jesus. Jesus asked her a question, not because He did not know the answer but because it was important for her to say what was weighing heavily on her heart: someone stole the body. She turned and saw Jesus, thinking Him to be the gardener.

Why was it that Mary assumed this stranger to be the gardener? Why didn't she recognize the stranger as Jesus?

First, because she was not expecting Jesus to be there. Some people cannot seem to find a vertically standing toothpaste tube in their medicine chest if they were expecting it to be lying horizontal. Mary was not expecting Jesus. The location was a garden, so this individual *had* to be the gardener.

Second, she was overwhelmed with grief. When we are sad we often spend our time looking down, not up, and looking back, not ahead, and so we miss what's right there in front of us, often a blessing God wishes to give us. Christian discipleship does not mean the denial of the difficulties of life, but neither does it mean blindness to the blessings God makes available.

Third, she was in a panic. The body was missing! Where is it? Could she find it?

Fourth, Jesus was in His resurrection body. While there were similarities to His previous body (we soon will discover He could talk and eat, and He had wound marks), there were also dissimilarities (He could pass through locked doors, and He could vanish and suddenly appear elsewhere).

There were these *logical* reasons why Mary did not immediately recognize Jesus. But, far more importantly, God's purpose was to reveal Jesus to Mary in a particular way, one that would teach both her and the church throughout the centuries important truths about the Christian faith. As we noted in the introduction to this book, one of the chief purposes of Jesus' forty-day post-Resurrection period on Earth was to teach the church a number of lessons about what church life should and could be like once He ascended back to the Father.

Mary told "the gardener" she would take the body of Jesus to where it should be (John 20:15). It is doubtful she was that strong. This is devotion—piety—talking, not logic. God honors and appreciates such adoration, such heart language, as long as it is consistent with Christian orthodoxy. Personal piety and theological orthodoxy must be complementary, not antagonistic.

There is interesting symbolism at work here. Adam was the first gardener (Gen. 2:15) and Jesus is the second Adam. Adam, after his sin, had to fight the weeds in his garden, but Jesus came to inaugurate a kingdom which, at its consummation, would

completion

have no thorns or thistles. Adam was the head of the human race and sinned. Because of Adam's sin all subsequent humans—those who are "in Adam"—will die. Christ was the second Adam and was obedient and sinless. Because of Christ's obedience and atoning death all who trust Christ as Lord and Savior, those who are "in Christ," will have eternal life (1 Cor. 15:21–22; Rom. 5:12). In this way Mary Magdalene was correct; this unknown individual was, indeed, the gardener.

Jesus called to her by her name, "Mary" (John 20:16). Harry Griffith reminds us that, "There are few things in life more precious than hearing our names uttered by a familiar voice. There is power, comfort, hope, and assurance in the moment."[22] Though His body was now different, we assume Jesus' voice was the same. The same voice that had commanded seven devils to come out of her (Luke 8:2) is the voice that calls her by name by the tomb. The sheep know the voice of their shepherd (John 10:3–5, 16). Mary knew His.

It is clear that the restored—not the "perfect ones"—are best used of God. This is true in the cases of David, Peter, and Paul. Those who have been forgiven much (and blessed much, healed much, delivered much), love much (Luke 7:47) and are used of God much.

Once again, in this book we are asserting that *how* Jesus makes Himself known is significant, both to the people directly involved and to Christians throughout the centuries, including to the church today. In this story Jesus makes Himself known by calling someone's name. From this we learn that God wishes to know His people *individually and personally.*

Yes, Christianity is about theological truths. It is, as Jesus taught, the truth that makes people free (John 8:32). Faith is not just trust in God; it is also "*the* faith…once for all delivered to the saints" (Jude 3, emphasis added). We must never, as some try to do, put into opposition personal relationship with God and theological truths about God. They are two sides of the same coin. Both are of God.[23]

Yes, Christianity is obedience to God's moral commandments. Anyone remotely familiar with the Sermon on the Mount (Matt. 5:1–7:29) would know that. Lest anyone think that a warm, emotional love of Jesus in one's heart is sufficient discipleship, Jesus states, "If you love me, you will keep my commandments" (John 14:15), and, "As I have loved you, you also are to love one another" (John 13:34).

Yes, Christianity is a call to help the least, the lost, and the lonely. Christian discipleship involves giving food to the hungry, drink to the thirsty, welcome to the stranger, clothing to the naked, care to the sick, and visits to the prisoner (Matt. 25:31–46). It is about working for justice in the world.

Yes, Christianity is collective. It's about the church, the new kingdom of God. Jesus says He is building *a church* and that discipline of individual believers is ultimately to be done by that church (Matt. 16:18 and 18:17). But Christianity is also a *personal relationship* with Jesus Christ. Jesus here focused on Mary's heart. The good news is not just that Jesus rose from the dead, but that He also loves His people personally, individually, and by name. He now, as the risen Christ, reestablished the relationship He had had with Mary before his crucifixion. What an incredible thing to have a personal, individual relationship with the God of the universe!

Why might some people not want that?

First, they may not know that a personal relationship with Jesus is possible because they do not know who God really is. They think that God is merely a pervasive force, like electricity, or the "unmoved mover" of philosophy and not one who is and wants to be personal.

Second, they may not know that a personal relationship with Jesus is possible because they so respect Jesus as the Christ, the Son of God, that they think that to have a personal relationship with Him would be presumptuous. I mean, one does not call up the president and say, "Hey, want to go out for coffee?" So then, why would a person think he or she could know God personally?

Third, they may have been hurt in relationships before and so now fear relationships with anyone, even with God. They do not know that He will never hurt them.[24]

While Jesus had other things He needed to teach the church in His post-Resurrection appearances, He needed to teach the people of the church this personal relationship, even intimacy, with Him. He wants to teach us this today.

Jesus, in previously describing Himself as the Good Shepherd, said that the Good Shepherd's sheep "know his voice" (John 10:4). Mary discovered the risen Christ when she recognized Jesus' voice (John 20:16). Therefore, we need to spend time listening to God in prayer and in private and corporate worship so we can know His voice. The occasional, quick prayer when we need or want something is insufficient to attune our ears to His voice. Believing correct doctrine, keeping the moral commandments, and helping others in His name are important but are never a substitute for working hard at a personal, intimate relationship with the Lord.

Sometimes we wonder why people fall for the most absurd theological assertions. One reason is they have spent so little time with the Lord they cannot recognize His voice from that of others. Believers who have spent many hours in intimacy with the Lord may not always know why a particular theological assertion is wrong, but they usually will sense something is not right with what has just been stated.

Matthew tells us the women came to Jesus, took hold of His feet and worshiped Him (Matt. 28:9). We are not told that Jesus refused this worship, so we assume He accepted it, just as He would later accept the statement of Thomas, "My Lord and my God" (John 20:28) and the worship of some of His closest followers (Matt. 28:17). As numerous Christian apologists have noted throughout the centuries, no mere good teacher would accept such worship and such a statement of divinity. An egomaniac would, a con artist would, but not a good teacher. The only one who could rightly accept such worship and such a statement would be the one who was God-made-human.

The penetrating logic of C. S. Lewis rules out a response to the person of Jesus that says Jesus is simply a good teacher:

> A man who was merely a man and said the sort of things Jesus said would not be a great moral teacher. He would either be a lunatic—on a level with the man who says he is a poached egg—or else he would be the Devil of Hell. You must make your choice. Either this man was, and is, the Son of God: or else a madman or something worse.... But let us not come with any patronizing nonsense about His being a great human teacher. He has not left that open to us. He did not intend to.[25]

Physical Expression in Worship

The women expressed their love of Jesus with a physical expression of worship. Some Christian denominations are afraid of physical expressions in worship. I grew up in a church where, except for standing for three hymns, the only accepted posture in Sunday worship was quiet sitting. Anything else was considered inappropriate. Why is this? Why are some Christians turned off to physical manifestations in worship?

One reason is some people have seen individuals who express their faith in physical ways but do not act that faith out with the fruit of Christian discipleship. In The Godfather movie people are being murdered at the very moment a baptism is happening. The murders are conducted on the orders of some of those making the various Catholic gestures of worship, such as the sign of the cross. In the movie The Apostle, one of the women making the various Pentecostal gestures of praise (such as hands up in the air in praise of God) is an adulteress. While we may be tempted to dismiss these comparisons because of an anti-Christian bias evident in some movies, these two illustrations track with events that too often happen in real life.

The superficial response to such blatant inconsistency is to blame the outward gestures, not the shallowness and hypocrisy of some Catholic and Pentecostal Christians. One might observe that people who, for the most part, sit quietly in church could also be hypocrites, criminals, and adulterers.

A second reason for dismissing outward gestures in worship is that we are too much influenced by a Greek, not Hebrew, understanding of the body. The Greeks stressed that what was best was the idea of something, not its physical expression. Such thought was at the heart of Gnosticism, an early rival to the Christian faith. Gnostic teaching was that the God reflected particularly in the Old Testament was either a very junior God or else a very bad God because He made physical things. The goal of religion, Gnostics said, is to get past the physical.[26]

But attitudes dismissing the physical are not biblical Christianity. Christians look to the God of Scripture who made the physical creation and deemed it "good" (Gen. 1:12, 18, 25, 31). We see that Jesus spent a lot of time performing physical miracles. He turned water into wine (John 2:1–11). He did not say, "Who cares if the wine runs out. Let's just praise God."

He healed the paralyzed man (Mark 2:1–12). He did not say, "Whether you ever walk or not is not important. Just believe in me."

He multiplied the fish and loaves (Matt. 14:13-21). He did not say, "The spiritual feeding I just taught you is the only thing that is important."

Dr. Robert G. Tuttle is an expert in the comparison of Christianity and other world religions. He comments, "The Hebrew body, mind, spirit is evidence of God's creation. God is creator and we are God's creation. Please do not confuse the two. The Gnostics had creation out of evil matter and wanted to come out of the body to be absorbed into some kind of divine blob. Most of the religions of the world have this dualistic understanding of creation (Hinduism, Jainism, Buddhism, Sikhism, etc.)."[27]

Over the past century, under the influence of post-Enlightenment positivism, some theologians have been demythologizing Scripture. That is to say, they believe that many of the Gospel accounts are myths—a made-up story to make a spiritual point. Thus, when we are told in John 9 that Jesus healed the eyes of a blind man, we are to believe that this is a myth made up by John to get across the point that Jesus healed *spiritual*, not physical, blindness.

That may make sense in a culture where the body was deemed a tomb to escape, not part of creation to restore. But the first Christians, as good Jews, were earthy and physical. The Scripture writers would not spiritualize what was in front of them. They wouldn't think in those terms. *Of course* Jesus literally made water into wine, healed paralyzed and blind people, and multiplied fishes and loaves. It's what God does. What He does not do is say the physical things of Earth are unimportant. Demythologizing theology is extremely shallow thinking and extremely poor scholarship. It projects onto Christianity a philosophical foundation quite foreign to it.

The psalmist lifts up his hands as an evening sacrifice of worship (Ps. 141:2). The twenty-four elders fall prostrate before the one seated on the throne in the worship of heaven (Rev. 4:10). Biblical believers understood the use of bodily gestures in worship. We should not dismiss such gestures as being Catholic or Pentecostal/ Charismatic. It's what *Christians* are to do.

Ironically, it is usually white Protestant evangelicals or fundamentalists ("Bible-believing Christians") who are the chief offenders against biblically using the body in worship. (The black church, thanks be to God, is traditionally much more expressive.) I say *ironically* for two reasons. First, white Protestant evangelicals rightly want to model their behavior on Scripture, yet they deny those Bible verses which describe the use of the body in worship. Second, when it comes to physical representative gestures in church they, of all people, should know better. Most of these brothers and sisters in Christ will doff their hats when the flag comes by. Are they worshiping red, white, and blue cloths? Of course not. What they are doing is acknowledging that the physical gestures bespeak inward convictions.

And, on those days when their minds are wandering and they are not thinking or feeling patriotically, they know that they are not being hypocritical for using patriotic gestures. They are customs—traditions, if you will—done because they are right. Often, observing these customs, even when their minds and hearts have wandered far off things patriotic, brings them back to what they should be thinking and feeling. I would simply say to them, apply what you know to do toward the flag to your worship of God.

Mary wants to hold Jesus (John 20:17), not unlike a little child whose daddy is going away on a business trip. Harry Griffith wisely notes, "When we find that which is lost, we all want to hold it close and make sure it is real and will not be lost again." Mary is saying, "Don't leave me again."[28]

Jesus' response was not, "Don't touch me," but rather, "Don't *hold* me." It was permissible to touch the risen Christ. He was not a ghost. Though He had and has a *resurrection* body, it is still a *physical* body, and Mary and Thomas (John 20:27) and anyone else could touch it. As Paul John Isaak explains, "Jesus does not want to be confused with false messiahs, false teachers or even ghosts (Luke 24:39). He wants to be experienced and touched as the Christ."[29] The Lord who took little children in His arms (Mark 10:16) has not ceased to value embracing those who love Him. Christians do not say in the Nicene Creed, "I believe in the immortality of the soul," but rather, "I believe in the resurrection of the *body*."

What Jesus was saying is, "Do not keep me here." When we encounter Jesus in a special way we want to freeze the moment, just as Peter did on the Mount of Transfiguration (Luke 9:33–35). Jesus was telling Mary He must move on, to make Himself visible to various individuals and groups, and, in forty days, to ascend back to the Father. He was also telling her that she, too, must move on in her work for Him. Yes, there are promised, guaranteed, and regular places of meeting the Lord—in Scripture, in sacrament, in the Christian community—but the *special* moments of meeting are just that, special. They occur when and how God chooses.

Henry Barclay Swete observed a century ago:

> It was necessary to make it clear at once that old relations were not to be restored, as Mary evidently hoped; that the Resurrection was the beginning of a new order....the intimacy of the life in Galilee is to be exchanged for a new fellowship of a closer kind. The Resurrection must, however, first be consummated by the Ascension; the visible presence must be finally withdrawn before the presence of Jesus in the Spirit can be realized....If Mary may not hold the prize which she thinks that she has won, it is only because to keep it would be to lose one immeasurably greater.[30]

Edward A. ("Ted") Schroder adds, "The message of the Bible is forward looking. 'I know the plans I have for you,' declares the Lord, 'plans to give you hope and a future.' (Jeremiah 29:11) That is the message of Easter."[31]

We must cherish those special moments when God is ever so real to us, but we must not try to prolong them when God says the moment has passed or try to re-create them so as to capture the same experience again. God will come to us again, in ways He chooses and at times He chooses, and quite possibly in new ways, lest we focus on the manner and not on Him.

Mary had just called Jesus Rabboni (John 20:16), which was the way she had known Him previously. Jesus is moving her along in how she relates to Him. The old relationship is now out of date. Something wonderfully new is now in place.[32] The Jesus whom she had known became the stranger in the garden so when she rediscovered Him it would be in a new way. The same Jesus wants us to know Him in deeper, newer ways as well.

After He tells Mary not to hold Him, Jesus tells Mary to go to His brethren to tell them this good news (John 20:17). Note Jesus calls these men His brethren. Martin Luther wrote that because the disciples had all fled they had no reason to think that they had any claim to be even His servants, much less His apostles or especially His brothers. But they are called brethren![33] Jesus is not ashamed to call them His brothers even now (Heb. 2:11). They and we may be immature brothers and sisters, but they and we are brothers and sisters nonetheless. What a comfort to us when we stumble.

Also in this passage Jesus uses the term *Father.* Yet He distinguishes "my Father and your Father" (John 20:17). Although God is Father to all, there is a distinction: Jesus is part of the Trinity, and we are not.

Matthew tells us that the two Marys departed from the tomb "with fear and great joy" (Matt. 28:8). We, understanding the words *fear* and *joy* in a secular way, might wonder how both could happen at once. But what do these words mean in Scripture?

Fear is often godly respect and being overwhelmed at something incredible that is being experienced and a reverential awe at it and the God who brought it about. When we read that the "fear of the Lord is the beginning of wisdom" (Ps. 111:10; Prov. 9:10), we are not being told to dread or run from the Lord as we would an enemy about to harm us; we are being asked to give godly respect, devotion, and obedience.

Joy is not merely happiness, because happiness depends on what happens. Happiness is out of our control. If things are good we are emotionally "up"; if not, we are emotionally "down." But joy transcends that. Joy is a gift of God and a fruit of the Spirit (Gal. 5:22). It depends on who we are in Christ, not on outward circumstances. We are, to quote a line in an Easter hymn, "victors in the midst of strife." Paul, listing various terrible things that could befall us, encourages us that "in these things we are more than conquerors" (Rom. 8:37). We can be joyful even when all hell is breaking loose around us *if we are centered on God.*

Mary and the other women certainly knew that the persecution of the followers of Jesus would only escalate when they testified to His being risen from the dead. But the joy of which no one could rob them was there because Jesus had risen. Mary knew she had to tell the others that she had seen the risen Christ (John 20:17–18). And yet, that was not exactly what Jesus had said to her. He did not say, "I have risen," but rather, "I am ascending to my Father." While John does not have an Ascension account like Luke does (particularly in Acts), it is clear John knows not only the Ascension but that the Ascension is different from and takes place at a different time than the Resurrection. As Rod Whitacre notes about Jesus, "He has finished the work (19:30) and can now return to the Father."[34]

She was to be a witness. This word *witness* has two meanings. We witness a car accident—we see the brown van run a red light and broadside the white sedan. We may also be called to be a witness in a court case to tell what we saw. In court we are not asked questions about the relative merits of a Detroit-made car versus a Japanese import. We are not asked about the relative merits of and possible problems with a diesel car versus a gasoline car or an electric one or a hybrid. We are simply asked to give witness to what we had witnessed. Mary is not asked to give specifics as to how the Resurrection may have occurred. She is simply asked to announce that it happened.[35]

Our Christian witness today is similar. What have we seen God do in our lives and in the lives of people around us? Most likely we are not experts in theology, but we do not have to be. We are to tell people about what God is doing.

Having said that, we *are* to tell people of the basic truths of the faith. It's not just *my* experience we're talking about but also the objective truths of the gospel. Otherwise someone listening to us could rightly say, "What happened to you is wonderful. Why should I expect anything like it to happen to me?" Or, they might respond, "Could I expect an experience similar to yours without a relationship to this Jesus you mentioned?" When John Wesley confessed he felt his heart "strangely warmed," it was in the context of him hearing a lecture on the gospel as outlined in the Epistle to the Romans. Wesley was not pumped up by a praise band playing a contemporary praise song louder and louder to work up the audience; it was in the context of solid theological teaching.

While we may start with a simple presentation of what Jesus has been doing in our lives, we must soon move on to present basic Christian truths. We do this to point people not to our own individual experience but to Christ, who may then encounter each person somewhat differently and who alone can save.

In one telling of the Resurrection story, the people that Mary and the other women told did not believe their words (Luke 24:10–11). The apostles thought it was an idle tale. This is not because the story was told by women but because the story was so unbelievable. Luke's word is *lēros*. David Jeffrey believes the term was "apparently used by physicians to describe the delirious babblings of very ill persons."[36] Thomas did not believe the story either, even though it had been told to him *by men*. Yes, Jesus had said on numerous occasions that He would be crucified and rise on the third day (for example, from just one Gospel: Mark 8:31; 9:31; 10:34). But what could that possibly mean? Hans Conzelmann says the phrase "idle tale" in Luke 24:11 means that the truth of the Resurrection cannot be deduced from the idea of Messiahship or from the life of Jesus. It is, in fact, something new. Only in retrospect can we see it is right. Only after it is explained (as Jesus would twice later do) can we see how the Old Testament teaches it.[37]

Because all of this—the Resurrection, the first appearances of Jesus to His followers—took place on Sunday, Sunday is now the day for Christians to worship. It is not wrong for Christians to worship on Saturday. Christians can and should worship God every day. But the principal, corporate worship of the church is on Sunday. Because it is the day of the Resurrection, Sunday is now the eighth day, the first day of the second week, the day of eschatological fulfillment, the day that inaugurates the kingdom of God. God is beginning the cycle of creation anew. It is, as John points out, "the Lord's day" (Rev. 1:10). (Because the Jews reckoned a day as beginning at sundown, Sunday begins on Saturday evening. Therefore, Saturday evening worship is Sunday worship, while Saturday morning worship is not.)

Jesus appeared to Mary and other women that first Easter morning. This is but the beginning of His post-Resurrection appearances. He will next appear to two people walking home to Emmaus. It is to that story we must now turn. But first, to review the most important part of this chapter: Each of the post-Resurrection appearances of Jesus teaches us something about what the church would be like after Jesus' Ascension and what the church should be like today. What do Matthew 28:1–10, Mark 16:1–10, Luke 24:1–11, and John 20:1–18 teach us? In the appearance to Mary Magdalene, God is telling us that Christianity is *personal*. It is not just sound doctrine. It is not just imperatives on how to be and do good. Though it is in the context of the church, our faith is about a personal relationship with this God who chose to be incarnate as a person, Jesus of Nazareth. In addition, God is telling us that we must tell others about Him, what He has revealed in Scripture, and what He is doing in lives today.

Discussion Questions

1. One major event and one major prophecy appear in all four Gospels: the resurrection of Jesus and baptism with the Holy Spirit by Jesus. How significant are these, and how are they related?

2. When have you encountered the risen Christ without recognizing him?

3. How and why is voice recognition often superior to eye witness and/or circumstantial evidence, and how does this apply in our own prayer life?

CHAPTER 2

ON THE ROAD TO EMMAUS

Luke 24:13–35

THERE ARE TWO things Luke likes to talk about: a journey and a meal. In the story of the two travelers on the road to Emmaus we have them both. Luke tells us that on the same day as the Resurrection two people were heading to Emmaus (Luke 24:13–35). Good Jews would make sure they were in Jerusalem for Passover, and these two had been there. Are they now heading home?

Biblical archeologists have debated for centuries where this village of Emmaus was located, with several possibilities being suggested. We do know it was seven miles from Jerusalem (Luke 24:13). Recently, however, the late Carsten Peter Thiede, sometime professor at the University of Basel, stated he had sufficient evidence to name the true location.[1]

If, Thiede notwithstanding, we do not know for certain where Emmaus was, neither do we know for certain who these two travelers were. One is named Cleopas (Luke 24:18). In the prologue to his Gospel, Luke promised to write an orderly account of what eyewitnesses had stated (Luke 1:1–4). Had Luke interviewed him? Thiede notes how Luke's account of the Emmaus journey is "remarkably restrained."[2] There is neither exaggerated language nor fanciful speculations. Luke is a physician (Col. 4:14), and as such highly educated and a cautious, careful observer and reporter of detail.

So who is this man Cleopas? Some Bible scholars equate him with Clopas, who, with his wife, Mary, stood near the cross when Jesus was being crucified (John 19:25). Matthew tells us that Mary is the mother of James the younger and Joseph (Matt. 27:56). The difference in the spelling of his name need not concern us. Until the early nineteenth century spelling had not been standardized as it is now. Many people spelled their names with variations.

If we do not have certainty about the identity of Cleopas, we have even less certainty as to the identity of Cleopas's companion. Was it his wife? This might be the case, because in offering Jesus hospitality, they said, "Stay with us," perhaps implying the place all of them later entered was their home (Luke 24:29). However, nowhere is it actually mentioned that Jesus was being invited into their home. They might have put in for the night at an inn and suggested Jesus do the same. They might have been friends, not husband and wife. We must be humbly dogmatic where Scripture clearly states something and reverently agnostic when it does not.

While such speculation as to the identity of the two Emmaus travelers may be interesting, the heart of the story is what Jesus said and did.

As the two were journeying to Emmaus a stranger came alongside them and wondered aloud why they were sad. Luke explains in this narrative that there were two primary reasons for their sadness: First, because the man they had come to know and follow, and perhaps even love, had been killed, and He had died in a most cruel way just three days previously. Second, because they had hoped that if He were the Messiah He would inaugurate the Messiah's reign, but with His death this now would not happen (Luke 24:21). They had thought, as many others had, that the problem facing the Jews was the occupying Roman government and its army, and the Messiah's mission would be to free Israel from that.

In Jesus' day, the various groups within Judaism attempted to deal with the problem of a pagan government and its occupying army in different ways:

- The Pharisees mostly ignored the political situation and, instead, concentrated on their own personal religious beliefs and practices and on moral purity.

- The Sadducees represented the religious authority that had compromised with the pagan establishment. They "got along by going along."

- The Essenes fled to the wilderness to practice a monastic, communal piety.

- The zealots sought a political overthrow of the occupying government and a defeat of its army.

Many in the populace were in expectation of the Messiah coming (Luke 3:15), but almost no one expected the cross to be the central part of the redemption of Israel.

These two travelers to Emmaus were sad and Jesus came to comfort them. Martin Luther noted, "See with what care Christ gave himself to these two weak believers, how he did everything to help their weakness and strengthen their faith, because he saw and knew why they were so troubled.... The Lord would not leave them in doubt and torment but went to their aid."[3]

In the last chapter we noted that Jesus' initial post-Resurrection appearance was not to the mighty or even to His core disciples, but to a woman sad because the Lord who had so wonderfully set her free was dead and His body apparently stolen. In this chapter we note Jesus appearing to Cleopas and a companion.

Cleopas was not a core leader. His companion is not even named. While Jesus will later appear to His core leadership group, here and, previously, to Mary, He ministers to people the world might call insignificant. We would think that if the Lord truly wanted to launch a movement to transform the world He would have first appeared to powerful, influential, and educated people, or at least to those He had spent three years grooming. But no! He appeared to Mary Magdalene and other women, to Cleopas, and to someone whose name we do not know. We can take comfort in this. He wants to come to *us*, and, when we let Him, He wants to deepen our relationship with Him.

Cleopas and his companion failed to recognize their fellow traveler to be Jesus, just as several of Jesus' followers initially failed to recognize Him during His forty-day post-Resurrection time on Earth. We are noting throughout this book that God the Father intentionally prevented their initial recognition of Jesus so that the eventual recognition would be coupled with both further disclosure as to who He is, and with what the church throughout the centuries should include as central aspects of her life.

In the post-Resurrection event under consideration here, we are told that the eyes of Cleopas and his companion were similarly kept from recognizing Jesus (Luke 24:16). Why was this?

William Barclay notes how some suggest it was because the sun was in their eyes. Emmaus was to the west, the direction in which they were walking. The sun was sinking and so their eyes were dazzled.[4] This is not a very likely explanation by itself. One would likely turn away from the sun and toward this incredible person with whom they were having such a fascinating discussion. They would wait until their eyes were able to focus on their companion, and, if they knew Him, they would recognize Him. Moreover, when they reached Emmaus the sun was low in the sky; hence the invitation of the two to stay with them "for the day is now nearly over" (Luke 24:29). Even if we could accept

Barclay's suggestion of the sun keeping them from recognizing Jesus early in the day, they should now have known Him since the sun was far lower.

Moreover, might they have not detected in His opening up of the Scriptures the style and depth of teaching He had previously evidenced in the various discourses they had heard Him give? And, wouldn't the sheep know His voice (John 10:4)?[5]

The best explanation is provided from Luke's commentary itself: "Their eyes were kept from recognizing him" (Luke 24:16). We are not told how this took place. No matter how it happened, we are told it was an intentional act on God's part, not something that happened by a normal event of nature or by chance.

One reason their eyes were kept from recognizing the stranger was so that the stranger could gradually unfold how the entire Old Testament Scripture pointed to, and was fulfilled in, Jesus of Nazareth. Had Jesus' identity been immediately known, the travelers would have been so overjoyed that He had risen that they would not have listened to a lengthy discourse about how for centuries God had been carefully preparing for this day and how all Scripture had just been fulfilled in Christ.[6]

The stranger we know to be Jesus asked the two travelers what they were discussing. They are incredulous that He does not know. It was the major event in Jerusalem in the immediately preceding days. How could He not know? As I have taught on the Emmaus road experience the past several years, numerous people have volunteered that it would be like someone living in America on September 11, 2001, and not knowing about the attack on the Twin Towers in New York. Jesus, wise teacher that He was and is, was utilizing a technique good teachers everywhere deploy: He was drawing them out. We learn far more when a teacher gives us hints and clues, forcing us to assemble the puzzle ourselves.

Cleopas and his companion refer to Jesus as "a prophet mighty in deed and word before God and all the people" (Luke 24:19).

This is not a bad start for one's discipleship. This is often how He appeared in His earthly ministry (Luke 7:16, for example). Unlike some Pharisees, who asserted Jesus did what He did because He was in league with the devil (Matt. 12:24), Cleopas recognized the godly nature of Jesus' ministry.

Cleopas correctly noted that Jesus' ministry was *both in deed and word*. A danger among some individual Christians and in some congregations is that ministry is didactic only. That is, there is good, sometimes even great teaching, but there is little demonstration of God's power either through the gifts of the Spirit or through the sacraments. On the other hand, there are other individual Christians and congregations where there are abundant manifestations of the Holy Spirit or faithful and zealous ministration and reception of the sacraments but not faithful or mature teaching of the Word of God. Scripture teaches both, and our Lord demonstrated both. Paul knew it was both as he wrote to the Thessalonians, "Our message of the gospel came to you not in word only, but also in power and in the Holy Spirit" (1 Thess. 1:5).

However, while Cleopas gave a good beginning testimony of his admiration of Jesus, it fell short. Cleopas at this stage of his spiritual journey was like many people throughout the centuries. They have some admiration of Jesus, but they do not see Him as the unique, incarnate, divine Son whom they must worship, nor do they see Him as the sovereign Lord whom they must obey. But Jesus could not be just a prophet. He must be either much more or much less.

We saw in the last chapter the wise insight of C. S. Lewis as to how Jesus cannot be merely a good teacher or prophet. Let us now examine this point more fully. How do we know Jesus saw Himself as one far greater than a prophet or a teacher?

First, Jesus presumed to forgive sin, a divine prerogative. While Jewish priestly leaders might assure people of God's forgiveness, they would never dare declare that forgiveness as if they were God doing it in person. No mere prophet would dare do that. But Jesus did exactly that (Mark 2:5–12). A madman might. A con artist might, but a prophet or a good teacher? Never! The only one who was in good mental health and of personal integrity who would dare do that would be the God-made-flesh, who, thus, is much more than a prophet.

Second, Jesus called God His Father in a way others would not. The Jews clearly discerned what Jesus was saying about Himself and sought to put Him to death as a blasphemer because, John tells us, in speaking of the Father in this way Jesus made Himself equal with God (John 5:18). Once again, no mere prophet or good teacher would do this. Madmen might, con artists might, but a mere prophet or a good teacher? Never!

Third, Jesus made Himself the center of His message. He who counseled humility in others made extraordinary statements about Himself. He said that no one could go to the Father except through Him (John 14:6) and that to see Him was to see the Father (John 14:9). Again, Jesus must either be dismissed as a lunatic or shunned as a bad man or worshiped and obeyed as God and Lord. He cannot be merely a prophet or a good teacher. He is much less or much more.[7]

Fourth, as Jacob Neusner so rightly points out, *Jesus treated the Law in a way that only God could do.* Neusner concludes that as a Jew (and a rabbi) he himself would not have been a disciple of Jesus. Again, we would assert, Jesus is a bad Jew or else He is God, but there's nothing in-between.[8]

Cleopas is on a journey, perhaps to his home. What he would soon learn is that he was on a spiritual journey as well. Are we on a spiritual journey, or are we content to stay where we are?

There are two important points about spiritual journeying we can learn from the story of the travelers on the road to Emmaus.

First, Jesus walks with us on the journey. We are not to be so focused on the distant goal that we do not enjoy His presence along the way. In your quest to be more holy in conduct and more effective in ministry, and in your desire to receive God's blessings, are you neglecting your present relationship with the Lord? He wants to know and love you *right now,* not just someday when you've become a holier and more effective person. The best blessing God can give you is not health or wealth but *Himself* in an ever-growing personal relationship.

Second, there is an actual goal. The travelers are not just out for a stroll. They are not groping along or wandering aimlessly. Cleopas and his companion were heading to a specific destination. They were going to someplace safe, a place to get away from the madness that surrounded the events in Jerusalem.

To be on a religious quest—a spiritual journey—could be quite harmful if you see it as self-directed or if you wind up in the wrong spot. Jesus did not and does not call people to be more religious. He did not and does not invite people just to dabble in Christian things from time to time. He called them and calls us to His person with a personal relationship to cherish, doctrinal truths to believe, and moral commandments to obey. Follow Him and His Word, be nourished by His sacraments, and be guided by mature, orthodox Christian believers in the fellowship of the visible church, and you will not stall on your spiritual journey or get lost along the way. Understand what God seems to be saying to you and your local church in the context of the consensus of what wise Christian leaders throughout the centuries have understood God to be saying, and you will not wind up in a spiritually strange place.

After he made his statement about Jesus being a prophet mighty in deed and word, Cleopas related the story of the women at the empty tomb earlier that day. It has been fashionable in some liberal theological circles to malign the early church leaders for some imagined chauvinism. They assert that the apostles and others dismissed what the women related about their experiences at the empty tomb simply because they were women. However, an examination of the biblical texts does not support this view. Cleopas first simply relates what the women said. There is no hint of patronizing, no sense of, "Well, you know how emotional and delusional women sometimes get." Then he notes that others went to the empty tomb, and their experiences verified the women's story. (We also note how Scripture tells us most of the men fled from the cross and how slow it was for the male apostles to come to certainty.)

When Luke related the event, he described the women as having been perplexed at the empty tomb (v. 4) and having been terrified at the appearance of "two men in dazzling clothes" (v. 5). These are reactions anyone would have, not just women. Luke noted the women told the eleven and others who then dismissed their witness as an "idle tale" (v. 11). Given the doubts they all had, what else would they conclude? How many people had previously risen from the dead? (See previous chapter for the listing of these.) Moreover, if Jesus had been raised like Lazarus, then He would return to the state He was previously in and would probably be killed one more time. No, the story of the Resurrection was dismissed because it seemed too incredible, not because it was told by women.

Jesus' response to their puzzlement over the day's activities and to the reports they had been told was quite strong. They should have known what it all meant. He chided them, "Oh, how foolish you are, and how slow [of heart] to believe all that the prophets have spoken!" (Luke 24:25, NIV). Interestingly, Jesus does not say they should have known merely because He had taught them about the resurrection, but because His death and resurrection were *necessary* steps in God's plan. It was there in the Old Testament Scriptures, and not just in a few places. The

Cross was not an accident; it was God's intent from the beginning. The Resurrection was not, therefore, Plan B. Jesus will repeat this statement again when He meets with the ten (the twelve apostles with Judas and Thomas absent) in Jerusalem later that very night (Luke 24:44).

We can understand the confusion His followers had about the event of His death and the accounts of His resurrection. People for centuries have wondered why the crowd that so heartily cheered "Hosanna" on Palm Sunday was so quick to cry, "Crucify Him," just a few days later. The expectation of many people—and not just of the zealots—was of a warrior Messiah who would liberate them from the occupying Roman army. When Jesus triumphantly entered Jerusalem, teeming with pilgrims for the Passover festival, would He not finally issue a call to arms to begin the revolution?

There is nothing strange about the idea of a warrior Messiah. When the children of Israel entered the Promised Land they had to wage war under the leadership of Joshua against the people occupying the land. Then, under King David, Israel finally achieved something approximating the borders promised to Abraham centuries beforehand. And is not Messiah "great David's greater son"? And had not the Maccabees, nearly two centuries before, liberated their land and purified their religion by a successful armed rebellion against the occupying Syrians? God was the author of these conquests, so does it not stand to reason that this is what He would do again? Would not Jesus be the successor to Joshua and David and Judah the Maccabee? Many Jews at this time were fascinated by the apocalyptic passages such as Daniel 7 and the apocryphal book of Enoch. None of these passages speaks of a Messiah who was a sacrificial victim for sin.

Many believe that Judas betrayed Jesus because Judas was trying to force Jesus' hand, to make Jesus act like the warrior leader that he had expected. While I do not accept that this was the sole reason Judas betrayed Jesus, I do believe it was an important factor.

Or, some in the crowd might have expected Jesus to eliminate the Romans with the same supernatural dispatch He did with disease and demons.

Yet, Cleopas and his companion should have known about a different kind of Messiah if they had really known their Old Testament, if they had been paying attention when Scripture was read in the synagogue. Could we not point to the suffering on behalf of the people taught in the latter part of the book of the prophet Isaiah? Here we find four "Servant Songs" that, variously, describe Israel as a people serving the Lord (for example, Isa. 44:1–5) and then as a representative individual acting on behalf of and for the benefit of those people (Isa. 49:1–7). In the third Servant Song (Isa. 50:4–11) the servant suffered in various ways. In the fourth song (Isa. 52:13–53:12), he vicariously bears the punishment of sin belonging to the people. Simeon and Anna seemed to understand (Luke 2:29–40).

Luke wrote that Jesus pointed to Himself in "all the Scriptures" (Luke 24:27). Jesus is saying that it is in not just a few passages that He is to be found. The Messiahship He brought was the continuity of God's plan, not a surprise or an innovation. It was from all eternity. Josh McDowell points out, "The Old Testament contains over 300 references to the Messiah that were fulfilled by Jesus."[9] Should Cleopas have not known at least some of these?

This is why it is significant when Luke tells us that Jesus, "Beginning with Moses and all the Prophets, he interpreted to them in all the Scriptures the things concerning himself" (Luke 24:27). Earlier Jesus had said, "You search the Scriptures because you think that in them you have eternal life; and it is they that bear witness about me" (John 5:39). What had just happened to Him had been foretold all over the Old Testament.

This is important for at least two reasons. First, the Old Testament is part of Christian heritage. In the second century a heresy arose, led by Marcion of Sinope (ca. 85–160). Marcion could not reconcile God as portrayed in the Old Testament with the life of Christ, so he concluded that there were two different Gods. He believed that the God of the Old Testament was a God of wrath, and the God of the New Testament is a God of love; so therefore, we should reject that Old Testament God.

This is nonsense. Anyone reading the pleadings of the prophets and noting the longsuffering patience of God with His wayward people will immediately know how God as revealed in the Old Testament loved His people. Anyone reading all the statements of eternal lostness coming from the lips of Jesus will immediately know how God as revealed in the New Testament will punish the unrepentant. The God of the Old Testament and the God of the New Testament are the same God. This God of both Testaments upholds both righteousness and love.

Marcion was the first to come up with a canon of Scripture, that is, a list of what books should be in the New Testament. He kept part of Luke's Gospel and several epistles of Paul. The entire Old Testament and that part of the New Testament which sounded Jewish were rejected. The church responded first by excommunicating Marcion and declaring his teaching to be heresy, and then, eventually, by coming up with the official New Testament canon we know today.

Christians must know and value the Old Testament. There can be no anti-Semitism, whether via direct persecution of Jewish people or by failure to share the Messiah with Jewish people. Nor can there be a rejection of our Jewish roots, because Gentile believers in Christ are people graciously grafted into the Jewish stock (Rom. 11:13–20).

Early church leaders did not hijack primitive Christianity to force foreign concepts into it. What we are told in the New Testament is the next and final step in God's eternal plan, which we see unfolding throughout the Old Testament.

Jesus had done things "that the Scriptures might be fulfilled" (see, for example, Mark 14:49; Luke 24:44–45; John 17:12). When Jesus had said, "It is written," He did not mean, "Somebody wrote it down once upon a time." The verse, in its original Greek, literally means, "It stands written permanently" (see, for example, Matthew 21:13). The Jews, especially since the return from exile in the sixth century, were called the people of the Book. In the Upper Room, Jesus taught there would be what we now call the New Testament to parallel and extend the Old (John 14:26 and *commentary* 16:12–13). God's church is to be a Bible-centered community, basing its doctrinal beliefs and moral choices on God's written word.[10]

John D. Witvliet comments:

> Indeed, the Bible that Jesus opened on Emmaus is just as powerful now as it was then. And while we don't have the just-raised human Jesus walking next to us in [the] same way as he was present at Emmaus, Jesus is surely present. Through the Holy Spirit, we have walking with us nothing less than the body of Christ the church, the place where Jesus' own disciples are called to offer companionship, truth-telling rebuke, patient teaching and fellowship meals.[11]

And this truth-telling is based on Scripture.

There are people today that note that Jesus was silent on this or that particular issue, and therefore, they conclude, Old Testament teaching is now set aside. This is simply not true. While the ceremonial law of the Old Testament was, in Him, fulfilled and thus set aside, the moral law was not. Jesus never spoke to the issue of homosexual behavior, chastity, idol worship, or several other issues because He did not need to. Where Jesus was silent about an Old Testament moral teaching, it is because He endorsed it. There can be no playing off of a tolerant Jesus against an intolerant Old Testament. Paul similarly does not mention homosexual practice when writing epistles to Jews who knew better but does mention it when writing epistles to Gentile audiences who did not. There can be no playing off Jesus against Paul, either.

Moreover, Jesus did not speak about some issues while He was on Earth because He would speak to us later through the Epistle writers. In the Upper Room our Lord said, "I still have many things to say to you, but you cannot bear them now. When the Spirit of truth comes, he will guide you into all the truth, for he will not speak on his own authority, but whatever he hears he will speak" (John 16:12–13). All of the New Testament is the word of Jesus Christ, equally reliable, equally authoritative. When the Epistle writers speak, Christ speaks. It is for this reason we must reject the patronizing attitude of some who say they accept what Jesus said but not what the Epistle writers (especially Paul) wrote. When the Gospels *and the Epistles* speak, Christ is speaking. As many churches say at the end of *any* Scripture lesson, "This is the word of the Lord." Obedience to Christ is obedience to Scripture.

G. D. Arnold reminds us that by "his very nature man cannot avoid living his life under an authority of some kind. It may be an external authority imposed upon him from without.... Or, a man may live his life under the spurious authority of the self: a course which leads only to the disintegration of personality through self-indulgence. Alternatively, he may accept the authority of an ideal, which is known and consciously followed.... But a life which is committed to the Risen Christ, present everywhere and timeless, is even better; in so far as it is in living contact with the ultimately Real, rather than merely obedient to a mental image.... The Risen Christ, eternally living, is the Authority who alone can command our full obedience. And only under this obedience is humanity set free for true service."[12] We will speak of obedience to Christ as Lord again in chapter 7.

As we read various letters written from early church leaders to local congregations and as we read various theological treatises penned by these church fathers, it is clear the early church saw the emerging New Testament as authoritative. In fact, Scripture was the ace of trumps, the authority which corrected all other—secondary—authorities. The emerging New Testament was not merely memoirs or helpful thoughts the way we might view Christian biography or helpful teaching books. The early church leaders saw the New Testament as the final word of authority in matters of doctrine and conduct.

We must do the same. In college I had been told by a number of religion professors that intelligent church people saw the Bible merely as a statement reflecting the views of a relatively primitive people two thousand years ago. It was the ignorant who treated Scripture as God-given objective truth. However, when I got to Oxford for graduate study in theology I discovered that some of the most intelligent people I had ever met were "Bible men and women." They had no trouble believing the Bible to be factually accurate and religiously truthful and to be God's word to the human race. They showed me how questions about "problems" with the texts that were supposed to disqualify intelligent people from believing the Bible could be answered in ways intellectually satisfying. The roadblocks to our honoring Scripture as God's authority in our life could be removed without sacrificing the use of one's mind. In other words, it was not intellectual suicide to believe the Bible. It was spiritual suicide not to. But, it's one thing to believe in the Bible. It's another thing to read it, learn it, and apply it. That we must do.

Jesus' explanation of why His life and ministry had been foretold all over the Old Testament is important for two reasons. First, as we have just seen, because the Old Testament is part of Christian heritage. Now secondly, because this demonstrates that "God plans far ahead."[13] We can take comfort that while evil may prosper for a season, God knows what He is doing, and things will be right *in the end*. When we are told in the Book of Revelation that Jesus, "the Lamb of God, who takes away the sin of the world" (John 1:29), was "slain from the foundation of the world" (Rev. 13:8, KJV), we know that this was the plan of God the Father from the very beginning. Believers can rest secure in God because God has everything under control. (While this should remove our anxiety, it does not remove our responsibility to act to make the world a better place and to be obedient to His commands.)

Jesus rebuked the Emmaus travelers (Luke 24:25), not to make them feel even more sad but so He could help them grow spiritually in Him. He was strict with them, but He continued with them on the journey. They were weak and immature, but they were neither bad nor hostile.

But what if they had been bad or hostile? The Holy Spirit convicts us of sin not to rub our noses in our sin but so that we can repent and be forgiven and then grow into maturity (see 1 John 1:8–2:2). We may reject His love and walk away from Him, but God will not walk away from us. He never stops loving us or offering us His presence. If we are intentionally rebellious, He will tough love us. If we are but ignorant or lazy, He will gently nudge us back to Him.

Why might have Cleopas and his fellow traveler not made the connection between those blood atonement practices of the Old Testament and what happened to Jesus on Calvary? We can only speculate.

First, perhaps the Emmaus travelers had only a moderate commitment to their faith. Many have a religious commitment somewhere between occasional observance (the Christmas and Easter church attendees) and a deep discipleship. Yes, the Emmaus travelers were coming back from observing the Passover in Jerusalem. Yes, they were discussing the events of the past weekend and were trying to make sense out of them. Yes, they seemed to be followers of Jesus because they referred to the women at the tomb as "of our group" (v. 22), and, yes, they would soon, as people of good will, offer the stranger hospitality. But—and this is only conjecture—how deeply committed to Christ were they truly?

We *do* know, however, that there are many today who can give all kinds of details about the present-day cultural packaging of the Christian faith and be quite active in the organizational business of the church but not really know Christ as Lord and Savior nor believe the truths of the Creed. We might ask ourselves what essential truths of Christian doctrine, observance, and moral conduct are we ignorant or non-observant of because our discipleship is too superficial.

Second, even if they were deeply committed disciples, they might have had blind spots in their understanding of their religion. For us this means, first, we must study Scripture. The average Christian really knows but a handful of Bible passages, yet he thinks he or she knows much more. We can certainly take joy and comfort as we curl up one evening to read the wonderful stories of God's Word, but we must also spend time studying Scripture with such tools as a Bible dictionary to look up the technical words, a Bible atlas to see where the places mentioned are located, commentaries to see what Christians wiser than ourselves have understood a given passage to mean, devotional guides to grasp what wise Christians have believed these passages to mean for our walk with God and our work for God, and, perhaps for some of us, a Hebrew Old Testament and a Greek New Testament.

Furthermore, it is easy to place greater significance on some biblical verses and less significance on others because of what we want the Bible to say. Sometimes this selective reading is intentional. More often, it is a product of cultural blinders we do not know we have. It is for this reason that it is wise to read the Bible in community and not just alone.

One way to read the Bible in community is in a group Bible study with other Christians, our brothers and sisters in Christ alive today living near to us. The danger, however, is our Bible study is likely to be composed of people just like ourselves.

Another way is in reading the writings of other Christians

outside our local church, outside our period in history, and outside our socio-economic, political, cultural group. Our tendency is to read materials from people just like us, from our same expression (or denomination) of Christianity, and from our own era; in short, from our own kind of people. In researching this book I was careful to read what was said about the post-Resurrection appearances of Jesus by men and women both; from Americans and from people of other places in the world; from Roman Catholics, Eastern Orthodox, Anglicans, Protestants, and Pentecostals; from middle-class, college-educated people like myself and by people whose culture is quite different; from people whose lives are quite comfortable and safe and from people who are in serious danger; and from people alive today and from people throughout Church history.

Reading the Bible by ourselves is quite important, but there is always the danger we will overemphasize some parts and neglect other parts. We need other Christians to point out to us what we, for whatever reason, may miss.

Third, it is often not until one experiences the fulfillment of a promise that one gains a fuller understanding of that original promise. For many years I had believed in the various gifts of the Holy Spirit of 1 Corinthians 12 simply because Scripture teaches them. It was not, however, until I came into Charismatic Renewal in 1973 that the various terms such as *speaking in tongues, word of knowledge, word of wisdom, discernment of spirits,* and the like, started to make sense to me.

Second-century apologists such as Irenaeus and Justin understood why many could not make the connection between the Old Testament and the life of Christ. Irenaeus wrote, "For every prophecy, before its fulfillment, is to men full of enigmas and ambiguities. But when the time has arrived, and the prediction has come to pass, then the prophecies have a clear and certain exposition."[14]

There is always, of course, more to know about God, but it

always must square with His written Word, the Scriptures. What Jesus unpacked on the road to Emmaus was Scripture itself. His message was core doctrine.

Observe how the preaching of the early church as recorded in the Book of Acts was basic doctrine about the person and work of Jesus Christ. Note, for example, Peter's Pentecost sermon and how it centers in Christ (Acts 2:14–39). In our witnessing to others we must be careful to point to Jesus, who He is, what He did, and the claim He has on each person's life. Personal sharing as to how all of this makes us feel, how our faith has given us a happier marriage, how we have experienced a miracle or two, and other kinds of personal experiences all have their place. These make people know that Christianity is real, contemporary, personal, and important. But without proclaiming Christ as the heart of the message we are not leading people to the one who alone can save them for all eternity. Jesus taught the Emmaus travelers core doctrine about Himself. We dare offer people nothing less.

As we watch Jesus challenge His companions on the walk to Emmaus, we must ask ourselves, if we were to walk along with Jesus on a similar journey, might He be warranted in calling us "foolish... and slow of heart to believe" (v. 25) either because of an overly skeptical mind or because of a mind that quickly wanders off to non-biblical ideas that tickle our fancy (see 2 Tim. 4:3)?

At the same time we should be encouraged that Jesus continues to accompany us as we walk the Emmaus roads of life. Malcolm Muggeridge (1903–1990), that most remarkable convert to the Christian faith, noted that "wherever the walk, and whoever the wayfarers, there is always this third presence ready to emerge from the shadows and fall in step along the dusty, stony way."[15]

Discussion Questions

1. John Wesley gave us four criteria for ascertaining spiritual truth: scripture, tradition, experience, and reason. How was the Wesleyan Quadrilateral applied in the Emmaus Road story?

2. Compare the experiences of the Emmaus road, the Damascus road (Acts 9), and the Bethsaida road (Mark 8:22–25).

3. How should we balance our attention between the journey and the destination?

2. The were either spiritually or physically blind
   b Jesus asked questions
   c. gave instructions

3. Keep centered on christ as you go forth to your destination

CHAPTER 3

BE KNOWN TO US IN THE
BREAKING OF THE BREAD

Luke 24:28–35

THE TRAVELERS HAVE now approached the village of Emmaus. The sun is about to set. To journey on further would be risky because brigands and highway robbers were regularly about at night. Cleopas and his fellow traveler, as good Jews, knew the importance and duty of hospitality, so they invite their friend to stay with them. We are not told whether this was their house or if this was an inn. *Selflessly,* they invite the stranger to stay in the safety of nighttime lodging with them so that this stranger would be safe. Perhaps *selfishly,* they have enjoyed continuing their conversation with the stranger, as they later admitted how their hearts burned within them as they talked (Luke 24:32). Might he have even more to say?

We are told in Scripture to be hospitable to the stranger because sometimes that stranger is an angel sent by God to bless, guide, encourage, exhort, or correct us (Heb. 13:2; 1 Pet. 4:9). We should take a broad understanding of the word *angel* here. The word literally means "messenger," and God can use both His orders of angels and His human beings in the role of messenger. I think of several times in my life when I later wondered if, in showing hospitality to someone I did not know, I had entertained such a messenger from God. Conversations with a number of my Christian friends have yielded similar stories about entertaining angels.

Similarly, there have been times when I have been invited to stay with someone where, certainly only by God's grace, I had been specially used as a messenger of God for their benefit.

Jesus "walked ahead as if he were going on" (Luke 24:28, NRSV). He had revealed to His companions God's plan as unfolded in the Scriptures. Now He was to reveal Himself as God made flesh.

He entered the building *only because He was invited in.* Many have commented on various artistic renderings of Revelation 3:20 where Jesus says, "Listen! I am standing at the door, knocking; if you hear my voice and open the door, I will come in to you and eat with you, and you with me" (NRSV). The door at which Jesus is standing is depicted as having no door knob on the outside. The door must be opened from the inside. Jesus will not enter uninvited.[1]

P. M. J. Stavinskas wisely notes:

> Jesus wants to be with us, to stay with us but we, like the disciples on the road to Emmaus, must ask him to do so. Let us resolve today to open our hearts so that they may burn with love as he explains the Scriptures and let us pray for the kind of eyes that can see Christ in the breaking of the bread. For then we will encounter him who is the fulfillment of all our hopes and dreams.[2]

Once Jesus has been invited into the life of a person, however, His desire is to establish ownership. He will not enter our house as a mere guest but only as landlord. What do we miss when we do not press Jesus to stay with us, and what do we miss when we do not obey Him? While the phrase "I love the Lord in my heart" is certainly wonderful, it is insufficient. He calls us to love Him with our minds, our wills, and our strengths as well (Mark 12:30).

Once the Emmaus travelers had invited the stranger into either their house or an inn, Jesus assumed the role of the head of the family. He did not merely sit at table with them. He presided at the meal, a rather extraordinary presumption, especially if this be their house (Luke 24:30).

At table Jesus "took bread, blessed and broke it, and gave it to them." This is exactly what He had done three days earlier in the Upper Room in inaugurating the Lord's Supper (Luke 22:14–23).[3] Cleopas and his fellow traveler suddenly recognized Jesus as He presided at this meal.

Had these two been present at the Last Supper? There is no reason to think it was just Jesus and the twelve apostles in the room. While Luke tells us that the apostles were with Him at the Last Supper (Luke 22:14), we are not told that it was *only* the apostles who were present. Jesus had just said He wanted to eat with His *disciples*, implying a larger number (v. 11). Jesus had spoken of a *large* room (v. 12), implying space was needed for more than Jesus and the twelve. We tend to think there were only Jesus and the twelve because we have often seen Leonardo Da Vinci's painting of the Last Supper in which there are only thirteen figures. By referring to "our group" (Luke 24:22, NRSV) Cleopas may be indicating that he was part of the circle just beyond that of the twelve. If that were the case, he and his fellow traveler may well have been present. If so, Jesus' gestures at table would immediately flash them back to the Upper Room.

Cleopas and his fellow traveler suddenly recognized the stranger was Jesus. "Their eyes were opened" (Luke 24:31). Fleming Rutledge notes that every time we see a passive verb (such as "were open") you know that God is at work.[4]

Some have tried to say that all that was going on was an evening meal. This is inadequate an explanation for two reasons.

First, Jesus' hidden identity was being revealed at significant moments in the forty-day post-Resurrection period in order to reveal important truths about what life in the church would be like after His Ascension. What is significant about having just a meal? People of every religion and none have had meals all throughout history. Jesus was revealed as He was presiding at a Communion service in the way He had presided at the Last Supper. William Dickson notes, "I just can't believe that Luke could have imagined his readers would have failed to see a clear and deliberate parallelism of expression and of meaning."[5]

Second, when we are told in Acts 2:42 four things to which the primitive church expectantly devoted themselves, "the breaking of the bread" is one of them. (The others are apostolic teaching, apostolic fellowship, and prayers.) We immediately grasp how central these three other acts were and are to the life of the church. Would eating a mere meal need to be added to the list to make it central? Why not add breathing and going for walks?

The phrase "breaking of the bread" does not just mean eating *a* meal; it means eating *the* meal, the Holy Communion. By choosing to make Jesus' identity known as He again presides at this sacrament, God the Father is saying to the church that Communion is central and highly important. Of course Jesus is with us always (Matt. 28:20), but Scripture tells us there are particular places where we can especially be certain of His presence. One of those is in the breaking of the bread. Robert Barron wisely observes that "the Eucharist is not a luxury, but a necessity, for without it, we would, in the spiritual sense, starve to death."[6]

N. T. Wright notes that there are but two places in the entire Bible where people eat and then find that their eyes are suddenly opened. In Genesis 3:6–7 Adam and Eve ate of the forbidden fruit and discovered they were naked. In Luke 24:30–31 the Emmaus walkers ate of the food offered by Jesus and discovered the stranger was the Christ.[7] We are invited by the biblical authors to see in this post-Resurrection appearance of Jesus a typological fulfillment, a reversal of the tragic situation of

having characteristics or traits in common

48

the Garden of Eden. One time of eating resulted in eyes being opened to their sin, shame, and estrangement from God. The other time of eating resulted in eyes being opened to recognize the risen Christ. Comments Arthur A. Just, Jr., "Just as Adam and Eve's eating of the forbidden fruit was the first meal of the fallen creation, so this meal at Emmaus is the first meal of the new creation on the first day of the week."[8]

Dane C. Ortlund suggests:

> When Adam and Eve were offered food by the serpent and ate, their eyes were opened and they knew good and evil. When the two disciples on the Emmaus road were offered food by the risen Jesus and ate, their eyes, too, were opened and they knew who their traveling companion was, that he had been raised, and that he was the focal point of all the Scriptures.[9]

There are several important truths that follow from this meal in Emmaus being a service of Holy Communion. First, from the very beginning of the church Holy Communion was observed at least weekly. Luke notes, "On the first day of the week, when we met to break bread" (Acts 20:7, NRSV). It has frequently been noted that John's Gospel has no narrative of the institution of the Lord's Supper. Bishop William Frey wisely notes, "John has no need to describe the Eucharistic action [in the Upper Room], since the 'breaking of bread' was already one of the distinguishing characteristics of the budding Christian community."[10] The Gospel of John was the last of the four Gospels to be written.[11] Frequent—at least weekly—observance of Holy Communion was already well established in the church. John Marsh adds, "It is far from fancy to think that John may well be making clear to Christians that it is with the risen and ascended, the glorified Christ that they have communion, on whom they feed, in the Eucharist."[12] This quote is notable because it comes not from a Roman Catholic or an Anglican but from a British Congregationalist theologian and sometime principal of an Oxford college.

Around the year AD 150—a mere sixty years or so after the death of the apostle John—a man named Justin (circa 100–circa 165) wrote a non-Christian friend describing what Christianity was all about. Justin, called "Justin Martyr" because he died for his Christian faith, told his friend, among other things, what Christian worship incorporates. Sunday worship was Holy Communion. There is no record in the history of the early church of a dispute about this, like we have about the Trinity or the divinity of Christ. There were no contending parties of weekly Communion and periodic Communion battling it out. Communion was conducted weekly in the early church, as we see noted in Justin and referenced in Acts 20. If we are to worship the way they did it in Bible times, we are to have Communion every week. There was no debate about this, nor should there be a debate about this now. Sunday worship the way they did it in Bible times is Communion every Sunday.

We have said that there are several important truths that follow from this meal in Emmaus being a service of Holy Communion. We just saw, first, from the beginning of the church Holy Communion was observed at least weekly. Second, there is a specific order to this service of Holy Communion. This is not surprising, because the Jewish worship the early Christians knew followed specific liturgical patterns. Justin outlined the order of service Christians used. It is the order liturgical churches follow to this day. Having such an order liberates people from being dependent on either the level of spiritual depth or of the whims of the local church's pastor, from the preferences and imbalances of the local congregation, and from the fads and prejudices of a given moment in time.

Daniel Eddy notes:

This order, this full, rich and balanced diet of the Eucharist has been at the center of who the Church is from the very beginning. The very earliest Christians did not yet have the New Testament.... They did not risk death because they were studying the written Word. They risked death with courage—with joy in their hearts, in fact—in order to gather together and have Holy Communion.[13]

In the words of Anglican liturgical scholar Gregory Dix:

At the heart of it all is the Eucharistic action, a thing of absolute simplicity—the taking, blessing, breaking and giving of bread and the taking, blessing and giving of a cup of wine and water, as these were first done with their new meaning by a young Jew before and after supper with His friends on the night before He died...So the four-action Shape of the Liturgy [the Offertory; the Consecration of the Communion elements; the Fraction, that is, the breaking of the bread; and the giving of Communion] was found by the end of the first century. He had told His friends to do this henceforward with the new meaning "for the anamnesis" [usually translated "for the remembrance"] of Him, and they have done it always since.[14]

Some people, particularly those who grew up in liturgical, sacramental churches but did not find Christ as Lord and Savior in them reject liturgical, sacramental worship because they have only encountered the liturgy in ways that seem spiritually dead. But we would assert that liturgy cannot be dead. The words of a particular service might be in conformity to Scripture or they might not be—they can be true or false—but liturgy itself cannot be dead. It is worship leaders and congregations of people that are alive or dead. So many have discovered how alive liturgy can be when they worship in a spiritually vibrant liturgical assembly.

I have been in worship settings that are intentionally anti-liturgical and have found some of these also to be dead experiences.

In the end, man is liturgical. That is, he is hard-wired for ritual and ceremony. Although many people use the word *ritual* to mean the actions expressed in ceremony, the word *ritual* properly refers to the words. Ceremony is the action expressing those words. They are intertwined and both are important. All of the truly important things in our lives are expressed with some form of traditional celebration: birth, education, marriage, death. All have their "liturgical" expressions. Daniel Eddy challenges us to attend the funeral of a police officer or firefighter and say that these "liturgies" are empty or unnecessary.[15]

We are creatures that cry out for ceremonial form, for liturgies to mark important times in the lives of individuals and the wider community. Why should the most important things we do—the worship of our Creator and Redeemer—be different? As Thomas Howard wrote:

> Ceremony assists us to cope with the otherwise unmanageable. Far from erecting a barrier between us and the truth, it ushers us closer in to the truth. It dramatizes the truth for us. Ceremony does what words alone cannot do. It carries us beyond the merely explicit, the expository, the verbal, the propositional, the cerebral, to the center where the Dance goes on.... To prohibit ceremony, or even to distrust it, and to reduce the worship of God Himself to the meager resources available to verbalism, is surely to have dealt Christendom a dolorous blow.[16]
> *grievous*

Sally Rowan comments, "There are times that ceremony itself gets us through dark days when any verbal reassurance is rejected."[17]

In describing weekly Communion according to a liturgical order Justin was not taking up a side in an ongoing debate, nor was he advocating something new. He was simply saying this is what Christians did as they worship. As a growing number of Christians today explore the documents of the first few centuries of the church and study both the theology and practice of those leaders discipled by the apostles or their immediate successors, they are wanting their churches to embrace what the early church did, including making Holy Communion, according to the historic order of service, the way they worship every Sunday.

Some people, however, dismiss all of this, saying, "This is Catholic." What do we say to this?

First, this is terribly prejudiced attitude. Is the objector saying that if Roman Catholics believe or do something it is automatically wrong and should, therefore, be dismissed? Are we so arrogant and bigoted as to believe we have nothing to learn from other Christian groups?

Second, there are groups as disparate as Anglican, Lutheran, the Disciples of Christ, and Plymouth Brethren who observe the Holy Communion every Sunday. As with infant baptism, weekly observance of Holy Communion is not Catholic versus Protestant, but Catholic and a number of Protestant groups versus some other Protestant groups. American theologian and journalist Martin Marty observed what he called the "Baptistification" of American Protestant Christianity in which the distinctives of Baptists, a small minority in the Protestant Reformation, have become seen as the norm for American Protestantism. As a result, many people, in contrasting Catholic and Protestant, allow just that one distinct expression of Protestantism to speak for the whole.[18]

One's question should not be, "Is this Catholic?" The real question is, "Is this what the primitive church—those closest to the teaching of Jesus and the Apostles—believed and did?" Mark P. Shea, an evangelical Christian who converted to Roman Catholicism, asks the question many such converts have asked in their journey to Anglicanism, Roman Catholicism, or Eastern Orthodoxy: "What about all these apparently unbiblical Catholic traditions?"[19] He notes that the earliest of church leaders, those whom God used to convert pagan Europe, Asia Minor, northern Africa, and Palestine to the gospel, whom God used to help discern which books should be included in the New Testament and whom God used to solve according to biblical orthodoxy the questions about the Trinity and the person of Christ, "believed a lot of [what to me, an evangelical, had been] rather questionable stuff."

We have said that there are several important truths that follow from this meal in Emmaus being a service of Holy Communion. We just saw, first, that from the beginning of the church Holy Communion was observed at least weekly, and second, there is a specific order to this service of Holy Communion. Now third, Holy Communion is much more than a mere memorial, that is, just thinking about what happened two thousand years ago but nothing more. The early church saw Communion as a means of grace, in some way beyond our ability to comprehend, a receiving of the body and blood of Jesus.

British Anglican evangelical Michael Green reminds us that we have a short Eucharistic prayer from the earliest Christian community, from the original Aramaic-speaking church: "Maranatha"! It means, "Our Lord, come!" (1 Cor. 16:22). Because the Lord was revealed in the breaking of the bread, because He had said, "This is my body, this is my blood," these first-generation Christians knew that when they met for Holy Communion, Christ would be present.[20] His presence was no more a mere in their hearts or in their recollections in Communion services than it was in Emmaus. In each case He was truly, literally, present.

Belief in Christ's presence in the Eucharistic elements is not a superstitious medieval corruption of what had originally been but a simple commemorative meal. Ignatius of Antioch, writing approximately AD 107, stated, "I have no taste for corruptible food nor for the pleasures of this life. I desire the bread of God, which is the flesh of Jesus Christ, who was of the seed of David; and for drink I desire his blood, which is love incorruptible."[21]

When it comes to the Holy Communion, Justin Martyr wrote:

> For we do not receive this food [his previous sentence names it "Eucharist"] as ordinary bread and as ordinary drink; but just as Jesus Christ our Savior became flesh through the word of God, and assumed flesh and blood for our salvation, so too we are taught that the food over which the prayer of thanksgiving, the word received from Christ, has been said, the food which nourishes our flesh and blood by assimilation is the flesh and blood of this Jesus who became flesh.[22]

Instead of unnecessarily repeating the account of the institution of Holy Communion from the accounts of Matthew, Mark, and Luke, the apostle John focused on what Jesus had previously taught about receiving His body and blood. Jesus had taught that people are to eat of His flesh if they are to have eternal life (John 6:48–71). His audience, good Jews utterly opposed to cannibalism, were shocked, angered, and, eventually, many of them walked out on Him. Jesus could have rescued the moment by simply stating, "You're misunderstanding me! I mean all of this *symbolically.*" He did not answer in such a way because He meant it in some physical, literal way. Christians, from the beginnings of the church, believed He meant what He said *literally.* In the Upper Room Jesus repeated this teaching: "This is my body" and "This is my blood" (Matt. 26:26, 28).

The opposition of some people to this teaching stems from unhelpful religious experiences in their formative years. Many former Roman Catholics testify they never heard the Bible taught at weekly mass, nor were they ever led to a personal relationship with Jesus. Episcopal renewal leader Everett L. ("Terry") Fullam frequently commented that the liturgical churches had done a good job sacramentalizing their people but not evangelizing them.[23] For many Protestants, what is believed to be the necessary correctives of the sixteenth-century reformers is still urgent, lest the evangelical faith again become corrupted. Some conclude from this, however, that good preaching is important, while receiving Communion weekly is either not important or an actual distraction.

However, such negative experiences do not demand we set Scripture and sacrament against each other. To believe Christ is truly present in the Communion elements—in a way we do not understand—is not Catholic as opposed to Protestant. Many Protestant groups believe Communion to be more than a mere memorial or the presence of Christ to be more than a mere spiritual one. The first great leader of the Protestant Reformation, Martin Luther, certainly did.

Because of differences between Luther and Swiss reformer Huldrych Zwingli over the real (and not symbolic or spiritual) presence of Christ in the Communion, Philipp I of Hesse held what is now called the Marburg Colloquy in October of 1529. Philipp wished to unite the various Protestant states in a political alliance against the armies of Roman Catholic states and saw theological differences to be an impediment. Although consensus was reached on many points, Luther held the consecrated bread and wine were united to the body and blood of Christ, whereas Zwingli considered the Communion elements to be only symbolic. At the colloquy Luther wrote in chalk on the velvet cloth covering a table the words *Hoc Est Corpus Meum* (in English, "This is my body.")

If sacramentalizing without evangelizing is a danger, the emphasizing of knowledge of the propositional truths of the faith to the virtual exclusion of objective sacramental grace is a danger as well. Presbyterian pastor Philip J. Lee warns that "the enemy of true religion today is a different enemy than that facing the Protestant reformers. Calvin's principal foe might well have been, as he apprehended it, Roman idolatry (the false materializing of the spiritual). The arch foe today, however, is Protestant Gnosticism (the false spiritualizing of the material)."[24]

Gnosticism was perhaps the chief spiritual opponent of early Christianity. Many scholars believe that the New Testament book of Colossians (among others) was written to oppose Gnostic ideas. Early church father Irenaeus, a student of Polycarp, who was a disciple of the apostle John, wrote his major work, *Against Heresies*, as a refutation of Gnosticism. Although there were various Gnostic groups, they had in common the belief that the physical world was inherently evil, the creation of a lesser and evil God. Salvation was through learning spiritual knowledge so that one could be delivered from the evil physical creation. Given that physical things are evil, there was no possibility that God could take a material body in Christ. Similarly, there was no way that such physical things as the sacraments could be of help.

Could opposition to the beliefs of objective grace and of Christ's presence in consecrated Communion elements be a failure to grasp a mystery, that is, something that is neither merely rational nor irrational but *suprarational*? Rationalist Christians—both liberal and fundamentalist—have challenged me, "How could God, in some way or other, inhabit bread and wine? It makes no sense." I would answer, How could God, in some way or other, inhabit flesh, blood, and bones? Yet, that is exactly what happened in the Incarnation. There, the second person of the divine Trinity, God who is Spirit, became human—flesh, blood, and bones (John 1:1–14). If you reject the Incarnation, you are a heretic and not a Christian. So, if God can inhabit flesh, why could He not inhabit the elements of Communion?

A supernatural God does supernatural things. A God who created the material world and called it good uses His created order as ways to dispense not just thoughts but blessings. Philip Lee's point is that Protestants are sometimes more Gnostic than they are biblical.

Why is this important? If Holy Communion is merely a

memorial, just a visual aid to remind us of events long ago when Christ died in our place for our sins, then much of the work of obtaining the blessing at a Communion service is on us. We have to do the mental heavy lifting to remind us what these elements are about. But isn't it true that the times when we need God's grace the most—when we are tired, sick, upset, troubled in faith—we are least able to do that heavy lifting? I'm so glad that when I'm really in need of divine blessing, of sovereign grace, God is there in a way far more than I can make happen by my recollecting of what these Communion elements (merely) symbolize. Or, stated in a very different way, when I'm hungry and go to a restaurant, I need a meal, not just a menu. When I am sick I may not appreciate the meal in the way I would when I was healthy, but when I am sick I need its nutritional value all the more. In some way, beyond our abilities to understand the depth of mystery, we are to feed on His body and blood more than just symbolically.

We think of time as linear only, while God, who does interact with us in linear time, is eternal, where time is not existent. Or, put another way, God exists where all times occur at once. Because of how think of time we, therefore, tend to think of Holy Communion mostly as something done "way back then," which we do in remembrance. To a much lesser degree we think of Communion's eschatological dimension, something we do "until He comes again," a foretaste of the Messianic banquet in heaven.[25] Unless we have been given good Eucharistic teaching based on the biblical concept of time-in-eternity, we do not think of Communion as having meaning for us today except as a reminder of the past and, secondarily, as a pointer to the future.

Our English language does not help us here. When Jesus said, "Do this in memory of me" (Luke 22:19) He meant much more than what we think of when we hear that word *memory*. Unfortunately, the word *anamnesis* is translated as "memory" when it means so very much more. In ancient Greek the word anamnesis is defined as "a calling to mind" or (significantly) a "reminder to the gods" or (perhaps even more significantly) "a memorial sacrifice." The same word is used in the Greek version of the Torah at Numbers 10:10, where it is used in the context of sacrifices and burnt offerings. Thus the word itself carries and implies not merely human recollection, but the eternal memory of God and the blood sacrifices offered to Him by the commandments of the Law.[26]

Gregory Dix discussed the deep meaning of *anamnesis* and the difficulty of a fully accurate translation into English in his work *The Shape of the Liturgy*:

> It is not quite easy to represent accurately in English, words like "remembrance" or "memorial" having for us a connotation of something itself absent, which is only mentally recollected. But in the scriptures both of the Old and New Testament, anamnesis, and the cognate verb have the sense of "re-calling" or "re-presenting" before God an event in the past, so that it becomes here and now operative by its effects.
>
> It is in this active sense, therefore, of "re-calling" or "re-presenting" before God (but, of course, not re-sacrificing) the sacrifice of Christ, and thus making it here and now operative by its effects in the communicants, that the Eucharist is regarded both by the New Testament and by second century church leaders as the anamnesis of the passion, or of the passion and resurrection combined.[27]

Anamnesis means not the ephemeral and fallible memory of man but the eternal reality (much more "real" than the modern notion of "memorial") which is the mind of the living God. As the Orthodox theologian Alexander Schmemann, wrote:

> Here we should recall that in the biblical, Old Testament teaching on God, the term memory refers to the attentiveness of God to his creation, the power of divine providential love through which God "holds" the world and gives it life, so that life itself can be termed abiding in the memory of God, and death the falling out of this memory. In other words, memory, like everything else in God is real, it is that life that he grants, that God "remembers"; it is the eternal overcoming of the nothing out of which God called us into his wonderful light.[28]

Does this mean we should believe in transubstantiation? I believe the answer is no. Transubstantiation is a medieval attempt to explain, using philosophical categories and language, *how* Christ is truly present in the Communion elements. It has been a doctrine of the Roman Catholic Church since 1215 but is not a doctrine of other sacramental churches. Anglican Bishop John Cosin (1594–1672), in agreement with the practice of the church for a thousand years, preferred to keep the mystery less keenly defined:

> As to the manner of the presence of the body and blood of our Lord in the blessed Sacrament, we that are Protestant and reformed according to the ancient Catholic Church, do not search into the manner of it with perplexing inquiries; but after the example of the primitive and purest Church of Christ, we leave it to the power and wisdom of our Lord, yielding a full and unfeigned assent to his words.[29]

I believe the church should ensure its Sunday worship follows the liturgical pattern of sacramental worship the early church knew and practiced, along with the early church's theological understanding of sacrament.

If we are correct in believing this meal in Emmaus is a

Eucharist, then it tells us the resurrection of Jesus means the kingdom of God is here. Jesus had said at the Last Supper He would not partake of it again until it is fulfilled in the kingdom of God (Luke 22:16), and here He is partaking. While the kingdom will not be truly and completely fulfilled until the new heaven and new earth are inaugurated and we sit down to the marriage supper of the Lamb (Rev. 19:9; 21:1), the kingdom has broken in now because of the atoning work and bodily resurrection of Jesus. No wonder the church gathered to worship on Sunday, the day of the new creation, a week after the day the creation began, the eschatological eighth day.

After this Communion service was over Jesus "vanished from their sight" (Luke 24:31). If His journeying with them had been subtle, His taking their leave was dramatic. We see, and will see in subsequent post-Resurrection appearances, how Jesus' resurrection body is similar, yet different. He is not a ghost because He can walk, eat, and talk. Yet His body is different because it can suddenly disappear, and, as we will see, immediately reappear seven miles away in Jerusalem. Part of our future hope in Christ is that He will transform our humble bodies so that they may be conformed to the body of His glory (Phil. 3:21).

I believe there are at least three reasons why Jesus left so immediately, so supernaturally.

First is to demonstrate that while God regularly gives spiritual mountain-top experiences, they are not designed to last long. As much as Peter had wished to build booths on the Mount of Transfiguration to keep that incredible experience going, God rebuked him for this desire and ended the moment (Luke 9:33–35). In our first chapter we saw that Mary Magdalene could touch the risen Christ but not hold Him in the sense of keeping Him from leaving (John 20:17). While there are many Christians who need to discover the incredible truth that God wishes to encounter them incredibly and personally, there are many other Christians who need to base their faith on the truth of the

Gospel, not on the exhilaration of spiritual experiences. Just as Mary Magdalene was not allowed to prolong the encounter with Jesus but instead was instructed to tell the others, so, too, the Emmaus travelers could not remain with Jesus at the place of the Communion meal but left in haste to tell the others in Jerusalem.

A second reason Jesus left immediately and supernaturally is to underscore the fact He would not be on Earth with them much longer. But, after His Ascension there would be ways in which He would especially be present. Christians can meet Him regularly at the Holy Communion, as well as in Scripture and the church community.

A third reason Jesus left immediately and supernaturally is to demonstrate the supernatural nature of the Resurrection body. Today, in our individual and corporate walk with the Lord, God works both subtly and dramatically, both naturally and supernaturally. While we may have our preferences in how He works in our lives, it is not our place to tell God how to conduct His business.

As one who regularly leads services of Christian healing in a whole variety of churches I sometimes encounter people who tell me that they would like to be healed by God giving wisdom to their doctors and efficacy to their medicines. Others consent to being prayed with, "but in a quiet and dignified manner." Indeed, God often works those ways. But I'm saddened when what's behind those statements is the attitude, "I'd really prefer not to have a dramatic healing." In trying to limit God in such a way they may well miss the day of God's visitation.

On other occasions, in quite different churches, I have been told by attendees that they expected God to do something in a most dramatic way because "it's the way He works!" Once I was praying for an individual who had a serious skin condition. As I prayed with her I felt God was giving me a word of knowledge (1 Cor. 12:8) that she was allergic to a food she was fond of and this food was causing her skin problem. I told her that and suggested she contact an allergist for tests. I added that I believed God was saying that as she identified the problem food and eliminated it from her diet her skin would clear up. She was furious! She wanted something dramatic and instantaneous, something that would awe her and all around her. (She was by no means the first person in history to demand that God does His healing in dramatic ways. Refer to the story of Naaman, the Syrian leper, in 2 Kings 5.) She was adamant that she would *never* go get an allergy test. I believe she, too, missed what God was trying to do for her.

God invites us to pray, in fact, to go boldly to the throne of grace (Heb. 4:16) and make our needs known as we perceive them. But we would be wise to let God act the way He chooses! Don't you think He knows more than we do?

The two Emmaus travelers, immediately after Jesus' vanishing, shared how their hearts were burning within them as the stranger now known to be Jesus opened up the Scriptures (Luke 24:32). We can compare this to the experience of so many throughout the centuries, including Anglican priest and founder of Methodism John Wesley (1703–1791), whose heart "was strangely warmed" as he heard the preface of Luther's commentary on the Book of Romans being read.

The hearts of the Emmaus travelers were warmed for at least two reasons. First, they were discussing godly things. To those who love God, such discussions are pleasing. Second, they were sharing personally and intimately with the Lord of the universe, even though they did not know it. John Maxwell points out that people don't care how much you know until they know how much you care, and it was clear this stranger cared. Jesus tells us He will be with us always (Matt. 28:20). T. S. Eliot's question in "The Waste Land"—"Who is the third who walks always beside you?"—should make us realize we are always on an Emmaus journey of spiritual growth, and Jesus is always walking with us to guide us.[30]

We have been noticing that Jesus' forty-day post-Resurrection period demonstrated what life in the church would be like. With Mary Magdalene we saw that church life, among other things, centers in a personal relationship with Jesus. With the two Emmaus travelers we see that church life, among other things, centers in Scripture and Holy Communion. And both must be kept together. Without the sacrament, a mere biblicism becomes wooden. Without Scripture, sacraments can become superstitions. William Dickson notes, "The sacraments simply cannot be detached from the ministry of the Word which ministry informs and instructs the people of God about the nature and the meaning of our sacramental experience."[31] In the following chapters we'll discover more.

It was late, Cleopas and his companion were tired, the road was dangerous, but they felt compelled to go back to Jerusalem to tell others of their group what had just happened. Now they have it right. Some have argued that the Emmaus travelers' journey was simply two people going home after the Passover. Others, however, have suggested that if they were indeed part of the company of disciples, their going away from Jerusalem was indicative of their status as "failed disciples."[32] They do not see Jesus until He appears in the Eucharist "because their lives are misdirected."[33] It is through the Eucharist that they saw the Lord. Francis J. Moloney notes, "Jesus drew the disciples who had lost their way at Emmaus back to Jerusalem through a Eucharistic table."[34]

This Communion service in Emmaus is the culmination of what Jesus had been teaching them along the way. They had heard the words, and it had moved them but they did not understand it. It was words—true words—but just words. Because Christianity is not Gnostic, nor is it about Platonic ideas but about reality incarnate, it was necessary for Jesus to repeat "the great gestures of the Last Supper... [to] present for them again the sacrifice of the cross, the act by which he offered his own body as reparation for the sins of the world."[35] He did not just need to talk about it; He needed to do it. He didn't just need to do some shallow ceremony, some mere memorial reminder. He needed to feed them with His very body and blood, even though that body and blood were sitting before them.

And with all of that, they ran back to Jerusalem. How could they not? When anyone encounters the Lord, he or she cannot help but share. Cleopas and his companion returned to Jerusalem right away (Luke 24:33). B. W. "Pete" Wait III comments, "The road was no less dangerous than when they felt compelled to stop for the night, but now they felt a need stronger than their personal safety to return and testify to their risen Lord."[36] They found the others gathered. This was the evening of the first Easter Day. It is the time, then, described in John 20:19–23. This is the subject of our next chapter.

The whole Emmaus experience parallels what Christians following the historic way of worship do every Sunday:

> As many commentators have pointed out over the centuries, this narrative is a symbolic presentation of the liturgy. We come to Mass, like these two disciples, often walking in the wrong direction. This is why we beg, in the Kyrie Eleison, for the forgiveness of sins. But Jesus, with infinite patience, comes to join us, opening up for us the meaning of the Scriptures, showing us once again how the Old Testament story culminates in and centers around him. This is the liturgy of the Word. Though this illumination is necessary, it is not sufficient. We don't fully understand who Jesus is until we sit down with him at the sacred sacrificial banquet that makes present his saving cross. In the liturgy of the Eucharist, in the breaking of the bread and the drinking of the cup, we see him in his real presence. Finally, having seen, we move, presumably in a more correct direction.[37]

Leander Harding describes it this way:

> First, the "stranger" walks with Cleopas and his companion towards Emmaus, unfolding the Scriptures to them. This parallels the first half of the liturgy, the "Ministry of the Word," with Scripture read and taught. Second, the stranger sits at table with them and becomes known as Jesus as He "breaks bread," that is, celebrates Communion. This parallels the second half of the liturgy, the "Ministry of the Sacrament." Then, the two run back to Jerusalem to tell the others. This parallels our being sent forth for witness and service. In the Anglican tradition this is expressed in a post-Eucharistic prayer which includes the words, "...send us out to do the work you have given us to do..." and in the dismissal, "Go in peace to love and serve the Lord" (*Book of Common Prayer*, page 366).[38]

We started the previous chapter by noting two of Luke's favorite topics are a journey and a meal and that this passage has both. A meal (unless it's fast food consumed in the car) involves stopping. A journey involves going. As we will later see, the disciples of Jesus were first to stop (wait in Jerusalem for the coming of the Holy Spirit) and then to go (make disciples of all nations). Our Christian discipleship, too, involves both taking time to stop (to be replenished by Word, sacrament, and prayer, and to enjoy precious moments with the Lord right now as they occur) and then taking time to go do the work He's given us to do.

Each of the post-Resurrection appearances of Jesus teaches us something about what the church would be like after Jesus' Ascension and what the church should be like today. In the appearance on the road to Emmaus (Luke 24:13–35) He is trying to tell us that both Scripture and Holy Communion are to be front and center in the life of the church.

To Protestants Jesus is saying that Holy Communion is to be celebrated at least weekly and to be seen as His body and blood, not just as a memorial meal to a past event. To Catholics Jesus is saying that church is not just having the mass, or a mass with but a brief homily, but it is to teach Scripture in depth and at length.

Discussion Questions

1. If the Eucharist is a sacrament and a sacrament is an efficacious means of grace, how would you explain this to someone who doesn't speak "churchese"?

2. In Communion what is the difference between remembering Jesus and recalling things you have learned about Jesus?

3. Can a sacrament bring a past encounter into your present experience? How about a future encounter, such as the marriage feast of the Lamb?

CHAPTER 4

BEHIND A LOCKED DOOR

Luke 24:33–43; John 20:19–25

JESUS HAD ABRUPTLY disappeared from Emmaus (Luke 24:31) and, though highway robbers frequented the roads at night, Cleopas and his companion immediately headed back to Jerusalem to a gathering of other believers. We could assume that, unlike their leisurely pace to Emmaus, they ran back to Jerusalem because they could not wait to tell the others the exciting news that Jesus had risen from the dead (Luke 24:33).

Their fidelity in witnessing to this incredible news was amply rewarded. They got to see the risen Christ a second time. Too often those of us who have been blessed by a special day of visitation from our Lord dwell on that event to the point where we do not expect Him to come in a powerful way ever again.

When they got to Jerusalem they found a core of Christian believers meeting together, ten apostles and companions. They, too, had heard the news of Jesus' resurrection, and they told how He had appeared to Simon.

A seeming problem emerges in the evangelists' telling of the story. We are told in John 20:24 that Thomas was not with this core group, and, of course, Judas was gone, meaning there were only ten apostles and their companions, not literally eleven, as we read in Luke 24:33. Some Bible scholars suggest that the phrase "the eleven" is a general term for the apostles remaining after Judas' betrayal of Jesus and not a literal head count. As a parallel to this, sometimes in the early days of radio there would be programs called *The Hour of [This or That]*, even though the shows lasted only fifteen or thirty minutes. We call our town baseball team "the local nine," even though the squad numbers several more. Therefore, we need not think that Scripture is erroneous for using the term eleven to mean ten people. It is how we often speak.

Jesus would soon appear to this frightened group. It is to this next post-Resurrection appearance we must now turn our attention.

It was Easter Sunday evening. John twice lets us know Easter is the first day of the week, first when Jesus appeared to Mary Magdalene (John 20:1) and second at the end of the day when He appeared to a number of disciples (John 20:19). N. T. Wright tells us to pay special attention when John says something twice.[1] Similarly, Jesus often used the repetitive phrase, "Verily, verily" (or, "Truly, truly"), to note that what He was to say was of particular importance.

We saw in our last chapter that New Testament worship is *sacramental* worship with Communion observed at least weekly, that it is liturgical worship following a set order, and that Communion is more than a mere memorial. Now we need to see how New Testament worship is *Sunday* worship.

Luke notes it was *on the first day of the week* they met "to break bread" (Acts 20:7). Paul tells the Corinthians to set aside money on the first day of the week, implying that is when the community met for worship (1 Cor. 16:2). John received a revelation "on the Lord's day," that is, the special day of Jesus, the Lord, the day He rose (Rev. 1:10).

From the very beginning of the church, Christians worshiped God-in-Christ on Sunday. While we certainly can and should worship God every day, (Friday night and) Saturday is no longer the principal time of worship for Christians. Because they were Jews, members of the primitive church continued to meet in the temple and in the synagogue on the Jewish Sabbath while gathering on Sunday for Communion. But within a few decades, believers in Jesus were no longer welcomed in those places, and Gentiles were coming to faith in Christ, leaving all of them with Sunday worship only.

At the end of the first century, with John the Apostle still alive, Ignatius of Antioch wrote to the Magnesian Christians that Christians are "no longer living for the [Saturday] Sabbath, but for the Lord's Day on which life dawned for us through him and his death" (Magnesians 9:1).[2]

Christ inaugurated the new covenant and, with it, new observances. Sunday is, indeed, the Lord's Day. On this day He rose from the dead. While it is the first day of the week, it is also the eighth day, the eschatological day, the day of the new covenant. Just as creation began on day one, God's new creation begins on the second day one, which is Sunday.

The disciples were afraid. Ten of the eleven remaining apostles had fled. Except for John, they were not present at the cross. Now they were huddled behind locked doors. Would the same combination of religious and civil authorities that crucified Jesus now come for them?

To their credit, they did not run away, but they stayed in town and met together. Woody Allen is considered the author of the popular quote, "Eighty percent of success is showing up." We may not understand everything the Christian faith teaches, and we certainly know how far short we fall from godly discipleship, but if we are actively in the game—through prayer, Bible study, corporate worship, receiving Holy Communion, and active fellowship with other believers—we give God room to move in us, through us, and for us. As a sailor friend of mine puts it, "You can't let the wind fill your sails and propel your boat if you are anchored in the harbor. You've got to do your part for the wind to do its."

There was excitement as evidence began to mount that the Lord was alive. The ten and their companions were discussing how Jesus had appeared to Peter (Luke 24:33–35). Though Paul also references Peter's encounter with the risen Lord (1 Cor. 15:5), there are no details provided. Mary Magdalene had already told them Jesus had appeared to her (John 20:18). The Emmaus travelers arrived to share their story as well. They, too, had heard the experience of "some women of our group" that morning (Luke 24:22–23, NRSV).

Yet, despite all of this, the experience of the ten was that "in their joy they were disbelieving and still wondering" (Luke 24:41). Why this ambivalence?

First, it is possible to be overwhelmed with news that is so incredibly good as to believe and doubt at the same time. This is why some people say, "Pinch me, I must be dreaming."

Second, just because God can and often does work supernaturally, we wonder, is He actually at work *this time*? While many of us have heard stories of the Lord miraculously saving those who should have perished in the capsizing of a boat, sometimes Christians drown. While the apostles had seen signs and wonders before, was God doing something now? It seemed so, but was He really?

Third, we can "sort of believe." We can be in that fuzzy area between true belief and true doubt. I find in the healing ministry people will ask me to pray that God would give greater efficacy to their medicines and give greater wisdom to their medical providers but are much less trusting that God could sovereignly take the illness away. Perhaps those gathered here would expect "something wonderful" might happen, but not the actual, literal presence of the Lord Jesus Himself in His resurrection body.[3]

Was this figure suddenly standing before them truly Jesus, or was this an apparition? The stories of restoration to life we have already cited were resuscitations to the state these people had previously been in. Now here is an unknown someone standing in their midst, having appeared inside a locked room, not just resuscitated but in a body of a different kind.

Fourth, it is not unusual for Christians in one breath to testify to incredible blessings the Lord has recently performed in our lives while in the next breath speak of fears we have that some other difficulty we are facing will turn out badly. We struggle to believe that the Lord who acted powerfully one time could act similarly once again. Sally Rowan reminded me that Elijah was like that. He triumphed over the priests of Ba'al, proving Yahweh was powerful and Ba'al non-existent (1 Kings 18), but immediately fled for fear of Jezebel (1 Kings 19:1–3).[4] Sometimes we need other believers to remind us yet again that God is not limited either in scope or in quantity in His acting on our behalf.

Those who were known to be the inner core of Jesus' followers were in great danger, and it is not faithless to acknowledge this. Yes, Peter was soon to be miraculously delivered from prison (Acts 12:3–11), but James would be martyred (Acts 12:1–2). There is no evidence that Peter was more godly than James. We are to have faith but not foolishness. Sometimes fear is the realistic acknowledgment that some people are truly out to get us! The apostles might be thinking that at any moment Roman soldiers would burst in and kill them.

Fifth, it is still pre-Pentecost. Long-time United Methodist renewal leader Harry Camp reminded me that they could not evidence the fruit of the Spirit because the transforming power of the Holy Spirit had not yet fallen upon them, as would soon happen on Pentecost.[5]

To their credit, Jesus' followers stayed in Jerusalem, and, also to their credit, they met together (or at least stayed hidden together). There is a place for the individual in Christianity. A person must personally come to the Lord to be saved. No one can be saved on our behalf. Nor are we so to lean on the community that we have no individual discipleship. But we in America so overemphasize the individual nature of our relationship with the Lord that we often underemphasize the corporate. We are to meet together (Heb. 10:25).

How do we know we need to be vitally part of the church? First, Jesus came to establish God's new *kingdom* of believers.

Second, in order for our corporate relationship with God and with one another to work, there needs to be structure. Therefore, God set up the church and a hierarchy in it. Three of the epistles (1 Tim., 2 Tim., and Titus) speak of the qualifications of orders of ministry leaders in Christ's church.

When Paul talks about the gifts of the Spirit the first thing he says is, "Now you are the body of Christ," and only then does he add, "and individually members of it" (1 Cor. 12:27). Because no one has all the gifts of the Spirit, we need each other. No one can go solo as a Christian, saying to those with other gifts, "I have no need of you" (1 Cor. 12:14–26). God calls us to be individual disciples *in the fellowship of the visible, organized church.*

Ted Schroder illustrates this point well:

> Arthur McKinstry who was the father of one of my congregants in Orange Park, and former Episcopal Bishop of Delaware, told me about a meeting he had with horticulturist Henry Francis DuPont of Winterthur during World War 2. He nominally belonged to the Episcopal Church but was not much of a churchgoer. He told McKinstry that he didn't feel that the church was necessary for him, and that he could be a good person without it. McKinstry said that if that was the case then he should call up President Roosevelt and tell him to disband the armed forces. DuPont was startled, and asked why? McKinstry said, "We don't need the army to fight

the war. Just arm each individual citizen and let him get on with the job of fighting Hitler in his own way."[6]

DuPont took his point. It's about individual disciples and it's about the church community.

Into this fearful community of believers, huddled behind a locked door, Jesus came (John 20:19). He had appeared to Mary Magdalene, to Peter, and to Cleopas and companion, but now He came to a group. Bonnell Spencer notes that the fact of the Resurrection "does not rest solely on the claim of certain individuals that somewhere, off by themselves, they had an esoteric contact with the Risen Christ. Such a claim might have been open to the charge that it was the product of self-hypnosis or self-deception.... The authority to which He appeals and through which He manifests Himself is the corporate witness of the faithful."[7] Later He would appear to over five hundred. When Paul adds, "most of whom are still alive" (1 Cor. 15:6), he is encouraging, perhaps daring, his listeners to go check it out for themselves: "You don't have to take just my word for it. I am not making this up."

Just as with our Lord's appearance to Mary Magdalene, to the Emmaus travelers and later to the disciples by the lake, we discover there are similarities and dissimilarities between the pre- and the post-Resurrection bodies of Jesus. On the one hand, He can immediately translate from Emmaus to Jerusalem and appear suddenly behind a locked door. On the other hand, He can speak and eat, and He is an individual, not some mere spirit soon to be absorbed into an undifferentiated, cosmic oneness. He is different enough from before His passion so as not to be immediately recognized, but, when God provides, there is no doubt it is He.[8]

Jesus noted their confusion and their fear about what they were seeing. He sought to show them it was He and that He had a body, albeit a new, resurrection one (Luke 24:39–40; John 20:20). They thought He might be a ghost (Luke 24:37).[9] There was a

Jewish folk belief at that time that ghosts could not eat, so to underscore the point that He was truly physical, He requested something to eat. Frederick Denison Maurice asserted, "Nothing clears our minds of the phantoms that are always floating between earth and heaven—not really approaching either—like this simple teaching."[10] The ancient world had no difficulty in believing in ghosts. What they were not expecting was a bodily resurrection, no matter how many times Jesus had taught on this subject.

Christianity teaches the resurrection of the body, not the mere immortality of the soul. Unlike Greek religion, unlike oriental religions, unlike many New Age groups today, Christianity does not deem the body to be a prison trapping the soul. We are corrupted because of sin, not because of physicality. God saw that His creation was "good" (Gen. 1:12, 18, 21, 25).

Those present were learning about what a resurrection body is like. Paul would later expand on this in 1 Corinthians 15:35–49, telling his readers they, too, would have such bodies.[11]

The risen Christ still bore the marks of His wounds (Luke 24:40; John 20:20, 27). More, He invited them to gaze on His wounds and even touch them. Some people wonder about this: Shouldn't the risen Christ have been perfect, that is, free from those marks? Why did He yet bear them?

He bore these marks, first, to prove to them it was really He, Jesus, the same one who had received those marks on Calvary just a few days previously. Jesus told them, "Look at my hands and my feet; see that it is I myself" (Luke 24:39). Jesus invited Thomas to see His hands and place his hand in Jesus' side (John 20:26–27) to prove to Thomas the reality of the Resurrection. Ignatius of Antioch, writing around AD 100, said, "The risen Christ was the very one who had been crucified."[12] It will soon be *this* Jesus that will ascended to heaven, and it is *this* Jesus Who will someday return, visibly, physically at His second coming (Acts 1:10–11). The body of Jesus during His time on Earth from His birth until

His being lain in the tomb is now His resurrection body. It is a transformed body, *but is not a different body*. Nowhere does Scripture teach three bodies for Jesus: one for His life on Earth, a second for the forty-day post-Resurrection period, and a third for His ascended state in heaven.

Second, to deny the wound marks on the ascended body of Jesus is to misunderstand what is being said. On several occasions when discussing the wound marks on the ascended Jesus people have told me this could not be, because nothing imperfect is allowed in heaven, including physical imperfections. If the wound marks of Jesus still hurt, it would be those hurts that would not be allowed in heaven. But think of the marks, rather, as ribbons or medals on a soldier's uniform. These marks are reminders to all of the glory of Jesus' obedience unto death on the cross for our sakes. Jesus' wound marks are, for Him and for us, not marks of imperfection, but rather the opposite—marks of perfection. They are visible reminders of the greatest love that life has ever known.

Some churches, alongside the crucifix and the empty cross, place a "Christus Rex," a carving of the exalted Christ wearing a crown and priestly vestments, reigning in glory from the cross, still bearing the wounds from Good Friday. Charles Wesley, probably the greatest and most prolific hymn writer who ever lived, wrote a second-coming hymn, usually sung during Advent, entitled, "Lo! He Comes with Clouds Descending." One of those verses refers to the returning Christ, bearing the wound marks of glory from Good Friday:

> Those dear tokens of his passion
> Still his dazzling body bears,
> Cause of endless exultation
> To his ransomed worshippers:
> With what rapture, with what rapture, with what
>   rapture

Gaze we on those glorious scars.

The message soon to be preached by the apostles would include the fact of Christ dying for our sins. The risen and ascended Christ even now bears those marks because they remind the watching universe what He did, dying in our place for our sins. John's apocalyptic vision includes seeing "a Lamb standing as if it had been slain" (Rev. 5:6). Some translations of Revelation 13:8 speak of the Book of Life that belongs to the Lamb slain "from the foundation of the world" (NRSV). How could John know the Lamb "had been slain" unless it bore some mark of that slaying? Inasmuch as the marks of that slaying were the marks of crucifixion, we can conclude that the Lamb bears these marks in heaven.

He bore these marks, third, to teach the disciples and us that God *transforms, not annihilates*, the created, material order. God called the creation good, and Christ's resurrected state is neither as a revivification of His old body nor as a non-material ghost but as a body made perfect, fit for heaven. Raised to our resurrection bodies, we Christians will still have our old characteristics, but they will be perfected. As with other examples of physicality (walking, talking, taking food) the wound marks demonstrate "the body is real as well as the spirit. The body is redeemed from death as well as the spirit."[13]

Patrick Henry Reardon trumpets the truth that "the Paschal mystery is not about the death and resurrection of a god," although Jesus was and is a member of the Godhead. Rather, "it is as a human being that Jesus was raised from the dead."[14] We, too, will rise, *and with resurrection bodies*.

Edgar Gardner Murphy stressed the continuity between Christ's divine and human natures, and between His pre-Resurrection and post-Resurrection ministries:

> The divine Christ taking the flesh not only to die to it but
> save it, not only to nail it to the cross but to raise it from
> the tomb, has made us to feel the bond of all seasons in
> the soul, has shown the marks of kinship between every
> past and every future, between even the immortal and
> the earthly.[15]

We might add, and between the Eden of Genesis and the City
of God of Revelation.[16]

He bore these marks, fourth, to teach the disciples and us that
Christians must focus on all aspects of our Lord's ministry, not
just certain ones we prefer.

> There are those who wish to wallow in Lent, stuck in
> the "woe is me, I am unworthy, Jesus died for our sins"
> without ever celebrating grace. And there are those who
> only want to celebrate—who do not want to acknowledge
> sin or confront pain. Jesus Christ challenges us to live in
> the tension between the two. Life is full of now and not
> yet. Advent and Christmas. Lent and Easter. Crucifixion
> and resurrection.[17]

Our true Easter joy should not blind us to the reality that there
is still pain in life. He has risen, but He has not yet returned to
make the new heaven and earth. Noting the wound marks in the
risen Christ ensures our Easter joy is grounded in gospel truth,
not in denial.

He bore these marks, fifth, because when He ascends and
offers in person the atoning sacrifice of His very self to God the
Father, the marks are an outward sign of that sacrifice. John of
Fidanza (1221–1274), known to us today as St. Bonaventure, the
Franciscan theologian of the thirteenth century, said that Jesus
ascended in part "so that, seated at the right hand of Majesty,
he might show to the glorious face of his Father the scars of the
wounds which he suffered for us."[18]

Some might see an inconsistency between Jesus' coming through a locked door to be with the disciples in Jerusalem and His knocking outside the fast-closed door of Revelation 3:20. Why doesn't He just come through the door in the second instance? Simply because the disciples in Jerusalem wanted Him in their midst, though they wondered how this might happen, while the inference in the Book of Revelation is the Christians in Laodicea were lukewarm (Rev. 3:16) and really did not want Jesus at the center of their lives. While Jesus will make every effort to come to those who want Him, despite their fears, He will not barge in where He is not welcome. Harry Camp notes John 20:19 is a historical event to be pondered, while Revelation 3:20 is a metaphor to be explored.[19]

I wonder what the ten must have been thinking as Jesus came into their midst. To the degree they believed He was their Lord they were overjoyed, but might they have wondered what He would do to them? Except for John, none of them had had an exemplary end of Holy Week. Peter denied knowing Jesus, and, except for John, none was at the cross. What would Jesus say to these who had vowed to follow Him but had turned and run? Would He curse them and tell them He was going to start a new community with others in the lead?

Not at all! What Jesus did was to bless them. The first thing Jesus said when He came into their midst was, "Peace be with you" (John 20:19; Luke 24:36, NRSV). It was a standard rabbinic greeting, *shalom alekem* in Hebrew. It had been a standard Jewish greeting for a long time, coming from God Himself. (See how when Gideon is frightened by seeing an angel of the Lord, God says this to him [Judg. 6:23].)

Although the numinous breaks into this world in powerful, dramatic ways, such an inbreaking is relatively infrequent, then and now. For this reason, at the birth of Jesus, the angel said to the shepherds, "Be not afraid" (Luke 2:10). C. S. Lewis discusses the mythological stories of the "miraculous" of various cultures

presence of divinity

80

and is glad they could not be literally true. The fun of the story would quickly become a nightmare, he points out, and would demonstrate the world "was being invaded by an alien power."[20] Beasts would become men and men beasts, he said, and a magic ring would "cause tables richly spread with food to appear in solitary places." Christian miracles, by contrast, "are what might be expected to happen when [the world] is invaded not simply by a god, but by the God of Nature: by a Power which is outside her jurisdiction not as a foreigner but as a sovereign." Be at peace. Just as Jesus had once said to them when they saw Him walking on the water (Matt. 14:22–36), once again He brings assurance of benevolence: "Take heart; it is I. Do not be afraid" (Matt. 14:27).

The Hebrew word *shalom* is a much fuller and richer word than the Latin word for "peace," *pax*. *Pax* simply means "the absence of war," while *shalom* means "God's presence to bless, to bring harmony with Him, with others, and with oneself." In the Old Testament the context is "the blessing of God, especially the salvation to be brought by the Messiah" (see Ps. 29:11; Isa. 9:6; 52:7; 55:12; Ezek. 37:26; Zech. 9:10).[21] His "*Shalom!*" on Easter evening matches His "It is finished!" on Good Friday.

On the cross Jesus paid the penalty price our sins deserved. When we receive Him and His atoning work by faith, we are justified in God's sight, and, therefore, "have peace with God through our Lord Jesus Christ" (Rom. 5:1). This peace is the richness of grace and blessing the risen Lord desires to bestow upon those who love Him. It is the peace which the world cannot give *but He can*. It is the peace which He gives to calm fearful hearts (John 14:27; 16:33).

For *pax* to occur, the conflict or difficulty or problem must go away. *Shalom* can be enjoyed regardless of circumstances. *Shalom* can happen even in the midst of the difficulty. Sometimes God answers our prayers and works His blessing by taking the problem away. But other times, to quote the hymn "Joyful, Joyful We Adore Thee," we are "victors in the midst of strife." Paul

rhetorically asks the Romans if "hardship, or distress, or persecution, or famine, or nakedness, or peril, or sword" would sepa-
rate us from the love of Christ. His answer is, "No, in all these
things we are more than conquerors through him who loved
us" (Rom. 8:35, 37, NRSV). Yes, sometimes these various difficulties are supernaturally prevented from happening, or else, if
they do happen, are immediately removed in response to prayer,
but sometimes not. Look at the various difficulties suffered by
Christians in the Book of Acts. Paul described the various beat-
ings; shipwrecks; and times of hunger, thirst, and exposure he
himself suffered for Christ (2 Cor. 11:23–28).

We are told the peace of God "passes all understanding" (Phil.
4:7). One reason this is so is that God's blessings are so wonderfully amazing. But another reason is that this peace makes no
sense: How can we have peace when the outward circumstances
are chaotic? It's not because we're in denial of these terrible circumstances. It's because God's grace is at work within us.

There is a false teaching being taught in some circles that says
if you are experiencing something unpleasant, all you have to do
is "claim the victory," and if you do it in perfect faith the problem
will go away. However, if the problem still remains, then you
either are not really walking in faith or else there is some deep
wickedness in you of which you need to repent. This teaching
echoes the wrong analysis of Job's problem by his friends. While
their motives were most likely sincere, their understanding of
the reasons for Job's misery were wrong. Eliphaz said Job was
being punished for some sin he had committed (Job 4–7), Bildad
that Job was a hypocrite (Job 8–10), and Zophar that Job was a
liar and hypocrite (Job 11–14). The substance of their charges was
rebuked by God (Job 42:7–9).

The tragedy here is that spiritually sensitive souls caught up
in this off-base teaching are sometimes left devastated when the
item "claimed" doesn't arrive. They are told it has to be their
fault. Yes, sometimes we can put roadblocks in the way of God

acting. He tells us we will be blessed if we take that job offer, but we do not and continue to be miserable in our old job. Or, a healing is blocked because we stay bitter toward someone. But sometimes the problem remains not because of anything wrong on our part but because it is God's will to work in a way different from simply removing it. We periodically see godly Christian leaders die young from disease or accident. Many are among the godliest people we will ever know. And, let's be honest, isn't this "claiming it" by using a "faith formula" actually the practice of magic, although covered with a thin veneer of Christian language?

Many of us know of individuals who were not healed of their disease but were brought to a saving relationship with Jesus, to a transformed character, and to reconciliations with loved ones. They were healed though they were not cured. God promises never to leave or forsake those who belong to Him (Heb. 13:5). He will be there with us as we face whatever problems arise. *That* is the promise—not that we will always glide through life.

While *shalom* peace often occurs in the midst of difficulty, it is always a rich peace. G. R. Beasley-Murray tells us, "All that the prophets had poured into [the word] *shalom* as the epitome of the blessings of the kingdom of God had essentially been realized through the death and resurrection of Jesus for the world's salvation."[22] Nor was Jesus just *talking* about peace; He was bestowing it: "Peace be with you" (John 20:19). Jesus can do this because He is the Prince of Peace. They certainly needed it. They were afraid, and rightly so. Jesus will bestow His peace on us when we ask Him to. We need it, too!

Then Jesus said to them, "Receive the Holy Spirit," (John 20:22). Some have wondered if this is John's version of Pentecost, but the details are significantly different. The outpouring of the Spirit which occurred in Acts led immediately to bold preaching and miraculous ministry. In the account John relates, one week following this bestowal of the Spirit the apostles were once again meeting in a locked room (John 20:26). Something else was going on here, but what?

Ben Witherington III sees this initial bestowal of the Holy Spirit "as a prophetic sign-act, much like his cleaning of the temple, which depicts and foreshadows in dramatic fashion what is yet to come."[23] The Coptic monk Matthew the Poor comments that seeing the risen Christ with the marks of the nails and spear "was quite enough to give them faith in the resurrection, but it was not enough, even with their faith, to give them the Spirit and the power of the resurrection."[24] For that "we must be given a spiritual gift."

Might we hear a strong echo from Genesis 2:7, where God breathed into Adam the breath of life? Pentecost will soon empower them to proclaim boldly and act mightily, but first they needed a re-creation. Westcott comments, "The same image which was used to describe the communication of the natural life, is here used to express the communication of the new, spiritual, life of re-created humanity."[25] John Marsh notes the symmetry: "John's gospel ends with an announcement of the new creation, as it also began."[26] The first Adam received the Spirit. Christ, the last Adam, "became a life-giving spirit" (1 Cor. 15:45).

The power for ministry would truly fall on Pentecost, but more had to happen first. Jesus had to reveal Himself a few more times, in part, to underscore important elements in the future church. He had to bring closure to Peter's Holy Week denials. He had to ascend back to the Father, and the inner circle needed to spend ten days together.

Discussion Questions

1. How have you responded when someone you trusted introduced a practice or told a story that was totally

foreign, or possibly repugnant, to your education and experience?

2. Can you think of some New Testament events that are both literally true and metaphorically profound? (A few Old Testament examples are the Passover and the crossing of the Red Sea.)

3. What do "Fear not" and "**Shalom**" mean to you?

4. Is there a difference between the faith of John 3:16 and the faith of 1 Corinthians 12:9, and how is such faith acquired?

CHAPTER 5

THE APOSTLES' COMMISSION RESTATED

Luke 24:33–43; John 20:19–25

JESUS HAD PREVIOUSLY called the apostles to ministry (Matt. 10:1). Now He was reconfirming that call. Why would He do this again? Had the previous call not been sufficient?

I believe Jesus issued this present call, first, because they may have wondered if He still wanted them as apostles after the cowardice they had exhibited during Holy Week. Here, as He would soon do in a more dramatic way with Peter (John 21:1–19), Jesus is reassuring them of both His love and His call. Sometimes we need reassurance after we've failed. God delights to restore and reassure the fallen Christian who humbly acknowledges his or her sin, confesses it, forsakes it, and works to do better—by his or her effort, by the help of others, and by the grace of God. (Please note: it's all three of these.) Satan may keep us focusing on the past, but God delights to move forward with repentant sinners.

I believe Jesus issued this present call, second, because at critical junctures, when something in us or in the surrounding circumstances has significantly changed, it is good to rededicate ourselves—both in our walk with and in our work for the

Lord—and to hear His call of us reaffirmed. When a person has taken a leap forward in giftedness, in spiritual maturity, or in academic qualification, or when a person has truly repented from serious sin, a special time of rededication and recommissioning may well be in order.

It is also good to do this periodically as a congregation. Some churches have an annual preaching mission or revival ending with a time of recommitment to Christ. Some churches have periodic altar calls at the end of worship. In many liturgical denominations people renew their baptismal vows at the Easter vigil each year. Sacramental confession is another way to start fresh.

Many have found John Wesley's Covenant Service to be very helpful. Wesley wrote in his *Journal* that he would hold these services as the situation warranted, but in the latter years of his ministry he usually celebrated them on New Year's Day or a Sunday at the beginning of the New Year.[1] The congregation I pastor, Trinity Church, Kingston, New Hampshire, makes use of this service the first Sunday of every year.

Jesus wastes no time in recommissioning them. It is done on the evening of the first Easter. He will not let them wallow in their failures committed during Holy Week. He will not let Satan rub their noses in it.

In Luke's Gospel Jesus gives a brief discourse that encompasses past, present, and future.

First, we find Jesus explaining how the Old Testament Scriptures pointed to Him (Luke 24:44–45). Skeptics might think that the inclusion of these verses is a scribal mistake in copying a new manuscript from an older version, because Jesus had just said these things to the Emmaus travelers (Luke 24:25–27). But why must the skeptics conclude that? Why would Jesus explain how the Old Testament pointed to Him to just the two walking to Emmaus but not to anyone else? Have any of these doubting scholars never repeated a point in a subsequent lecture?

All along Jesus had taught that the Son of Man would suffer (see, for example, Luke 9:22, 44; 17:25; 18:31–33) and that this had been foretold in the Old Testament (for example, Isa. 50:6; Isa. 53). Now He would help His closest friends understand this truth more fully.

Second, He reminded them that it was the Father's plan for Him to be crucified and raised on the third day, an event that had happened early that very day (Luke 24:46).

Third, in words similar to those that soon would be uttered again (the Great Commission of Matthew 28:19–20), Jesus spoke of their future work in proclaiming repentance and forgiveness to all nations, starting in Jerusalem (Luke 24:47). We will say more on this shortly.

Jesus came to them to bless them and alleviate their fears but not so they could remain a small, inward-looking "holy huddle." They had work to do. While they would need to get over their fear, and while they would still need to grow in wisdom and knowledge, they were to start the work as soon as they were baptized in the Holy Spirit on Pentecost. Their walk with Christ and *their work for Christ* would proceed simultaneously. So must ours. If we wait until we are perfect in our discipleship we will never serve God or His people.

They are "witnesses" (Luke 24:48). As we saw in our first chapter, this word *witness* has two meanings here, as it does in our own lives. First, we see a car running a red light and crashing into a van. We witnessed it. Secondly, we may be called upon to be a witness during a trial. Hearing the account from someone else would not make us witnesses. Simply to have seen the accident but not testify would not help justice be served. To be a witness we must *see it and say it*.

The same is true here. Jesus had done many signs and wonders in their midst during the three years His closest disciples walked about with Him (Acts 1:22). In His post-Resurrection appearances He is doing the same, so there is firsthand testimony to the Resurrection. Then, once they have been empowered by the Holy Spirit, they are to go evangelize. Part of their appeal is that they are not giving mere theory or secondhand testimony; they had witnessed and experienced these incredible things *personally*, and now they would witness them to others (Acts 3:15; 5:32; 10:39; 10:41; 13:31; 22:15; 26:16).

Our Lord's commission to them indicates their ministry will be an extension of His: "As the Father has sent me, so I send you" (John 20:21, NRSV). We need to examine this commissioning from two different angles.

First, the scope of the work. Scripture tells us Jesus came "teaching...preaching...and healing" (Matt. 4:23, KJV). That is the ministry of the church today, both literally in those three specific ministry tasks and, more broadly, in what each represents.

Teaching is, of course, instruction in the content of the faith, important because it is the truth that makes you free (John 8:32). Christianity is not just relationship with God; it is theological content, "the faith that was once for all delivered to the saints" (Jude 3). Teaching also involves training people in ministry. Jesus sent seventy of His followers out two by two and then debriefed them and gave them further instruction when they came back (Luke 10:1–20).

Preaching, understood more fully, broadens from pulpit exhortation into testifying to others, giving spiritual direction, training people in personal discipleship, offering godly counseling, and the like. Paul said that his job was to present each person "mature in Christ" (Col. 1:28).

Many people assume that Jesus' ministry prior the cross was simply one of preaching and teaching. Many pastors preach that this is what He did. The surprise is how central the ministry of healing was to Jesus. Try this: count the number of verses in the four Gospels, then go back and note every verse that has to do with the subject of healing, either Jesus teaching about healing or Jesus healing someone, Jesus teaching His disciples about healing, or Jesus sending them out to do it. Now divide that number into the first one. You will discover that approximately 18 percent of the four Gospels has to do with healing. When we consider the various subjects about which Jesus needed to teach and exhort, and the various events in His life that the evangelists needed to describe, the fact that just one subject—healing—comprises such a large percentage should convince us this is important to God. Since we are sent out as the Father sent out Jesus, we must make the healing ministry something we and our church do. The healing ministry of the church is not something only for those who might be interested in it. It is not just for those churches that emphasize either the sacraments or the gifts of the Spirit. It is for the church as a whole. It is for each local congregation or parish or fellowship.

Moreover, in some way each Christian is called to be part of this work of healing. While *presbyters* (elders, pastors, priests) have this ministry by virtue of their office (James 5:14), and while some people have one or more of the "gifts of healings" as a char-ismatic endowment (1 Cor. 12:9), each Christian can, from time to time, expect God to use him or her in praying for a person's healing. The longer ending of Mark's Gospel, present in some of the ancient manuscripts, tells us "those who believe" are to lay hands on the sick so the sick would recover (Mark 16:17–18).

Healing is expressed in two different but complementary modes. The first is through medicine, as people use their God-given intellect to discover new medicines and procedures. (We can add osteopathic and chiropractic manipulation, massage, instruction in sound nutrition, and more.) The second is as God works supernaturally. Sometimes a supernatural healing is dramatic and instantaneous. Other times not. Sometimes God heals by the medical and the supernatural working together. Sometimes the healing needed is physical; other times it is psy-chological or spiritual.[2]

These three functions of preaching, teaching, and healing are to be prominent in the church today.

So, first, the commissioning of the disciples for ministry is to extend the scope of Jesus' work.

Second, the power behind the work. The disciples were faced with the prospect that the just-risen Christ was also the soon-to-be-ascended Christ. He was leaving, and they would carry on the work. How could they possibly do this? For the most part they had not distinguished themselves in the week just past, and now they were going to do *His* work? Perhaps they were about ready to ask Him, "But how can we do this?" when He "breathed on them and said to them, 'Receive the Holy Spirit'" (John 20:22). This was a preliminary bestowal of the Spirit, I believe for their own souls' sake—the necessary next step—but not yet for empowerment for mission, because they were also told to wait in Jerusalem for the bestowal of the Spirit (Luke 24:49; Acts 1:4), which would begin that mission.

Everett F. Harrison writes, "This is a crucial point in redemption history, the beginning of the new creation."[3] As we saw in the last chapter, this event bookends the original creation when, in Genesis 2:7, we are told "the LORD God...breathed into his [Adam's] nostrils the breath of life." In Genesis God breathed upon the first Adam to culminate the original creation. In the Gospels the final Adam breathes upon His closest disciples to make them the beginnings of His new creation.

In addition, the nation of Israel is likened in Ezekiel 37 to a valley of dry bones. Under the re-creation of God, the bones received flesh once again, but they were not animated until God breathed life into them (Ezek. 37:9–10). Now, on Easter evening, Jesus breathed upon His disciples—bones, flesh, and human spirit—to make them a new creation, fit for life in the new covenant. Once again we note that at Pentecost this new creation would receive full empowerment for service.

Some scholars believe that John has confused the outpouring

of the Spirit on the Day of Pentecost with this particular bestowal of the Spirit on Easter evening. This skepticism is not new. Roman Catholic scholar Raymond E. Brown reminds us that the fifth ecumenical council of the church (the Second Council of Constantinople) held in AD 553 "condemned the view of Theodore of Mopsuestia that Jesus did not really give the Spirit on Easter but acted only figuratively and by way of promise."[4] Such skepticism is unwarranted. The details of the two stories are significantly different.

Brown agrees with the belief that the Easter bestowal was for individuals for themselves personally, but the Pentecost bestowal was for missionary work. He notes that some contemporary conservative scholars teach that the Easter bestowal was so the leaders could recognize the risen Lord, while others see a quantitative distinction between the initial bestowal on Easter and a much greater bestowal on Pentecost. John Chrysostom (AD 347–407, patriarch of Constantinople from AD 398 onwards) said the gift of the Spirit in John 20:22 was to enable the forgiveness of sins and that in Acts 2 was for the power to work miracles and raise the dead.

Whatever the distinction, the fact is we cannot accomplish God's work unless we work in God's power. Note how Jesus did not begin His earthly ministry until His human nature had been baptized in the Holy Spirit in the River Jordan at the hands of his kinsman, John the Baptist (Matt. 3:13–17; Luke 3:21–22). The followers of Jesus would not begin their ministry in earnest until they, too, had been baptized in the Holy Spirit. Jesus never calls us to do something without first either bestowing upon us the power to do it or else by telling us to seek that empowering.

Important as this infilling of the Holy Spirit would be, it would not give them a lifetime's supply of grace! When Paul exhorts us, "Be filled with the Spirit" (Eph. 5:18), he uses what is called the present continuous tense. A more literal translation would be, *"Keep on being filled with the Spirit."* Holy Spirit empowerment is spent when we minister. We need to be replenished again and again.

Many years ago I read a great phrase by James K. Wagner: "Blessed to be a blessing." We are neither just to be blessed without being a blessing to God and others, nor are we to try to be a blessing before we receive God's empowering grace. This was true for our Lord as well. Go through the Gospels and note this alternation between Jesus taking in empowerment from His Father and then giving out in ministry to others. You can try this. Take a red pen and a blue pen and work through the four Gospels. Every time you read a transitional verse saying Jesus went off to a quiet place to pray, or went to commune with His Father—anything implying that He was off recharging Himself—underline it in red. Then every time you read a transitional verse indicating Jesus left that place of empowering and re-engaged with the public to teach or minister, underline it in blue. Then go back to the beginning of each Gospel and note your marks: red, blue, red, blue, red, blue. He was blessed so He could be a blessing. Being a blessing drained Him so much He needed solitude and prayer to be blessed again. And then He emerged once again to be a blessing. We will take a look at just the first part of Luke's Gospel to demonstrate this point:

- Jesus launched His ministry by identifying with us as His cousin John the Baptist baptized Him. The Holy Spirit descended upon Jesus, empowering Him for ministry (3:21–22). *Taking in.*

- Then, after His temptation, He engaged people "in the power of the Spirit" (4:14). Jesus cast out evil spirits and healed the sick (4:31–41). *Giving out.*

- Jesus went to "a lonely place," no doubt to pray and be empowered by His Father (4:42). *Taking in.*

- Jesus healed, taught, and did other forms of ministry (5:12–9:17). *Giving out.*

- Jesus then prayed alone (9:18a). *Taking in.*

- Jesus taught important truths (9:18b–27). *Giving out.*

- Jesus went up the Mount of Transfiguration to pray (9:28). *Taking in.*

- Jesus came down the Mount of Transfiguration to minister (9:37–10:42). *Giving out.*

- Jesus "was praying in a certain place" (11:1). *Taking in.*

- Jesus taught and ministered (11:2 and following). *Giving out.*

So, just as the Father had sent Jesus, He now sends them, first in terms of the scope of the work, and second in terms of the power behind the work.

Jesus then dealt briefly with the subject of forgiveness of sin (John 20:23; Luke 24:47). Scholars commenting on these two passages diverge, depending on their church affiliation: those from sacramental churches (Eastern Orthodox, Roman Catholic, Anglo-Catholic) will focus on the church's power to absolve (or not absolve) penitents, while evangelicals and Pentecostals will focus on the need for individual Christians to forgive and to seek forgiveness as individual disciples. But both are true and both are important. Luke brings out the point that the church is to proclaim repentance and forgiveness (Luke 24:47) while John, writing later when the structures of the church had been more put in place, focuses on the role of church leadership in disciplinary authority (John 20:23).

I have often heard people wax nostalgic for the early church. They state, "If only the church today were like the church in the earliest days of the church where everything was so simple and unstructured." But even a cursory reading of the New Testament should dispel that notion.

First, read the Epistles. The early church had serious problems of doctrine and behavior. Do we really want our churches to be like that? From the beginning church discipline was needed.

Second, church discipline was not something added on later, when the church moved from being an informal, loving family of believers to a hierarchical, impersonal structure. Jesus Himself taught the steps on what we should do when a fellow Christian sins against us (Matt. 18:15–18). The final step when a person remains hardened to our entreaties is to turn the situation over *to the church* for discipline. The church has the role of disciplining offenders, and God honors the leaders' ministry of binding and loosing. And, as for hierarchy, note how 1 and 2 Timothy and the Epistle to Titus all deal with the various offices of the hierarchical ministry of the church. While this hierarchical ministry is something that must be done with great humility, care, and sensitivity, it is a ministry that is of God and that must be done. If a hierarchical ministry done wrongly has bad consequences, so does not having such a ministry. While the church is not a breathless corpse, neither is it a skeleton-less amoeba. To those who say, "I do not like organized religion," I respond, "Do you really want disorganized religion?"

Special care must be taken to maintain biblical balance both by Christian individuals as we share the Christian faith with others and by the church in her proclamation of the Gospel more widely.

Some individuals and churches emphasize repentance to the point where God seems harsh and where forgiveness appears to be infrequently granted. To emphasize that people are lost sinners is not the gospel's "good news," because such a message is neither good nor news.

Others, by contrast, skip repentance altogether, proclaiming God to be loving when in fact they're really making Him permissive and enabling. Rowan Williams, recent Archbishop of Canterbury and active in international peace and justice issues, comments, "Salvation does not bypass the history and memory of guilt, rather it builds upon it and from it."[5] Pope Paul VI said that reconciliation "never offends against true justice or denies the rights of the poor."[6] Later in this book we will see how Jesus ministered in such a complete way during the painful but necessary process of rehabilitation of Peter (John 21:15–17.) Any other way—any less painful shortcut—would not have been effective.

The tough love balance of the gospel involves two things:

- The first is in taking sin seriously. This involves acknowledging sin (and sin is what God in Scripture says sin is), confessing sin, repenting of sin (desiring to turn from it and not repeat it), asking people to hold us accountable in those areas in which we are prone to sin, making amends and restitution to those against whom we have sinned, and taking intentional, regular steps that lead to holiness.

- The second is in taking God's forgiveness seriously. This involves acknowledging that what Jesus did on the cross to pay the penalty price of our sins truly made our being forgiven possible, and believing that God has truly restored us to fellowship with Him when we repent.

Anything less than all of this is not the gospel. Anything less than all of this does not work. God's pleasure is not in pointing out people's sins. He does this because it is a necessary first step to their return to Him (Ezek. 18:23). John noted this balanced completeness in his first epistle (1 John 1:7–2:2).

We, corporately as the church and individually as a Christian disciple, are to replicate Christ's ministry—"As the Father has sent me, even so I am sending you" (John 20:21). Since Jesus preached and ministered both the call to repentance and the bestowal of forgiveness, so must His church. So Luke and John, writing from different perspectives, touch on Jesus' brief conversation with the ones gathered in Jerusalem on the evening of that first Easter.

Each of the post-Resurrection appearances of Jesus teaches us something about what the church would be like after Jesus' Ascension and what the church should be like today. What do Luke 24:36–43, and John 20:19-25 teach us? Three things, I believe.

First is the importance of Christian community. The ten, with others, were together despite their fears. Cleopas and his companion instinctively knew to head for this core group when they met the risen Christ.

Second is the church as a redemptive community in its role of binding and loosing, of forgiving sin (and sometimes not forgiving if there is no genuine repentance).

Third, that Christianity is both supernatural and physical. Jesus can quickly relocate from one place to another and can pass through locked doors. Soon after these events the Holy Spirit would fall on believers at the day of Pentecost, and the church would manifest signs and wonders, that is, supernatural workings of the Spirit. And yet, Jesus still had a body, He could speak and He could eat. Lester Durst reminds us: until Jesus returns at His Second Coming the Church would still be in the world.[7] Christians would sometimes accomplish great things for God not by watching Him perform something supernatural but by rolling up their sleeves and going to work. Sometimes people will be healed miraculously, and sometimes, like Timothy, who was instructed to take wine for his stomach ailments (1 Tim. 5:23), we'll have to take our medicine.

In the conclusion of his gospel, Luke briefly touches on the Ascension, a subject with which he would begin his second volume, the Acts of the Apostles. When verse 50 of Luke 24 begins with the word *then* we are not to add the word *immediately* and conclude Luke has misremembered the chronology. It is Luke himself who tells us the period between the Resurrection and the Ascension was forty days (Acts 1:3). He's leaving it to others to give accounts of further post-Resurrection appearances of Jesus. One week later, Jesus appears to "doubting Thomas" (John 20:24–29). It is to that story we must now turn.

Discussion Questions

1. When we say that the church is the body of Christ and that we are members, does that mean that we are the
 * incarnation in the world today? *yes*

2. What are our roles in preaching, teaching, healing, forgiveness, reconciliation, and absolution?

3. St. Irenaeus wrote that "the glory of God is man fully alive." What are the implications of this?

* a person or thing regarded as embodying or exhibiting some quality, idea, or the like.

2. Jesus' commission indicates that our ministry will be an extension of His — teaching, preaching and healing.

3. According to Taylor Marshall, "God is truly glorified when we live the life of grace here on earth."

CHAPTER 6

"DOUBTING THOMAS"

John 20:24–25

Thomas wasn't with the other ten remaining apostles that first Easter evening. He had "skipped church" and in doing so missed Jesus' appearance (John 20:24). (We might ask ourselves what we miss when we skip church [Heb. 10:25].) Why was Thomas not there? Scripture provides no reason, but we could speculate. I would like to suggest nine possible negative reasons, reasons that put Thomas in a bad light, and two very positive possible reasons for his absence that first night.

First, perhaps Thomas was not there because he was frightened and wanted to hide. If this was his motivation, it did not differ from that of the other apostles who, except for John, abandoned Jesus at the Cross. Although the ten did meet that first evening, it was behind locked doors (John 20:19).

How often do we who love Jesus hide our discipleship so others will not ridicule or persecute us? That is not who we should be and that is probably not who we want to be, but it is where many of us presently are and will be until God increases our trust in Him. However, we are not to wait until every last bit of fear has disappeared before we stand boldly for the Lord. One quote often attributed to the actor known as John Wayne (née Marion Robert Morrison, 1907–1979) puts it this way: "Courage is being scared to death—but saddling up anyway."

Or, second, perhaps Thomas was not there because, like many people who pull into themselves when they are sad, Thomas wanted to stay by himself that night. The man he had followed for three years had been killed. Thomas undoubtedly had grown quite fond of Jesus, even loved Him. Now Jesus had died, and Thomas became despondent. Though we can empathize with Thomas, and although sometimes it's wise to be alone, we should not stay too long in our solitude. We need the consolation of others. Our sadness can trick us into harming ourselves when we are alone. Moreover, after a while, such solitude, understandable and even acceptable at first, can become a self-indulgent excuse for not getting on with life.

Or, third, perhaps Thomas was not present because he was disillusioned as a disciple of Jesus and embarrassed to have followed along. Perhaps Thomas never actually understood what Jesus was saying. The Messiah was to be like David or like the Maccabees—a warrior—wasn't he? Yet for all the teaching, praying, and even miracle working that Jesus had done, Pilate was still the governor and Caiaphas was still the high priest. Nothing had really changed. Perhaps Thomas was too ashamed to admit his credulity to the other apostles, even though they, too, had exhibited the same seeming misplaced trust.

In our day we observe individuals blindly following some impressive leader. When disillusionment occurs, many no longer find it possible to believe anyone or make a commitment to anything for fear they would be betrayed again. This is one more reason why active participation in a balanced Christian community is essential: it can keep us from the toxic extremes of credulity and cynicism. We want to "test the spirits" (1 John 4:1), but we do not want to miss the time of God's visitation (Luke 19:44).

Mature Christians can keep us in balance. They keep us from going gullibly into the kind of extreme that, when reality sets in, often leads to an opposite and equally imbalanced cynicism.

Or, fourth, perhaps Thomas realized he had seen Jesus as a father figure and felt this father figure had now abandoned him. Ted Schroder points to a book by New York University psychology professor Paul Vitz in which the author discusses his study of the childhood of several well-known atheists. Vitz notes strong evidence that their rejection of God is directly related to pain not dealt with over the death of, or abuse or abandonment by, one's father.[1]

Part of Christian healing ministry is the healing of one's emotions damaged by tragic events. One application of the inner healing ministry is to the wounds caused by an absent or abusive father. In the process of being healed, a person comes to the place of forgiveness of that father. In addition, the child realizes that God the Father is not at all like those earthly fathers who neglected or abused their children. Instead of rejecting our heavenly Father, renaming Him with gender-neutral or feminine terminology, or reimaging Him as impersonal or feminine, we can embrace God the Father for who He truly is, one who can supply what we were denied by our earthly father.

Or, fifth, perhaps Thomas was ashamed for having run away after originally vowing that he would die with Jesus (John 11:16). He could have taken comfort, however—and we can take comfort—in how Jesus restores those who fail Him, as we will soon see in our Lord's restoration of Peter.

Sixth, perhaps Thomas was not present because he had insufficient faith. True, he had seen Jesus do many incredible things, but then Jesus was crucified. The accounts of Jesus' resurrection may have been just too much for Thomas to believe. In this he is like many Christians. We have experienced answered prayer, but when something terrible strikes, like the diagnosis of a life-threatening illness, an unexpected job loss, or tragedy in the life of one of our children, many of us discover our faith is not that strong after all. As we noted previously, we may have a "sort of" faith, a belief in a God who is real but is too small.

How do we build faith?

Of course, we pray for stronger faith. Like the father of the demoniac boy, we can ask, "I believe; help my unbelief!" (Mark 9:24).

Further, we review Scripture, noting how God's promises came true in the lives of so many people in Bible days.

We also examine the lives of Christians throughout the centuries. The value of reading what is variously called Christian biography or the lives of the saints is that these accounts demonstrate God's fidelity to His promises and His active love to His people throughout the centuries, some of whom are people much like ourselves.

Next, we note how God is still active today as we hear the witness of Christian believers whom we know and trust.

Finally, we remind ourselves of those times God answered our own prayers. We do this by asking God to bring back to our conscious memories those times when He clearly intervened, where it would take more faith to believe it was all a coincidence than it was God at work. We ask our pastor and Christian family and friends if they remember such times in our lives. Then we give each occurrence a title such as, "When I was down to my last hundred dollars with bills coming due, a check came out of nowhere," and then make a list of those titles. We make copies of the list and place them in our Bibles, in the glove compartment of our cars, on our night stand, in our wallet or purse. When doubt creeps in we don't wait for some special divine assistance—though we pray for it—nor do we try to conjure up faith emotionally. We simply review the evidence.

Or, seventh, perhaps Thomas was not there because his conception of discipleship was that of the "lone ranger" believer. We have already noted the problem of the individual, just-me-and-Jesus believer. Let's now look at it again.

Various opinion polls have indicated that there are millions of people in the United States who claim to be born-again Christians but are not actively a part of a local Christian congregation. I recently spoke with a Pentecostal pastor who told me he would no longer be giving altar calls because too many of those who responded thought that a momentary experience of Jesus was all that would ever be required of them as believers. He now takes those inquiring about the Christian faith and disciples them as to the duties and doctrinal/ethical content of Christianity, with baptism as the eventual culmination of this rigorous process. This is what the early church did.

Even in the earliest days of the church there were people who thought that just having Jesus in their lives was enough without the necessity of the corporate church. That is why the author of the Epistle to the Hebrews told his readers and tells us as well that Christians are not to neglect "to meet together, as is the habit of some" (Heb. 10:25). God designed the church as part of the package of discipleship. Jesus talked about building His church (Matt. 16:18).

God definitely seeks to reach individuals, but He also wants a new people. Let us look at four reasons showing the necessity of having the church.

First, as we saw in the last chapter, Jesus taught that a stage in disciplining a wayward Christian was to lay the matter before the church (Matt. 18:15–17).

Second, God distributed the gifts of the Spirit to various people so one cannot say to another, "I have no need of you" (1 Cor. 12:12–26). They—we—are to come together in the church for the good of all.

Third, 1 Timothy, 2 Timothy, and Titus lay forth the names of and qualifications for various types of ordained ministry in the church.

Fourth, it is often in the Christian community that souls are won and built up. As David Baumann wisely observes, "Rarely someone may be converted by a vision, and occasionally someone may be converted by one's own study, but the overwhelming method by which someone comes to Christ is by testimony, by living in a community of believers whose lives have been changed by the risen Jesus."[2]

Or, eighth, perhaps Thomas was not with the others because there were relationship problems between him and one or more of them. Maybe the ten had a reason to be upset with him, or he with them, or both. There was at least one recorded disagreement among the apostles when the others were indignant at James and John for their ambition (Matt. 20:20–28). Later on there would be a strong disagreement between Peter and Paul (Gal. 2:1–14). Was this now happening with Thomas?

As we will see in chapter 13, reconciliation between members of the core Christian group was one reason why they had to wait in Jerusalem for a week and a half before the Holy Spirit would be poured out on Pentecost. *Dunamis* (spiritual power) in the hands of immature people can hurt others and hamper the cause of Christ. Before that power fell the disciples needed reconciliation with each other.

Reconciliation between believers is one of the ways the world is attracted to Christ. Jesus told us to be reconciled to our brother before we would offer our gift at the altar (Matt. 5:24). When a non-believer sees Christians exhibiting genuine love to each other, he sometimes responds with a statement of, "I want that for myself!" In the early years of the church non-believers would often say, "See how those Christians love one another."[3] Jesus prayed believers would be one so the world would know the Father had sent Him (John 17:21). The world does not expect Christians to be perfect. It does—and should—expect us to be better than non-believers.

Or, ninth, perhaps Thomas had a family concern that caused him to be absent at this time. These men had left their families to follow Jesus, but, now that He was gone, the responsibilities they had left behind may have weighed heavily on them. In this time of confusion, perhaps Thomas, always a practical man (John 14:5), felt the time had come to go back to his family. But Jesus had made it clear that allegiance to Him was superior even to that of allegiance to family (Matt. 12:47–49).

Those are nine possible negative reasons for Thomas' absence from the apostolic gathering that first evening. Now for a few possible positive ones.

First, do you remember that time around the death of Lazarus when Jesus had said He would return to Judea (John 11:7)? Several of Jesus' closest followers tried to dissuade Him, knowing the dangers lurking there (v. 8). Thomas, however, had yet a different response: "Let us go also, that we may die with him" (v. 16).

It could be that Thomas was identifying with the dead Lazarus: let us be like Lazarus in his death so, with Lazarus, he could experience some great action of the Lord. But it could also be that Thomas was identifying with the mortal danger Jesus would be placing Himself in if He were to return to Judea. In either case, Thomas was trusting in the Lord unto death. He was not opting for the coward's safe way out.

That being so, might then have Thomas' absence from the group on Easter night been an example of bravery? The ten were afraid and behind a locked door. Thomas was out and about, where those known to be followers of Jesus were in grave danger. Could it be possible that Thomas' absence was indicative of not weakness but strength?[4]

Second, could the reason for Thomas' absence be that he was gathering supplies for and bringing comfort to the Christian community? There were followers of Jesus other than the core leaders huddled behind locked doors. With the leaders sequestered away, who would help the weaker members of the flock? Perhaps it was Thomas.

We do not know why Thomas was off by himself. Nevertheless, we do know when the ten told Thomas that they had met the Lord (John 20:25), as he had done previously (John 11:1–16, especially the last verse, and John 14:1–6), Thomas blurted out a statement expressive of confusion and doubt. There is no record, either in Scripture or in the tradition of the church, of the others chastising him or trying to straighten him out. The next thing we read is Thomas being present with full acceptance by the ten the following Sunday evening.

What happened during the intervening week? Had the community reached out to him? A sound Christian fellowship should be a community of love that demonstrates trust, acceptance, and accountability. It is not always so. James Cirillo told his congregation:

> Problems in a marriage or with kids or with parents, financial difficulties, struggles at work or with an addiction of some sort—who wants to share any of this when there is not an environment of trust and acceptance? That's why [Alcoholics Anonymous] was formed, because the church didn't know how to love, accept, and help those struggling with alcohol dependency.[5]

No, love does not come at the expense of truth. Love without truth excuses and enables bad behavior. False love does not set people free, nor does it build people up. It does not make the world a better place. Holding someone accountable is as much a part of love as is consoling that person or offering that person understanding. But before you demand accountability from someone, make sure of your own sincerity and humility. Often the phrase, "I'm saying this because I love you," rings hollow because the other person clearly sees love is lacking.

Whatever the cause of Thomas' absence, and his doubts notwithstanding, he was present the next Sunday (John 20:26).

Craig Kallio comments, "Thomas may have had his doubts, but he has them in the very midst of the community. Thomas does not walk away from the other disciples disgruntled about his doubt.

Nor do the disciples ask him to take his questions elsewhere. Thomas was with them, his friends, in the midst of his doubts."[6]

British Church leader Russ Parker suggests it was "more about Thomas deciding to belong to the fellowship of faith even with his doubts, than to live on the margins of the community of believers and hide his doubt."[7] Was not Jesus teaching Thomas in all of this that the church is an essential part of following Him? Is He not saying that to us?

Thomas has been given the nickname "Doubting Thomas" over the centuries. This is unfortunate. We don't call Peter "Denying Peter" for his threefold denial of knowing his Lord (John 18:15–18, 25–27). We don't refer to John as "Ambitious John" for his aiming for an exalted position in the kingdom of God (Matt. 20:20–23). We don't refer to Andrew as "Runaway Andrew" because he absented himself from the cross while his Lord was being crucified (John 19:25–26). Scripture records that the ten others, though full of joy at seeing Jesus in their midst, were "disbelieving and still wondering" even though they were in His presence (Luke 24:41, NRSV). David Baumann notes, "No one believed that Jesus was risen until they had seen him: not the women who went to the tomb, not the eleven, not the two on the road to Emmaus—no one. Thomas was not unique in that."[8] All he wanted was the same evidence the others had been given. But poor old Thomas has been stuck with nickname "Doubting."

David Montzingo points to the transparent discipleship Thomas had exhibited previously. He offered his loyalty to Jesus (John 11:6), he evidenced his honesty in not knowing what Jesus had meant (John 14:5), and, having been given the evidence he needed, he professed his certainty about the true identity of Jesus (John 20:28).

Honest doubt is part of a maturing faith. Scripture encourages us to help, not ridicule, those who have doubt. The Epistle of Jude commands us to "have mercy on some who are wavering" (v. 22, NRSV). The psalmist was not rebuked when he asked God, "O Lord, why do you cast me off? Why do you hide your face from me?" (Ps. 88:14, NRSV). Frederick Buechner says that if we don't have any doubts, we're either kidding ourselves or are asleep.[9] Doubt is not the opposite of faith. The opposite of faith is fear. Kevin Martin puts it this way: "Doubt is the anvil on which belief is formed."[10]

A faith that never wrestles with the hard questions is untested and remains shallow, making one vulnerable to loss of faith when encountering the hard parts of life. Fyodor Dostoevsky notes, "My hosanna has passed through a great furnace of doubt."[11]

Ted Schroder writes:

> If faith never encounters doubt, if truth never struggles with error, if good never battles with evil, how can faith know its own power? How can it enhance its power if it never exercises its perception? A faith that struggles with doubt becomes strong through that struggle.[12]

Pope Benedict XVI's Easter message of 2007 speaks of the mature faith that has passed through the struggle of doubt:

> We may all be tempted by the disbelief of Thomas. Suffering, evil, injustice, death, especially when it strikes the innocent such as children who are victims of war and terrorism, of sickness and hunger, does not all of this put our faith to the test? Paradoxically the disbelief of Thomas is most valuable to us in these cases because it helps to purify all false concepts of God and lead us to discover his true face: the face of a God who, in Christ, has taken upon himself the wounds of injured humanity. Thomas has received from the Lord, and has in turn transmitted to the Church, the gift of a faith put to the test by the passion and death of Jesus and confirmed by meeting him risen.[13]

Over the years I have seen the negative impact on the discipleship of people who did not ask questions when they experienced doubts, ignorance, or confusion. All the questions with which we struggle have been asked many, many times through the centuries, and wise Christians have given satisfying answers. But how can people get those answers if we do not foster a climate in which they can, without penalty, ask those questions? A good church will allow questions, not in the sense of encouraging people to play games or letting insincere questioning undermine the faith of others but instead as a place where honest questioning is wed to the commitment to look for answers, particularly in the writings of the authors who stand strong with the faith and who have brought comfort to so many in doubt. Those of us who have come to certainty on issues of the faith would do well to prepare to help those who are still struggling.

I came into the Charismatic Renewal in 1973 as a graduate student at Oxford. Many things were being promoted as part of the Christian experience with which I was unfamiliar. I did not expect the Christian faith to be bland, but neither did I think it should be weird. I needed to ask questions to make sure what was being offered was truly from God. I did not want to miss what God had in store for me, but neither did I wish to be hoodwinked. Faith is not *blind* faith, but neither is there divine approval for sitting lazily in one's doubt. I put to the test those claims made by those encouraging me to embrace the Charismatic Renewal in general and various aspects of it in particular.

Thomas was told by the others that the resurrected Jesus had appeared to them physically, not as a ghost or as some mere spiritual idea. Thomas wanted to believe this, but he knew there had long been fanciful stories circulating, and there had been too many "wonder workers" in recent Jewish history, people who had eventually disillusioned their followers. As Allen Quain notes, Thomas was called the Twin (John 11:16, 20:24) and was therefore quite familiar with the problem of mistaken identity. Had the others *really* seen Jesus, or had they seen someone who reminded them of Him?[14] If this was the case, Thomas was not doubting Jesus but rather doubting what people were saying about Him.

Thomas needed reasons to know that the one who had appeared to the ten was truly Jesus. To come to that knowledge Thomas needed to see the Lord's wounds.

William H. Willimon states:

> There are those who hear the historical reports of the gospels and, despite the two-thousand year space between our time and their time, they hear and they believe.
>
> There are other people who need something else.... They need touch. For those people, the good news is that Jesus gives them what they, you, need.[15]

He adds, "Thomas desired proof. No, what he wanted is presence, embodiment. He wanted Jesus."[16]

Jesus, far from rebuking Thomas, invited him to place his fingers in His wounds (John 20:24–29). Christianity centers in Jesus who is God-made-flesh. While a Christian's discipleship does involve spiritual feelings, it is centered in concrete facts; while it involves intellectual assent to truth, the truth is fleshed out in physical, tangible ways. Jesus offered Thomas graphic, physical, literal proof.

How did Jesus know Thomas needed this kind of proof? There is nothing in the text that tells us. There are at least four possible reasons why, each quite different from the others but each equally important to our Christian life.

Perhaps someone who had seen Jesus after His resurrection had told Jesus of Thomas' demand to see the wound marks. We do know Mary, a few women, and the ten had seen Jesus. Perhaps there were others. Thank God for the ministry of brothers and sisters in Christ on behalf of each other.

Or, second, perhaps it was because Jesus, knowing human nature well (John 2:24), knew that at least one of His closest would need such proof. Thank God He knows what human nature is like so He can minister to people well!

Or, third, perhaps it was because Jesus knew the individual Thomas well. Each one of us has a fallback position to which we go when we're scared, tired, or overwhelmed. Thomas had been close to Jesus, and so Jesus was aware how Thomas was likely to act under pressure. If it is wonderful that God knows people in general, it is even more wonderful that He knows us individually and by name.

Or, fourth, possibly Jesus had a word of knowledge. Jesus is God-made-flesh, and in the River Jordan His human nature was baptized in the Spirit. Throughout His adult ministry He often exhibited divine power not because He was and is God (although He was and is) but because He had a human nature that was filled with the Holy Spirit. One of the gifts of the Holy Spirit is called "knowledge" (1 Cor. 12:8). It is the supernatural granting to someone of information that either cannot be learned in the normal way one learns things or else could be, but wasn't learned in that way.[17]

It could be for any or for all of these reasons why Jesus knew Thomas' demand for tactile proof. Christianity is both the mundane and normal, and it is both the spectacular and supernatural. Christianity involves the loving ongoing work of the community, and it also involves divine wisdom and intervention. One of these reasons is not any more of God than the other, even though we may prefer, variously, that God would act gently, following more understandable procedures; or else act dramatically and supernaturally. (While God honors the personality type He has given us, with some of us preferring the quiet and the routine and others of us enjoying the dramatic and spectacular, we all need to be stretched. God may just want to bless us in ways we might deem boring or else seem overly dramatic.)

How far will God go to bring us closer to Him? Here we have the example of Jesus giving Thomas a second chance. Jesus is the Good Shepherd who leaves the flock to go rescue the lost individual (John 10:1–18). However, Jesus did not go chasing after the rich young ruler (Mark 10:17–31) or the nine healed lepers who did not come back to say thanks (Luke 17:11–19). While we can rejoice that God gives people additional chances to come to Him to be saved, we are not to presume upon this. The chances God offers are not limitless.

It seems that Thomas was rewarded because he was willing to express his doubts *as he sought answers.* As many have noted over the centuries, "Doubting Thomas" should rather be called "Thomas, the Apostle of faith." He doubted but he did something about that doubt. And, when sufficient facts presented themselves, he put his trust in Christ. He did not indulge irresponsible doubt.

Too many people believe the point of the Thomas story is that it is OK to doubt. This is a false assumption. We note in the New Testament that doubt is often challenged, and sometimes even faulted. In a previous chapter we saw how Jesus called those on the road to Emmaus "foolish" and "slow of heart to believe" (Luke 24:25). In the prelude to the Christmas story, Zechariah's skepticism of the angel Gabriel's announcement was punished by his being temporarily striken mute (Luke 1:5–23).

When Jesus challenges Thomas, "Do not doubt but believe" (John 20:27, NRSV), He clearly is not glorifying doubt but issuing a challenge: "It's OK to doubt, provided you do what is necessary to address your doubt, and, when the evidence presents itself, come to believe and manifest that belief in actions." The story of Thomas is not so much about doubt as it is about faith.

Harry Emerson Fosdick (1878–1969) provided a good illustration a half century ago that dispels any sentimental notion of the spiritual superiority of lazy doubt. He wrote:

> To be sure, in every realm the believers are commonly accused by the skeptics of being crazy. A friend of mine, operating in Arabia during the First World War, ran upon an Arab sheik who, hearing talk about telegraphy, was dogmatic that no message could possibly travel from

Basra to Baghdad faster than his swiftest horse could run. He refused to be credulous. He was one of those shrewd, hardheaded men, not to be fooled. No one was going to pull the wool over his eyes. What he failed to see was that skepticism can be just as mistaken as credulity.[18]

While there may be various emotional or personality type issues underlying one's doubt and one's faith, doubt and faith are actually based on definite decisions that we make. Jesus said to them, "Do not doubt but believe" (John 20:27). If doubt and faith were based on emotional or personality type issues He would not have said that. To give a command implies we can do something about it.

Ted Schroder comments:

> Feelings of uncertainty or doubt should not prevent me from making the decision to believe in Jesus and to follow him. Sometimes I have to act on my choices before the feelings will follow. The habit of keeping company with Jesus will result in a secure relationship of love, which fosters faith. Walking in the way of Christ each day can gradually dispel doubt, until it withers away through lack of attention. Faith needs to be fed, and doubt needs to be starved, through prayer, study, service, witness, and worship.[19]

Faith will grow and doubt will diminish as we take time to review the evidence. We have already seen that faith is made possible or else is strengthened as we read what God had done in Bible times and throughout church history, and in what He continues to do in the lives of Christians alive today. We also noted our need to renew the evidence of God working supernaturally in our own lives.

Thomas heard the testimony of the ten, "We have seen the Lord" (John 20:25). Perhaps, although John does not note this, he had also heard the secondhand account of Jesus' appearance to Mary Magdalene and of His appearance to Peter. Thomas had obtained some secondhand evidence, but it was still not enough. He needed evidence that was personal and firsthand.

Thomas' faith may have seemed weak, but he was still a follower of Jesus. German theologian Helmut Thielicke, commenting on artwork depicting the still-doubting Thomas, states that, "Although he stands outside in a state of unmastered doubt, Thomas is encircled by a halo, the aura of a saint."[20] Again recall how the father of the demoniac boy said to Jesus, "I believe; help my unbelief!" (Mark 9:24). We might hear Thomas say, "I have doubts, but I do believe in Jesus." John underscores this point for us by calling Thomas "one of the Twelve" (John 20:24).

In our next chapter we will see how Thomas' "hanging in there" was rewarded.

Discussion Questions

1. Can you compel yourself to believe something that your intellect knows is not true?

2. Can you walk by faith and not by sight without some experience upon which to base your faith?

3. Does faith come to you from outside sources (hearing, seeing, touching, being touched) or from the inside out (being impregnated by the Holy Spirit)?

Jesus is authority – "all authority ... has been given to me." Matt 28:18
obedience – Our love for Him is partly fulfilled by our obedience.

CHAPTER 7

THOMAS' FAITH: "MY LORD
AND MY GOD!"

John 20:26–29

WHEN JESUS HONORED Thomas' request for proof by inviting him to touch the wound marks, Thomas did not say, "That was nice. I now want to see you turn water into wine, multiply fish and loaves, and walk on water." Thomas had all the evidence he needed, and he committed himself to Christ immediately. God will give us enough evidence to believe. He will not honor our playing games.

How was Jesus' response to Thomas different from His response to Mary Magdalene? As we saw at the end of the first chapter, Jesus said to Mary, "Do not hold on to me" (John 20:17, NRSV). By contrast, He invites Thomas to touch the nail marks and to place his hand in His side (John 20:27). What is the difference? Russ Parker suggests:

> For Mary to touch Jesus in the garden would be to go back to how it all used to be. She would have Jesus where she wanted Him. For Thomas to touch Jesus would be

117

to step out of his routine of living on the margins and to face his fears. For Thomas to touch Jesus meant that there was no going back to living the way he used to.[1]

Then Parker challenges us: "We need a fresh contact with Jesus so we do not go back to old patterns."[2] Jesus graciously offered Thomas the opportunity to touch the marks of the crucifixion but challenged him as well: do not be faithless, but believing (John 20:27). There can be only two choices: "Faith in Him as the risen Lord who still bears the scars of His atoning death"[3] or no faith. A mere warm regard for a beloved teacher is too much or not enough.

Kenyan scholar Samuel M. Ngewa holds up Jesus' tempered challenge to Thomas as a model to African church leaders.

> Due to our tradition of a chief being a person of power, pastors in Africa tend to issue authoritative rebukes. But when we rebuke others, we must not lose sight of our goal, namely bringing those we serve to confess Jesus as their Lord and God.[4]

I believe that God will provide the evidence we need to come to faith but not necessarily all the evidence we desire. With Thomas having been given all that He needed—secondhand testimony and, now, firsthand experience—the ball was firmly in Thomas' court. Thomas acquits himself well. His comment was extraordinary. He did not just say, "I believe Jesus is truly risen from the dead," essential though this belief is (Rom. 10:9). What Thomas said was, "My Lord and my God" (John 20:28).

Can we identify what prompted Thomas' confession of faith? Philip Yancey is a contemporary writer particularly sensitive to the question of theodicy (how a powerful, loving God allows evil in the world). Yancey believes it was the presence of Jesus' wound marks.

In a flash of revelation, Thomas saw the wonder of Almighty God, the Lord of the universe, stooping to take on our pain.[5] [See chapter 4 for a thorough discussion of Jesus' wound marks.]

"My Lord and my God." Sir Edwyn Hoskyns reminds us that this combination of "Lord" and "God" is not new. It is how one honored God the Father in the Old Testament period (2 Sam. 7:28; 1 Kings 18:39; Ps. 30:2; 35:24; 86:15; 88:1; Jer. 38:17). Thomas had been present in the Upper Room when Jesus answered Philip by saying, "Whoever has seen me has seen the Father" (John 14:9).[6]

Thomas, then, by God's grace, connected the dots. To see Jesus is to see the Father. One calls The Father "Lord and God." Therefore, Jesus must be, as Thomas ascribed, "Lord and God." Kevin Martin wisely asks, "Isn't Thomas' confession the punchline of the Gospel of John?"[7]

Jesus corrected neither Thomas' oath of obedience nor his ascription of divinity. Christian commitment is to the person of Christ as both Lord to be obeyed and as God to be worshiped. It is both. It is much more than just "being good," being active in a church, being excited about having spiritual experiences, or about receiving blessings. God's church is to be marked by obedience and piety, and both of those at an advanced level. Many people tend to emphasize one of these much more than the other, but New Testament scholar C. K. Barrett reminds us they overlap.[8]

First, "Lord." It means we obey what He taught. Jesus is not a religious advisor from whose teaching we can pick and choose as we like. He claimed, "All authority...has been given to me" (Matt. 28:18).

Jesus challenged His followers, "Why do you call me, 'Lord, Lord,' and not do what I tell you?" (Luke 6:46). The story goes that the humorist known as Mark Twain (born Samuel Langhorne

Clemens, 1835–1910), was once asked, "Do you have trouble with the parts of the Bible you don't understand?" He responded, "It ain't those parts of the Bible that I can't understand that bother me; it is the parts I do understand." What God demanded of Twain was clear; Twain just didn't want to do it. Some churches have dropped the term *Lord* from their services of worship because, as they have stated, "The term *Lord* sounds authoritarian, as if Jesus were telling us what to do." Indeed! (And yet note how unafraid these same churches are to quote Scripture authoritatively on matters and causes dear to them.)

Just as most parents love their children despite their bad behavior, God loves us unconditionally, even though He must correct bad behavior. Salvation can only be received humbly as a gift from God because we can never be good enough and never do enough to merit it (Eph. 2:9–10).

However, once a person is saved—by God's grace, received through one's faith—obedience to God is expected (Eph. 2:10). Our salvation is proven by our growth in obedience and service. If a person has invited the Lord of the universe to live within him or herself, while that person will not become perfect in this life, he or she will become noticeably different. If no difference is observed, should we not wonder if that person has truly come to Christ? We do this not to judge but to help.

One of the ways we thank God for the free gift of salvation is by being obedient to God. (So is working hard for His kingdom. In response to our "abounding in the work of the Lord" [1 Cor. 15:58], God will give us a good reward [Mark 9:41; Luke 6:35].) Obedience is necessary for our joy. Disobedience causes destruction, misery, and disease, both in ourselves and in others. Obedience is required, not just as a mark of discipleship but also as a condition of our continued well-being and that of the world around us.

Three things are necessary for our obedient growth in personal holiness and in obediently abounding in good works.

First, obedience to God demands our hard work. Notice all the commands given in the New Testament; nearly all involve our active participation. When we are told, "Put to death therefore what is earthly in you: sexual immorality, impurity, passion, evil desire, and covetousness" (Col. 3:5) we are not to think, "Should God wish to act to make me be a holier person, I'd like that, but there's really nothing I can do." Not at all. We have a definite part to play; we are *actively, intentionally* to put these bad attitudes and actions things to death. Paul told the Philippians, "Work out [the ramifications of] your own salvation with fear and trembling, for it is God who works in you" (Phil. 2:12–13). You work; God works. Both. And with the help of others.

Second, obedience to God also involves the involvement of other believers in our lives. Mature brothers and sisters in Christ teach and model good discipleship for us. On behalf of others, believers are exhorted to "admonish the idlers, encourage the fainthearted" (1 Thess. 5:14, NRSV). Tough love ministry is taught in many places in the New Testament, such as Galatians 6:1: "Brothers, if anyone is detected in a transgression, you who have received the Spirit should restore such a one in a spirit of gentleness" (NRSV). James 5:16 emphasizes this point, saying, "Confess your sins to one another and pray for one another, that you may be healed."

Third, obedience to God cannot happen without His grace, because only God can give the increase (1 Cor. 3:6) and only the Spirit can cause us to bear fruit (Gal. 5:22–23). We can neither be good nor do good without the grace of God, with us praying for it and seeking it day by day. We receive that grace by humbly asking for it and by making use of the God-appointed means of grace in Scripture reading, prayer, corporate worship, in the Christian community, and in the sacraments—especially Holy Communion. While obedience to God does not *merit* further grace, obedience to God *prepares* us to receive further grace.

Three necessary things to grow in obedience: our efforts, the help of others, and the grace of God as we actively pray for it and make use of the means of grace. If little or no change in spiritual maturity is observed in by others, it is most likely because either we are not doing anything to foster it or else because we are making use of only one or two of these three necessary things, not all three.

When Jesus said our love of Him is fulfilled in part by obedience, the original Greek of John 14:15 could be read in two ways. Jesus could be saying, "If you love me you will find that you are keeping my commandments because my grace is at work in you." Or, He could be saying, "If you love me you must do your part to keep my commandments because your love is proven in your obedience." In reality, both translations are correct and both meanings are needed.

Jesus does not offer Himself as *a* Lord to obey, but as *the* Lord Whose teaching trumps that of all authorities. Many Christians in the early centuries of the church were martyred because they would not say "Caesar is Lord" in contradiction to the earliest Christian creed, "Jesus is Lord."[9]

First, then, Jesus is the Lord to obey. And second, Jesus is God to worship. In His infancy the Magi, in paying Him homage, offered Him frankincense, which is an offering presented to God (Matt. 2:11). After seeing Him walk on water, some disciples worshiped Him, saying, "Truly you are the Son of God" (Matt. 14:33). No one ever called a mere mortal God. It was blasphemy, as the Jews who took up stones to throw at Jesus knew only too well (John 10:33), that is, unless it were true. Here, Thomas, as a Jew, knew what he was doing when he called the resurrected Jesus "My God" (John 20:28).

This designation evidenced more than the physical observation of the risen Christ. Merely to see Jesus again would demonstrate a resurrection but not demand the ascription of divinity. Thomas could easily say, "My Lord," but for Thomas to say, "My God," something had been deeply at work in Thomas' soul.

Jesus accepts Thomas' ascription of divinity. He did not say, "Thomas, I'm just a human being, and no more than that. I'm just a good teacher. Do not worship me." Jesus accepted Thomas' worship because Jesus knew Himself to be God-made-flesh. If this were not the case, then Jesus was either a crazy person or else the most egocentric person ever. In either case we must reject Him and not even deem Him a good teacher. As many writers have pointed out, He is either much more than a good teacher— or else much less. (Once again note C. S. Lewis' comment on this from chapter 2 of this book.)

Whether one believes Jesus to be right or not, it is abundantly clear that Jesus knew Himself to be God. R. C. Sproul speaks to those who have to ignore numbers of New Testament passages to deny Jesus' self-knowledge as divine, in particular the one in which Thomas calls Jesus "God."

> Those who deny the deity of Christ and insist the New Testament does not teach it much contort themselves in pain over this passage....If John did not want to convey the idea that Thomas' confession was sound, he would have been quick to add an editorial disclaimer, as he frequently did. Yet John's silence on the matter is nothing compared with the silence of Jesus. Jesus offered no rebuke to Thomas for calling Him 'God.'[10]

The belief that one should worship Jesus came gradually to His followers over the three years they knew Him, as indeed it should have. Just before His Ascension Jesus gave the eleven the Great Commission. Matthew tells us "they worshiped him, but some doubted" (Matt. 28:17). Only as the Holy Spirit fell upon them on the Day of Pentecost were they able to understand.

How did Thomas come to understand Jesus was divine? There was no expectation in Second Temple Judaism of God appearing in human form. The Pharisees believed that resurrection was to happen to everyone, or at least to the righteous, but there was nothing of divinity attached to that belief. No one imagined Lazarus or Jairus' daughter or the son of the widow of Nain to be divine just because they had been brought back from the dead. The Emmaus travelers thought Jesus to be a prophet, mighty in word and deed but not God. There is nothing in the Resurrection accounts or in the story of Paul's conversion that demanded divinity of the one being raised now.[11] It is the inner work of the Father through the Holy Spirit that then enabled and now enables people to know the truth of who Jesus is. It was because Thomas refused to abandon Jesus that Thomas was able to come to the truth.

The divinity of Christ was one of John's major themes. His prologue speaks of this Word who was both with God and was God. Stated differently, this Word was divine but not the same as God the Father. Reginald Fuller enumerates the various ways John instructs us in how Jesus is God. In addition to the prologue of John 1:1 and 1:14, Fuller points us to:

- How Jesus made himself equal with God (John 5:18).

- How He said, "Before Abraham was, I AM." Had Jesus simply said, "I had already been," people would have understood priority, however that may have happened, but nothing more. By saying, "I AM," Jesus is claiming for Himself the sacred name of Yahweh (John 8:58).

- Jesus saying, "I and the Father are one" (John 10:30).

- How His enemies were on to Him, saying, "You being a man, make yourself God" (John 10:33).

- Jesus saying, he "who has seen me has seen the Father" (John 14:9).

- And Jesus saying, "even as we are one" (John 17:11).[12]

Thomas, the doubter rewarded for his persistence, got the point. It is not that John is putting words into Thomas' mouth. Rather, John brings out those aspects of the story that serve his most important theological point, that Jesus is God made flesh.

Our being good people and our doing good for others are important. Our correct understanding of the doctrines of the Trinity and of the Person of Christ is definitely important. But they are not substitutes for the active, regular, intentional worship of God, Father, Son, and Holy Spirit, in the community of the church following the patterns of worship God gave to the church in the church's infancy.

Jesus then said to Thomas, "Have you believed because you have seen me? Blessed are those who have not seen and yet believe" (John 20:29). John's Gospel was the last of the four Gospels to be written, written at a time when an ever-growing number of converts had not been alive when Jesus was on Earth. Perhaps they thought belief must have been easier when people were able to see the physical Christ on Earth. John brings them assurance this is not so. John Marsh notes how Thomas is "the link between the experience of the apostles and that of the later Church, making plain to all believers there was no advantage to the apostles in 'seeing.'"[13]

Raymond E. Brown draws a comparison with the Jews who had come out of Egypt and those of succeeding generations. His research discovered that in Midrash Tanhuma, Rabbi Simeon ben Lakish (ca. AD 250) said:

> The proselyte is dearer to God than all the Israelites who were at Sinai. For if those people had not witnessed thunder, flames, lightning, the quaking mountain, and

the trumpet blasts, they would not have accepted the rule of God. Yet the proselyte who has seen none of these things comes and gives himself to God and accepts the rule of God. Is there anyone who is dearer than this man?[14]

And God offers us hope. R. William Dickson asks:

How can reasonable people attempting to live reasonable lives find hope that our lives are not so easily just swallowed up by the ravages of time in its passing? How can those with lives very much grounded in time, aspire to a life which is beyond time, indeed eternal? The answer lies in the greatest of all miracles, the literal, bodily resurrection of Jesus Christ from the dead. The one who had been dead and buried within a tomb has risen.[15]

In the introduction to this book we noted how each of Jesus' post-Resurrection appearances points to a different but equally vital part of Christian discipleship present since the beginning of the church. What does John 20:26–29, the story of Thomas, teach us?

First, it teaches us that doubt is not wrong as long as we doubt honestly, with a diligent search for the truth and no playing of games.

Second, we see that Jesus is Lord to be obeyed and God to be worshiped.

It is not how we start that counts; it is how we finish (Matt. 10:22; 24:13). Thomas may have been the last of the eleven apostles to believe, but look what actions followed. The tradition of the church tells us that when other disciples headed into the Roman world to spread the good news, Thomas headed east. The first Portuguese explorers who reached India in the fifteenth century were astonished to find Christians already there. This small community of believers told them they had been established by

Mark went to africa in AD 49 and founded the Church of alexandria.

126

Thomas himself. Thomas believed, and this belief manifested in great fruit for God's kingdom.

Discussion Questions

1. Discuss the tension between the concept of "walking by faith and not by sight" and the concept of being graciously given the personalized experience necessary to instill faith.

2. To what degree is Christianity propositional (specific doctrinal truths) and to what degree is it relational (a believer's walk with the Lord)?

   the act of offering or suggesting something to be considered

   only meaningful relative to other objects

3. Obedience is a major theme throughout the Bible. What does biblical obedience look like in terms of attitude, contemplation, and action?

CHAPTER 8

JESUS AND THE SEVEN BY
THE SEA OF GALILEE

John 21:1–14

JESUS BY NOW had appeared several times since His resurrection, but there was still some unfinished business with the apostles. Jesus had met with them as a group at least twice before (Luke 24:36–43; John 20:19–29). On the first of these occasions He gave an initial bestowal of the Holy Spirit and the beginnings of a recommissioning for ministry in His name. There remained to be given, however, a full-fledged call to service, different from previous calls because Jesus was about to ascend back to heaven in anticipation of the Father sending the Holy Spirit. (And, as we will see in our next chapter, there was unfinished business with Peter.) This second call took place in the dual context of a night's fishing and a simple meal.

There are two focal points in this appearance of Jesus, and they are quite different from each other. First was the supernatural way in which Jesus made Himself known to them. Second was personal, intimate fellowship with Him at a simple meal.

Some scholars doubt the Johannine authorship of John 21

because the last verses of chapter 20 sound very much like the end of a story. When we are told, "Now Jesus did many other signs in the presence of his disciples, which are not written in this book" (John 20:30), the implication is that we will not be told any more of them in John's Gospel. And yet, there is John 21 following.

To the skeptics of Johannine authorship of this additional chapter, I say, first, there is no manuscript evidence that this Gospel ever circulated without chapter 21.

Second, even if chapter 21 had been appended, that action was to ensure the inclusion of this significant post-Resurrection appearance, which had circulated either in a short story form, or orally, or both.

And third, have these skeptical scholars preached much? I do not know a preacher who does not say, "Finally," and then goes on to make more than one final point!

John tells us that several of the disciples were fishing up north in Galilee (John 21:1–8). John uses the term "Sea of Tiberias," the term better known to his Greek audiences. (See John 6:1, where the range of names for this body of water is listed.) John does not inform us why they were in Galilee, but Mark records that Jesus had told them to return to Galilee, where He would meet them (Mark 14:28). An angel had said the same thing to the women (Mark 16:7).

There seems to be a tone of frustration in Peter's saying, "I am going fishing" (John 21:3). Jesus had already appeared to Peter once individually (1 Cor. 15:5) and twice to Him with other apostles present (John 20:19–29), yet there is no record of any personal reconciliation necessitated by Peter's recent denials of knowing Jesus. If Peter was just keeping busy supporting himself and his family while awaiting further orders perhaps he wondered if those orders would ever come.

Many of us also have a call from God and are waiting for it to unfold. As we will see more fully in the last chapter of this book, while waiting we are to keep busy in the usual spiritual duties of prayer, worship, sacrament, Scripture reading, service, and fellowship, and also in the normal duties and responsibilities of our personal, family, and work lives. "The daily round, the common task" is not all God has in store for us, but while we are awaiting something more specific and, perhaps, more spectacular, we must be about our simple duties. Waiting for the Lord to call us does not mean *idly* waiting.

They were fishing at night. Fishing was usually better then, and fishermen could sell their catch fresh the next morning. Fishermen though they were, they caught nothing until an unknown individual on shore told them where to drop their nets.

These disciples had previously been called to fish for people (Matt. 4:19), but until they had further evidence of the reality of the gospel, a further call to service, and an empowerment to be successful in that service, they would not try to catch those people. Right now, they were not even having success catching fish![1]

Once again, they did not recognize Jesus. Was it simply because they were one hundred yards off shore—the length of a football field—and because the light was limited as it was dawn (John 21:4)?

Or was it that Jesus, in His resurrected body, was somewhat different now, even though they had seen Him in this body at least twice before (Luke 24:35; John 20:19)?

Or was it something God the Father was doing for a specific purpose, as He had done first with Mary Magdalene and then with Cleopas and his fellow traveler? While the text does not say that their eyes were kept from recognizing Him, chapter 21 does begin by saying, "Jesus revealed himself." The Greek word can carry the sense of disclosure. Jesus is going to do more than just appear here. He is going to disclose something more about what life in the church should include. The church is to move in the supernatural, and here Jesus is manifesting the gift of the Spirit called a word of knowledge.

When the Holy Spirit fell on the disciples on the Day of

Pentecost, they started speaking in tongues (Acts 2:1–13). As we continue reading in the Book of Acts we see other charismatic gifts in evidence, some of them later enumerated by Paul in 1 Corinthians 12 and 14. One of these charismatic gifts is called knowledge (1 Cor. 12:8). The person manifesting this gift has been divinely given information that he or she either could not know except supernaturally or else could know naturally but did not in this instance learn in the normal ways of acquiring information.

A Manifestation of the Word of Knowledge

Many years ago when temporarily living in St. Louis, I had a most profound experience of God manifesting this gift through me. My wife was doing three months of rotations toward her medical degree. Since my full-time ministry at that time was leading conferences around the United States, I could easily be in St. Louis with her, needing only a nearby airport and a church that would offer me office space in which to work.

I was asked to lead the Friday noon service one week at a church, a service which included laying-on-of-hands and anointing for healing. After administering Holy Communion to the twenty or so people present I went back down the altar rail and prayed for each person. I prayed that the first one would receive a healing for the emotional hurt she was experiencing from the betrayal of a close friend. I prayed that the son and daughter-in-law of the second person would reconcile and that their marriage would be saved. I prayed that the cousin of the third would be healed of his heart ailment. I prayed with that kind of specificity for about half the people present.

After the service one of them asked me, "How did you do that? You don't know us and you don't know our problems and needs. You prayed for us as if we had told you what to pray for but we didn't. How did you do that?"

Before I could answer one of them blurted out, "He must be psychic." It was so sad that the only explanation she could think of was from the occult and not from the Bible. As I explained the operation of the gifts of the Spirit in general and the one called word of knowledge in particular, another woman exclaimed, "It's true, then!" I thought she meant that the present-day manifestation of the gifts of the Spirit were true and not some religious con job or something relegated to the early days of the church, but her newfound belief was much more significant than this. She added, "Jesus really rose from the dead! I believe it now." In Scripture and throughout the church's history we often find that it is when people see the signs and wonders of God manifested that they can believe the contents of the doctrinal message (Mark 16:20).

This congregation was a good one and led by a godly and biblically sound pastor, so these two people must not have been paying attention for one to confuse a gift of the Holy Spirit with an occult operation and for the other one finally to be converted to Christ after having attended the church for years.

To other churches and clergy I would suggest that if we ignore some aspect of the Christian faith because we don't like it or because we have been turned off to it by the antics of some who have twisted it or because we fail to see that the essence of that aspect can be expressed in ways more consistent with our church's particular style, some of our people will find another source for their spiritual education. What they embrace may be way off base. To put it another way, if you don't want your dog to raid the garbage pails of the neighborhood, make sure you feed it good food.

I suggest it was Jesus' manifestation of a word of knowledge in His human nature that caused Him to know where the fish were located. *You* try seeing fish below the surface of the water. A hundred yards ahead of you. In the faint light of dawn!

Is there symbolic meaning in what has just occurred? I like the speculation of Harry Griffth, who sees the throwing of the net over the side of the boat as proving the importance of obeying Christ in all things, the unbroken net as symbolizing the church, the water from which the fish would eventually be removed representing sin and death, and the large catch demonstrating there is room in the church for believers from all nations.[2]

Jesus' Supernatural Manifestations Are Examples of His Spirit-filled Human Nature

Jesus was and is God made human. Therefore, He had and has both a divine nature and a human nature. We might quickly conclude that our Lord's supernatural manifestations came from His divine nature, but did they? I believe they came from His spirit-filled human nature. How might this be so?

First, He did not start His earthly ministry until His human nature had been filled by the Holy Spirit in the River Jordan (Luke 3:21–22). There are fanciful pseudo-Gospels, never accepted as true by the church, in which the little boy Jesus, out of His divine nature, does such things as turn His playmates into stone statues and then back into living children again. The real Gospels will have none of that! Jesus starts ministering only after His human nature has been empowered, and when it is He does not do stunts. (It is sometimes said that various writings were kept out of the canonical Scriptures because the church wanted to keep aspects of the truth from people. Rather, it was because the church wanted to keep falsehood away.)

Second, He often is drained by ministry. When the woman with the hemorrhages touched Him, Jesus noticed "power has gone out from me" (Luke 8:46). What kind of puny divinity would He be if only one person could thus drain Him? What Jesus experienced is what we all experience when we've been ministering for a while: not only are we physically and emotionally tired, we are also spiritually drained.

Third, as we noted in chapter 5, He needed periodically to recharge His batteries by going off to pray before He could minister with power again.

Fourth, when Jesus met with the ten on the first Easter evening, He said, "As the Father has sent me, even so I am sending you" (John 20:21). He would not send His followers out in their own strength, because Jesus did not minister in His own strength. He would not tell them to minister through their divine nature, because they did not have one. He told them to wait in Jerusalem for the "power from on high" to fall upon them (Luke 24:49). They were to minister, just as He had done, in their Spirit-empowered human nature.

Jesus came to them in their frustration and disappointment, just as He comes to us in our daily lives, with our frustrations and disappointments. Jesus came, and their nets were quickly filled. By suddenly catching a large number of fish after an evening of frustration, might they have recollected a similar experience—when Jesus first called them as disciples (Luke 5:1–11)? Then, too, they had also toiled all night and caught nothing (v. 5). Jesus then called out to them, instructed them to drop their nets, and the nets were filled with fish. Afterward Jesus told them that from then on they would not be catching fish but people (v. 10).

While fishing was routine for them, the timing of these two amazing catches was at significant moments in their lives. These were times of transition from what they had known to what Jesus was calling them to be and to do. The first occasion, described early in Luke's Gospel, was their call to leave fishing and follow Him. This second occasion, recounted in this last chapter of John's Gospel, was their re-commissioning. They were not to go back to fishing now that He had risen but were to lead the church after He ascended and the Holy Spirit fell upon them. In both cases, their empty nets symbolized that they were being called away from something unfulfilling to something significant.

Sometimes before we can hear God's call to enter a new way of serving Him or to continue what we are doing but in a new place, we first have to hear the call to leave what we are doing or where we are living or both. Often we must leave behind what is comfortable and secure. Sometimes God's new call comes as we see a significant reduction in our bearing fruit for Him in what we have been doing or as we perceive an increasing sense of uprootedness in where we have been living, or both. Often before we hear the call *to*, we have to sense a call away *from*.

Sometimes people ask me if they need to be **Charismatic** in order to have an effective ministry for God. It depends on what you mean by *Charismatic*. There is both a cultural definition and an ontological definition for this word. Or, put another way, there's Charismatic packaging and there's Charismatic content.

If by *Charismatic* a person means informal as opposed to formal, spontaneous as opposed to carefully planned, loud as opposed to soft, new as opposed to traditional, and new music accompanied by a praise band as opposed to classic hymns accompanied by the pipe organ, then, no, one does not have to be Charismatic, because these ways of expressing the faith are simply cultural packaging, personal preference, or personality type. There are myriad people moving in the power of the Spirit whose spirituality is quite traditional and formal, and there are also countless numbers of people who are loud and spontaneous and who love contemporary music who are not moving in the Holy Spirit.

But if by *Charismatic* a person means praying for and receiving Holy Spirit empowerment, and seeking, receiving, and manifesting various of the supernatural gifts of the Spirit (including but not limited to the more spectacular ones mentioned in 1 Corinthians 12 and 14), then, yes, one needs to be Charismatic, because these are essential to our bearing fruit for God. The gifts of the Holy Spirit are not *toys* to play with, although it is often quite fun and rewarding to see God use us in powerful, supernatural ways. (Real Christianity is far from boring.) Nor are the gifts of the Holy Spirit *trophies* to boast of, because it is God who accomplishes the good results as He works through us. The gifts of the Holy Spirit are *tools* to use in the Master's service.

And, again, the cultural packaging—the tool boxes—can vary. While writing the first draft of this chapter, I was in England ministering at Burrswood, one of the oldest and unquestionably the largest of healing centers in the British Isles. It was founded by

Dorothy Kerin, who had received a dramatic, sudden healing in 1912. Her healing made the national press. Dorothy was a formal, cultured, upper-middle-class Anglo-Catholic. There was no doubt her style of personal spirituality and ministry were culturally light-years away from contemporary American Pentecostalism, but she was used of God in just as powerful a way as any contemporary "Spirit-filled" Christian. For fun when rereading her autobiography, I swapped some of her traditional Anglo-Catholic terms for the supernatural experiences of God she had been experiencing and substituted contemporary Pentecostal-speak. The essence of Holy Spirit empowerment and activity was clearly present in her, even though the cultural packaging of it was quite different from contemporary Charismatic expression.

We could similarly note how spiritual fruit was borne in the lives of numerous Christians throughout the centuries—people who were clearly Holy Spirit–empowered and Holy Spirit–manifesting, even though their style and terminology was significantly different from that of the contemporary charismatic movement.

When God calls us to Himself He does not ask us to repent of our personality or our style—just our sins. We do people an injustice if we force them to change things that are not wrong and are central to who they are. When Simon matured he became Peter, not John. When Saul was converted, he became Paul, not Timothy.[3]

When the Scriptures tell us "be filled with the Spirit" (Eph. 5:18), the best translation of this phrase is, "Keep on being filled with the Spirit." Put politely, Holy Spirit power is expended as we serve so we need replenishment. Put less delicately, "We need ongoing replenishment because *we leak.*" The reason that we cannot bear fruit for God is that we are not regularly re-empowered by the Spirit, irrespective of how dramatic an encounter with the Holy Spirit we may have had at one time. But though we need regular replenishing, as Paul and countless disciples ever since have discovered, "I can do all things through him who strengthens me" (Phil. 4:13).

"The disciple whom Jesus loved," that is, John, recognized it was Jesus calling to them from the shore (John 21:7). Perhaps the sudden catch of fish after a night of failure triggered a memory in John. Triggers often bring us back—cognitively, emotionally, or both—to a previous event, either painful or pleasant. Triggers can sometimes cause us to act or feel strangely, or they can elicit pleasant memories. We wonder what's come over us and why. Triggers can be activated by any of the five senses.

Sometimes we remember the past event that is triggered. Years ago one of my high school youth group girls would cry whenever a certain song was being played on the radio because it was the song playing when her boyfriend broke up with her. The song triggered an emotion, and she knew exactly why. On other occasions we may experience the emotion but do not know its source in an event that hurt us in the past.

We need to recognize that triggers are always present in our lives, often bringing to the surface something powerful, either a bad memory to be healed or a good memory to be celebrated. In the Scriptural event presently under consideration, the memory triggered was a pleasant one. In our next chapter we will examine a few negative triggers in the life of Peter and how Jesus ministered to him accordingly.

Peter, upon hearing it was Jesus, abandoned the others so he could quickly get to Him. Impetuous, yes, and so like Peter. Here again is Peter acting before thinking, and thinking only of himself, not of the others who would now have a heavy net to drag ashore, minus one man to accomplish the task. This is Peter, not yet filled with the Spirit, not yet mature. But Jesus chose him as he was, and He also chooses us in our raw, green, immature state. There's encouragement here for us. If God would call Peter and would continue on with him, there's hope for each of us.

However, we should not make excuses for our wrong behavior. We are to ask for forgiveness and then take the necessary steps to continue our growth toward maturity. But we do not wait until we are mature before we start serving otherwise we might never start. We do our part, receive help from others and rely on divine grace in order to grow in our walk and in our work, both at the same time. Peter, as we see in the Acts of the Apostles, would continue to mature.

What might Peter have been feeling when He heard that it was the Lord calling to those in the boat from the shore? Excitement and happiness, to be sure, but might there have been other emotions as well? Jesus had still not spoken with Peter about his three-fold denial during Holy Week. In his previous encounters with the resurrected Lord there was no mention of his cowardly behavior, but wouldn't it eventually happen? It is normal human behavior to have mixed emotions when you expect at some point the other shoe will drop.

Yet, why would Peter now head toward and not away from Jesus? D. A. Carson understands that Peter's behavior here "does not read like the action of someone who is running away."[4] Aware of his sinfulness and Jesus' holiness, Peter had said to his Lord, on the previous occasion Jesus had helped them catch fish, "Depart from me, for I am a sinful man" (Luke 5:8). Why not now?[5] Was he acting like the prodigal son, expecting there might be discipline but so wanting to be home that he rushes toward him nonetheless? Peter knew that though he let Jesus down, Jesus still loved him. The past three years of being with Jesus had assured him of that.

When we know we've done wrong, we need not try to flee from God. God knows where we are anyway, so how can we escape Him (Ps. 139:7–12)? And also, our previous experience with the Lord's discipline of us should remind us His discipline is often light and always loving.

When they all got ashore, the disciples found a fire ablaze with breakfast ready (John 21:9). This meal, unlike the one in Emmaus, was not a Communion service. There is no wine and no indication of the gestures and words of the Upper Room. What is revelatory here for the future church is the fact that the Lord wants to have fellowship with His people in the ordinary things of life.

(Some denominations now call the Sundays in the summer and fall "Ordinary Time" to remind us of this fact.) Jesus' cooking them breakfast should also remind clergy that while we have authority over our flocks, we also have a servant ministry to them. Like Jesus, we preside at Communion yet sometimes need also to cook the breakfast.

Yes, He's the Lord of the universe, but He also likes to hang out with us personally. (Remember how he called Mary Magdalene by name in chapter 1?) He's concerned with both global issues and also with little things in the lives of individuals. Jesus raised Jairus's daughter from her deathly slumber yet at the end of the story remembered to tell the family to "give her something to eat" (Luke 8:55, NRSV). Regarding the disciples, He had just recently died on the cross to pay the penalty for their sins so they could have eternal life, and now He is making them breakfast. He gives Himself to us in the consecrated bread and wine of Holy Communion, and He also wants to be a table guest at every meal we eat.

Jesus directed them to supplement what He was cooking with some of the fish they had just caught. So the net, heavy with the overly large catch, had to be hauled ashore.[6] Christianity sometimes centers in a miracle, but often it focuses on plain hard work. God does not expect us to do it all, but He won't do it all for us. This cooperative balance is evident in many of the miracles related in the New Testament. In John 2, the men had to fill the jars with water, but only Jesus could turn it into wine. In Mark 2, the friends had to carry the paralytic to Jesus, but only Jesus could forgive and heal. We can't do the Lord's part, but He expects that we do ours. Merrill C. Tenney contrasts the instance when Jesus multiplied the fish and loaves that a boy had supplied (Matt. 14:15–21; 15:32–39) with the coming situation where it is the disciples who will multiply His ministry.[7]

Michael Brecht whimsically suggests that we could expect the now-risen Lord to show up back in Jerusalem wearing a great big "I told you so" sign or appear in Pilate's locked chamber and "mess with him, appearing and disappearing," or even be in Rome sitting in Tiberius's seat, saying, "'Now who's boss?' No, our great High Priest had more important things to do—just a little morning barbecue with His friends."[8]

We're told they caught 153 fish (John 21:11). Commentators over the centuries have tried to find symbolic meaning in that number. Cyril of Alexandria thought the number represented the conversion of 100 heathen and 50 Jews, with the three persons of the Trinity added. Several ancient writers such as Jerome declared there were 153 species of fish in the world, so we are to understand that the Gospel is for everyone, a lesson repeated in Peter's vision in Acts 10.[9]

As to the significance of the number 153, my response is that the Scriptures record the number as 153 simply because that's how many fish they caught. Period! The apostles counted them because men especially like to look at something they've done and think, "Could that be a record?" We catch a big fish and out comes the yardstick and the camera to record for posterity that on such and such a date we caught a big fish and here's how big it was. A friend of mine once couldn't wait to tell me he made nineteen free throws in a row. He counted! I want to tell you that a few years ago I set my personal best record by growing 64 butternut squashes in my garden. I, too, had counted! Jesus had said, "Without me you can do nothing" (John 15:5), but with Jesus they can do all things (Phil. 4:13). Jesus helped them catch a lot of fish, so of course they counted them.

Curiously, though they knew it was the Lord, they did not press the point. He was real and physically present, capable of talking and cooking breakfast, but something was different. Commentators point out that the word used here—*exetazo*—is best translated as they are "aware" it is He. Many commentators say it means that the apostles knew the person was Jesus, but they were uncomfortable. They had seen Him before in His resurrected body, but only on a few occasions. They are not yet used to "the new Jesus."

Jesus had been the friend of the disciples, and He was serving them here. But He was clearly now someone different. If it is true they were fishing while waiting for the next stage in their relationship, wouldn't they be wondering if that next stage has now started?

Each of the post-Resurrection appearances of Jesus teaches us something about what the church would be like after Jesus' Ascension and what the church should be like today. The events of John 21:1–14 teach us that:

- Jesus is recognized through His Spirit-filled human nature supernaturally knowing where the fish were to be found. Christianity includes the present-day manifestations of the gifts of the Spirit. Christians are to be supernatural instruments in the hands of a supernatural God.

- There was a miraculous catch of fish. Christianity means the church and individual Christians are to work so that people may come to faith in Christ.

- The seven have fellowship with Jesus around a simple breakfast meal. Christianity is apparent in fellowship with God and other believers in ordinary moments, not just on special occasions.

Discussion Questions

1. Jesus' favorite appellation for Himself was "Son of man" or "the human one." Some of his favorite things to do were healings and casting out demons. He told the disciples that they would do the same works and even greater. How do you fit all of this together?

2. Rabbi Zusya was deeply disturbed by a vision in which he heard the question he would be asked at the end of his life. "I have learned that the angels will not ask me, 'Why weren't you a Moses, leading your people out of slavery?'.... 'Why weren't you a Joshua, leading your people into the Promised Land?'.... They will say to me, 'Zusya, there was only one thing that no power of heaven or earth could have prevented you from becoming.' They will say, 'Zusya, why weren't you Zusya?'"[10] What are the implications of this for you?

3. What is the biblical definition of the word *charismatic*?

CHAPTER 9

JESUS RESTORES AND HEALS PETER

John 21:15–19

I F JESUS HAD unfinished business with the apostles as a group, He especially had unfinished business with Peter as an individual. The risen Christ had already met previously with him at least three times.[1] The accounts we have of those meetings give no indication of our Lord raising the subject of Peter's threefold denial. In one account Peter was given ministerial authority, but it was limited and it was given to the group as a whole (John 20:23). Gordon Bridger speculates Peter was then "probably...assured of forgiveness" at the individual meeting Paul and Luke briefly reference, but it does not seem this forgiveness was specifically about his denials.[2]

Peter would need a more individual, specific reconciliation with Jesus and a more extensive recommissioning in his work for Jesus because, though all but John had fled the cross, Peter was the one who had specifically denied the Lord. Jesus accomplished reconciliation and recommissioning in a way that also brought healing to Peter's inner being.

Gregory the Great (540–604) asked rhetorically why Peter was specially singled out when an angel told Mary Magdalene and the other women to tell the disciples Jesus was going before them to Galilee (Mark 16:7). Gregory answers his own question, "He was called by name so that he would not lose hope as a result of his denial."[3] Sir Edwyn Hoskyns points out that Jesus cares not just for the lost Gentiles but also for the dejected Peter.[4] Unlike some task-oriented people who care almost entirely about the project itself, Jesus also cared and still cares about those who are working on that project.

Jesus asked Peter, "Do you love me more than these?" (John 21:15). While John is often deliberately precise in his word choice, sometimes he is intentionally broad, speaking in ways that would admit to several understandings, each of which is true or at least possible. This question of Jesus has three possible meanings: First, "Do you love me *more than you love these men*?" Second, "Do you love me *more than these other men love me*?" Third, "Do you love me *more than you love these things*" (the components of the fishing occupation which you have now resumed)?

If it is the first—"Do you love me *more than you love these men*?"—could Jesus be asking if Peter really loved Him? But, though Peter often messed up his implementation, there was never a doubt in the Gospels that he really loved Jesus more than he loved anyone else. Therefore, we should probably not conclude this first theoretical possibility to be what Jesus meant.

The second theoretical possible meaning is, "Do you love me *more than these other men love me*?" Some scholars have suggested that if this is the intended meaning, Jesus would be encouraging a rivalry in the apostolic band that He had previously discouraged (Mark 9:33–35, 10:35–44) and would soon need to discourage again (John 21:20–22). Peter's boasting was not godly, and it got him into trouble. So, these scholars suggest, it is doubtful Jesus would be encouraging it. On the other hand, it could be that Jesus was tackling head on Peter's two-fold problem of boastfulness and denial. Peter had bragged that,

"Though they all fall away because of you, I will never fall away" (Matt. 26:33). How would Peter respond to Jesus' question here? If Peter responded in a way typical for him—"Of course I love you most"—Jesus could now tell Peter that his actions indicated to the contrary and that even if his actions were superior, he should not boast. But if Peter responded with in a different way—"It is obvious I don't, Lord, because look how I let you down"—Jesus would then get to the heart of the matter of Peter's boastfulness, receive Peter's confession, and begin Peter's restoration. If this is Jesus' intent, I believe it is possible that Jesus meant, "Do you love me more than these other men love me?"

If the meaning was the last—"Do you love me *more than you love these things?*—was Jesus asking Peter if he was going to go home and pick up his life where it had been before he met Jesus and not give his life to preaching the gospel? Peter and the others had left everything to follow Jesus once before (Luke 5:1–11). Was Peter prepared to do this again? He had just now gone home and gone back to the fishing that he knew, but arguably this was while he was awaiting further orders. Those were now coming. Would Peter again choose to follow Jesus? Would he now humble himself, continuing to do his part to grow into personal and spiritual maturity while, of course, needing the help of others and the grace of God? Or, like with so many throughout the centuries and today, was Christianity primarily the garnishing on the salad of successful, enjoyable middle class life? N. T. Wright asks, "Those who don't want to face that searching question and answer may remain content to help the world with its fishing."[5]

Do you love me more than you love these things? I believe this is most likely what Jesus was asking Peter, although there is certainly merit to the second possibility.[6]

But before Peter could once again choose to follow Jesus unconditionally, Peter needed to be restored to a full relationship with Him and receive what is called inner healing. Please note that there are three aspects to this restoration.

Jesus restored Peter formally, or what some call positionally. Jesus gave Peter three chances to affirm his commitment to Him, one each for the three times he had denied knowing his Lord (John 21:15–17). Far from Jesus rubbing Peter's nose in those denials, Jesus, in asking Peter for his commitment, was bringing closure. Additionally, Jesus gave Peter his ministry back when He said, "Feed [tend] my sheep [lambs]."

Peter might have assumed forgiveness and restoration from the way Jesus treated him in previous post-Resurrection appearances, but this time Jesus made it very clear. Peter was forgiven and restored, and he now knew it. What lessons can we learn from what Jesus was doing here?

First, God starts with us where we are but doesn't leave us there. Jesus started the reconciliation process with Peter by calling him Simon. Jesus had previously bestowed on him the nickname of Peter ("rock") when He first met Simon (John 1:42), knowing what Peter would become. By the transformation by the Holy Spirit, Simon will truly become Peter. But Simon is not there yet, so Jesus starts with him where he really is. God does not ask us to clean ourselves up before we can come to Him. Apart from His work in our lives, we can never get clean enough. Once we come to Him in faith and surrender, He will always love us, though He will not allow us to stay immature. He accepts us where we are and then compels us to take a walk with Him into maturity. God is definitely merciful, but He is not indulgent.

Second, we may not bypass dealing with error and sin on the way to reconciliation and restoration. While Jesus is not recorded as saying, "Simon, you really let me down a few weeks ago," it is clear that this recent event was not ignored. There can be no reconciliation until there is acknowledgement of sin, confession, and repentance. A relationship with others or life in a local church cannot go forward until the past has been appropriately addressed.

When apartheid ended in South Africa there needed to be an

addressing of the injustices that had previously occurred. The phrase often used was, "There cannot be peace until there is justice." It is frequently my politically liberal friends who quote this statement to me, but it is a truth that addresses evil all across the political spectrum. There cannot be peace against racism as long as racism is evidenced, but neither can there be peace against abortion until abortion no longer happens.

Years ago a staff member of mine made a careless mistake. I had forgiven her in my mind quite soon thereafter and the rest of the day smiled at her every time we passed in the hall. I assumed that she would somehow sense that all was forgiven. The next morning she approached me and said, "Are we OK?"

I gave an offhanded comment of, "Yeah, of course. Why do you ask?"

"I need to know if I'm forgiven for yesterday's mistake."

"Yes, you are," I told her. That was all she needed to hear, *but she needed to hear it.*

Jesus is too wise to think that Peter knew he was forgiven and restored just because Jesus didn't bring up the subject of the denials. Jesus made it clear by addressing the matter directly. He brought closure.

Rowan Williams, recent Archbishop of Canterbury and active in international peace and justice issues, comments, "Salvation does not bypass the history and memory of guilt, rather it builds upon it and from it."[7] Jesus figuratively took Peter back to the place of his denial so Peter could get it right. Any other way— any less painful shortcut—would not have been effective.

The psalmist said, "Mercy and truth are met together; righteousness and peace have kissed each other" (Ps. 85:10, KJV). But it is not easy. Everett L. Worthington, Jr. shrewdly observes that "knowing that God redeems does not mean that the kiss between righteousness and peace will be without bumped noses and mashed lips. Sometimes the embrace occurs only after a painful bear hug or a strenuous wrestling match."[8]

Peter needed to face his failures so that he would have humility requisite for a church leader. Later, when he wrote his first epistle, he exhorted other leaders to be in charge of others "not as domineering over those in your charge, but being examples to the flock" (1 Pet. 5:3). Jesus, the Good Shepherd, taught Peter how to be a shepherd in the apostolic church.

The third thing we can learn from what Jesus is doing as He restored Peter formally is that it is very important that when a matter is dealt with, unless it happens again, it is over. God tells us, "If we confess our sins, he is faithful and just to forgive us our sins and to cleanse us from all unrighteousness" (1 John 1:9). He removes our transgressions from us "as far as the east is from the west" (Ps. 103:12). Peter's sin was not thrown up in his face again and would not ever again be unless Peter repeated the mistake. Compare this to some people who say they have forgiven someone but keep bringing the matter up. With them we never experience actual closure, and therefore with them there is no opportunity to move forward.

So, first, Jesus restored Peter *formally*, or what some would call positionally. Second, Jesus also restored Peter *emotionally*. Sometimes just a statement of forgiveness will affect this. One knows he or she has been forgiven and also feels it. There are no residual, lingering guilt feelings.

This is not always the case, however. Sometimes something deeper is at work. Our conscious mind is only about ten to fifteen percent of our brain, and even some of that is more emotional than logical. There were numbers of triggers going on that could still trip Peter up emotionally even though he had been truly forgiven and knew it intellectually.

Jesus had told Peter that "before the cock crows, you will have denied me three times" (John 13:38, NRSV). When Peter did deny Jesus (John 18:17, 25, 27), a rooster crowed (v. 27). Now move forward to the scene here at the Sea of Tiberias. Peter and others had been fishing all night when Jesus appeared "just after daybreak"

(John 21:4, NRSV). This would be the time when the roosters of the villages all around the sea would be making their chanticleer morning wake-up calls. What might Peter be thinking or feeling as he heard their crowing? Would roosters crowing trigger something deep within Peter for the rest of his life unless Jesus brought healing?

In addition, Peter had denied Jesus by a charcoal fire (John 18:18). The New Testament uses the Greek word *anthrakia*, "charcoal fire," only twice.[9] The sight, sound, and smell of a charcoal fire differ from that of a wood fire. In the future, would a charcoal fire likely trigger in Peter a mental recollection or a visceral feeling stemming from that time, by a charcoal fire, when he let his Lord down? It quite possibly would unless Jesus were to change the significance of charcoal fires for Peter.

Therefore, when Jesus came to forgive and recommission Peter, it was not just with words. It was, I believe intentionally, both at dawn (John 21:4) and by a charcoal fire (John 21:9). Inner or emotional healing for those who have sinned is positional—dealing with our formal standing before the Lord—but it is also often emotional, dealing with the triggers which might bring back bad recollections and feelings. (Inner healing can also move people forward when they have been the victim of the sin of someone else.)[10]

I wonder what the future would have been for Peter if Jesus had forgiven him without taking into account these triggers. Cognitively, Peter could have known that he had been forgiven and commissioned for ministry, but what would have happened emotionally deep within him when he heard roosters crowing or encountered charcoal fires? Might these experiences have made him question his standing with the Lord and his authority to serve as a church leader? It's easy for us to say, "He should just own what Jesus said and believe it." Maybe he should have, but triggers are powerful things. If we ignore them, they sometimes pop up to hurt us, and, through us, others. And we're often not aware we are doing this. I believe Jesus deliberately picked a moment involving roosters and a charcoal fire for His asking Peter for a commitment.

So, first, Jesus restored Peter *formally* or positionally. Second, Jesus also restored Peter *emotionally*. Lastly, Jesus restored Peter *gradually*.

We just saw how Jesus went back to the name with which He addressed Peter when He first met him, Simon. When Jesus first asked Peter if he loved Him, Jesus used the word *agape*, a self-sacrificial love (John 21:15–16). Peter would not use Jesus' word in reply because Peter knew his previous boastful statements about his level of commitment had not been realized. Peter uses the word *philia*, meaning "brotherly love, friendship, profound admiration," because he was ashamed and embarrassed. The third time Jesus asked Peter the nature of his love Jesus used Peter's word (v. 17). Peter felt hurt, perhaps because Jesus decided He needed to ask Peter three times, perhaps because the three times reminded Peter of his three denials, perhaps because Jesus changed the word He used from *agape* to *philia*, or perhaps for all of these reasons. Jesus came down to Peter's level and restarted their relationship where Peter was, though of course He would not leave him there.[11]

Jesus told Peter to feed His lambs and sheep. Peter had also been told to fish for men. Fishing is evangelism for lost souls. Tending a flock of lambs and sheep is oversight in the community of believers, perhaps *lambs* being used to mean young people or adults who were new believers and *sheep* older people or people who are more mature in their faith. These are different tasks, but each is important.

We are blessed to be a blessing. Father Raniero Cantalamessa, official preacher to the papal household, comments on the initial call of the disciples in Luke 5:1–11:

Ordinarily in fishing the fisherman is after his own good and not that of the fish. The same goes for the shepherd. He shepherds and cares for his flock, not for the good of the flock, but for his own good because the flock furnishes him with milk, wool and food. In the Gospel we find just the opposite: the fisherman who serves the fish; the shepherd who sacrifices for the sheep to the point of giving his life for them.[12]

Jesus calls them "my sheep." They are His, not Peter's. Jesus provided the model of ministry by being Lord, but a foot-washing, self-sacrificing Lord. The danger in hierarchical churches is for leadership to dominate the flock. The danger in "democratic" congregations is for the flock to be rebellious to authority. Both ministers and congregations need to understand the balance.

Peter will come to understand the balance. When he later wrote to fellow church leaders, he styled himself as a "fellow elder."[13] He encourages them to be "shepherds of God's flock that is under your care, watching over them....not lording it over those entrusted to you, but being examples to the flock. And when the Chief Shepherd appears, you will receive the crown of glory that will never fade away" (1 Pet. 5:1–4, NIV).

Gregory the Great believed that God allowed the painful process of Peter's denying Jesus and having later to be reconciled to teach Peter the compassion that must go with church leadership. It was done, Gregory noted, "So that he who was going to be shepherd of the Church might learn from his own fault how he ought to have mercy on others."[14]

After Jesus tells Peter to feed the sheep, He restated the basic call: "Follow me" (v. 20). Because Peter had walked with the Lord for three event-filled years, this call has a greater meaning.

Many who truly desire to serve are disappointed when they don't get a specific vision to do a great ministry for the Lord. They may often try to force something, thinking they hear a call that isn't actually there. Or, erring in the other direction, if they do not get a notable vision of or a profound call to something, they may believe they have been relegated to a second-class discipleship and become lackadaisical in their prayer life, Bible reading, church attendance, and witness. He says to all who will listen: "Follow me." He says that to us.

Now that Peter has been forgiven and reinstated both positionally and emotionally, he is going to start becoming that new man, that "rock" which his name implies. But that transformation is only beginning. Immediately after this time with Jesus at the charcoal fire Peter expressed jealousy of John. Jesus rebuked Peter, telling him it was none of his business how Jesus deals with John. Peter's job was to follow Jesus (John 21:20–22). Yes, Peter has been restored, but he still is not perfect. God is not done with us yet either. We are to thank God for His merciful patience, but we are not to presume upon it.

We tend to focus on the faults of Peter because his misbehavior is so loud and dramatic. But remember, James and John plotted for a powerful position and involved their mother in their scheme. Their ambition was no less wrong just because it was done quietly and stealthily. "Timid Timothy" was not like Peter, James, or John, but he had to be nudged forward. Each of us has areas where we particularly let the Lord down. By God's grace, with the help of others, and with our own hard work—again please note, all three are essential—we are to continually work toward holiness until we see God face to face.

Each of the post-Resurrection appearances of Jesus teaches us something about what the church would be like after Jesus' Ascension and what the church should be like today. The events of John 21:15–19 teach us that:

- Peter was restored. Christianity is about redemption, forgiveness, reconciliation, and restoration. It is through restoration and healing that we are empowered to do those things God has called us to do, both individually and corporately.

- Peter was ministered to. Christianity involves God's tender care of us, including but not limited to inner healing of our past hurts.

God does not give up on us. If we are willing to let God work, if we humbly receive the ministrations of others, and if we work steadfastly to do our part, then that ongoing process of maturation towards genuine holiness will take place. Similarly, so will that gradual, often painful, process of restoration when we have fallen. So will that healing for where our inner being has been wounded.

Discussion Questions

1. How can triggers be sacramental?

2. Consider the differences between forgiveness and reconciliation.

3. Reflect carefully on the metaphorical implications of sheep–shepherd, fish–fisherman, washing Jesus' feet or letting Jesus wash yours. Who does the work and who gets the benefit in each?

CHAPTER 10

RESCUING AND DEFENDING THE CELEBRATION OF THE ASCENSION

Luke 24:50–53; Acts 1:9–11

THE FORTY DAYS of Easter have now come to an end. Jesus, as Luke asserted, had "presented himself alive...by many proofs" (Acts 1:3). In the sight of the apostles Jesus visibly ascended into the sky. Two men in white robes told them He was going to heaven (Acts 1:11). After a period of preparation the Holy Spirit would fall on them. One phase of salvation history had come to an end; another would soon begin.

Stop by many church buildings on Ascension Day and you will either find them locked, or if open and with a service in progress, you will most likely discover there's just a handful of people at worship. You won't find a reference to Ascension Day in Eerdman's *Handbook to the History of Christianity* or even a footnote in Williston Walker's *A History of the Christian Church*. J. G. Davies noted half a century ago, "Of all the articles in the Creed there is none that has been so neglected in the present century as that which affirms our Lord's Ascension into heaven."[1] Why is this?

Is this because Ascension is always on a weekday? Christmas is usually on a weekday, and in most churches Christmas services are the most attended services of the year.

Or is it because non-liturgical Protestantism once removed most holy days from the church's calendar—even Christmas at one point—as being "Papist," and this has set the tone for most Protestant congregations ever since. (By comparison, the *Book of Common Prayer* accords it priority status as a principal feast in Anglicanism, and Lutherans deem it a major day.)

Or might the reason why Ascension Day is often ignored be that there is no secular parallel culture of it (at least in America), no equivalent of Santa or the Easter Bunny, nothing akin to presents under the tree or hunting for eggs, no enticement to drag us into the malls to shop or gather with loved ones for a special meal? Unless a congregation goes way out of its way to emphasize the Ascension, unless there's a skit or the releasing of balloons to give a sensory illustration, there's nothing to help people anticipate this Holy Day or be excited about it when it arrives. And in those European countries where Ascension is a holiday, it is mostly observed as a "bank holiday," that is, a time to do other things than what the day is about (compare with how few Americans do anything to honor war dead on Memorial Day).

Or is the reason that the Ascension is generally ignored is that it is clearly about Christ and not, at least in an obvious way, about me? Some of church life in contemporary America is about how I can "claim my blessing" from God and about how Christ is a means to the end of my having physical health, financial prosperity, and happy family life. Rather, the Ascension speaks of Christ in glory, and the focus is on Him. Note how Paul tells the Colossians to "seek the things that are above, where Christ is, seated at the right hand of God," and to "set your minds on the things that are above, not on things that are on earth" (Col. 3:1–2).

This me-centered twisting of the Christian faith is not new

to our generation, however. The risen Christ spent parts of the forty-day post-Resurrection period going over basic themes with His closest followers, and yet on the verge of His Ascension they still were focusing on the political restoration of Israel (Acts 1:6). Jesus quickly attempted to force their attention away from themselves and their desires to what He wanted from them: they were to receive power and to be His witnesses to others (Acts 1:7–8).

Or could the reason there is little emphasis on the Ascension be that it celebrates Jesus leaving us?[2] We do not wish Him to leave any more than Mary Magdalene did when she tried to hold on to Him (John 20:17).

Or could the reason the Ascension is generally ignored be that it means we must focus on the Holy Spirit, who will come after Jesus departs, and many who believe in and love Jesus Christ are skeptical of the person and work of the Holy Spirit? Such persons might so love order and control they do not want to focus on the Holy Spirit, who, like the wind, blows where the Spirit wills (John 3:8). Or, might such persons have been frightened by the excesses of some who call themselves Pentecostals or Charismatics? Better, then, they think, to focus on Jesus' teaching, atoning work, and bodily resurrection and leave it at that.

Or could another reason for the lack of emphasis on the Ascension be attitudes ranging from skepticism to ridicule on the part of liberal theologians? Adolf Harnack claimed that the Ascension story was a myth made up by the post-Apostolic church under the influence of Greek ideas.[3] Even if we do not believe what he and others like him have said, many people are nonetheless left subtly influenced by their denials. Let us take a look at this theological skepticism.

Reasons Given for
Disbelieving the Ascension

**There are only two brief accounts of the story, and they are
both by the same writer.**

Skeptics of the Ascension point out that Luke affords the
Ascension but one verse in his Gospel (Luke 24:51) and only
three verses in Acts (1:9–11). The reference at the end of Mark
should be discounted, the skeptics assert, because many scholars
(including some conservative ones) do not believe Mark 16:9–20
is part of the original. Even if this passage from Mark is accepted,
the one-verse reference to Jesus' Ascension (Mark 16:19) is not
preceded by any discussion of post-Resurrection appearances,
possibly suggesting Mark saw the Resurrection and Ascension
as one event. There is no Ascension story in Matthew or John.
Thus, skeptics conclude, there is such scant biblical evidence as
to make belief in the Ascension unwise.

But such a conclusion is reached only by ignoring key pieces
of evidence.

As we note all throughout both his Gospel and the Book of
Acts, Luke is, as is befitting a physician, a careful, keen observer
of details. John Stott noted:

> Luke tells the story of the Ascension with simplicity
> and sobriety. All the extravagances associated with the
> Apocryphal so-called Gospels[4] are missing. There is no
> embroidery such as we find in legends. There is no evi-
> dence of poetry or symbolism.[5]

Douglas Farrow notes the significant difference between the
restrained story Luke tells with the fanciful stories of other cultures. He adds, "Nor does Luke attempt to match the much
more dramatic story of Elijah's departure, e.g., even though that

famous prophet is closely linked to Jesus by the transfiguration episode and the forty-days motif."[6]

Nor is what is described something that happened at a distance or in the peripheral vision of those witnessing the Ascension, nor was it something that happened in but a millisecond. Luke uses several phrases and words to indicate otherwise: "they were looking on" and "gazing" (Acts 1:9–10).

Although there are but a few *accounts* of the Ascension itself, the *fact* of the Ascension is well attested to by the major writers of the New Testament.

John

In John 6:62, Jesus says, "Then what if you were to see the Son of Man ascending where he was before?" In John 20:17, after His resurrection, Jesus tells Mary Magdalene not to hold Him because "I have not yet ascended to the Father." Jesus had a home to which He wished to return, and that is the same one He had left to be born of the Virgin Mary. His resurrection brings Him back to Earth but not to His home. Only the Ascension does that, when He will "go to the Father" (John 16:17, NAS).

Peter

In his Pentecost sermon Peter spoke of Jesus' resurrection and exaltation to the right hand of God, contrasting this with David, who "did not ascend into the heavens" (Acts 2:34). Peter further referenced Jesus' ascent into heaven in his first epistle, chapter 3, verses 21–22.

Paul

Richard Zepernick comments that Paul's repeated emphasis on Christ crucified (for example, 1 Cor. 1:23 and 2:2, Gal. 2:20) could convince some that Paul did not believe in the Ascension. Yet, Zepernick reminds us that the apostle noted how Jesus was "taken up in glory" in 1 Timothy 3:16. Without mentioning the Ascension *per se*, Paul spoke of Jesus being in heaven (Phil. 3:20) and of Jesus' session, that is, His sitting at the right hand of the Father, which assumes His Ascension (Eph. 1:20, Col. 3:1). More directly, Paul cites the Ascension and the various gifts with which the ascended Christ equipped the church (Eph. 4:8–13).[7]

The author of the Epistle to the Hebrews

Jesus has passed through the heavens and entered the holy place (Heb. 4:14; 9:11–12) and sits in heaven at the right hand of God (Heb. 1:3; 8:1).

Matthew

In Matthew the Ascension is assumed, with the setting of the mountain and the final commissioning of the disciples. For Jesus to conclude, "And remember, I am with you always, to the end of the age" would hardly be necessary if Jesus were not about to leave Earth (Matt. 28:16–20, NRSV).

The skeptics fail to see that there are many more biblical references to the Ascension than just the two brief Lukan accounts.

A second reason skeptics offer for not believing the Lukan account of a literal bodily Ascension is that it expresses a cosmology we know to be false.

The skeptic says, "No one believes in a three-story universe with heaven above, Earth in the middle, and hell below. How then can we take literally Luke's account that Jesus went *up*?" Episcopalian Bishop John Spong scoffs, "If Jesus ascended physically into the sky, and if he rose as rapidly as the speed of light (186,000 miles per second), he would not yet have reached the edges of our own galaxy.... Space is incomprehensively vast. The Bible is incredibly limited in terms of the knowledge available to us today."[8]

What can we say to comments like this? In going up— *literally*—Jesus was acting within a symbol system the people of His day understood. While He never accommodated Himself to bad teaching about theology or morality, He did accommodate

Himself to the symbols His viewers and hearers could grasp. Although God has always known about computers, Jesus did not use analogies based on computers because they would not have been understood. He spoke of sheep because His hearers immediately knew what He was saying. Jesus went back to heaven by *going up* because, to their understanding, it's how you go to heaven. It is the symbol of exaltation. If you want to speak to prescientific people you use prescientific metaphors and illustrations. If it had been in the plan of God for the Ascension to occur today, might Jesus enter a transporter, because we all have watched *Star Trek* and understand that symbolism? Might Jesus have said, "Father, beam me up"?

N. T. Wright comments that for the first-century Jews to speak of "going up" no more demands they believed in a fanciful, three-decker universe (with heaven literally above) than it means that when we speak of the sun "rising" we are ignorant of the fact it is the earth turning relative to the sun.[9]

Moreover, "going up" is a phrase that was understood in the ancient world when one went to visit a temple, even if the temple had been below one's starting point in terms of altitude. It was also a term understood to mean God was about to act, as in Psalm 47:5, "God has gone up with a shout."

Early second-century church leader Ignatius of Antioch, who died in approximately AD 110, student of the Apostle John, understood the necessity of the literal bodily Ascension of Jesus. Quoting Acts 1:11 ("This Jesus, who was taken up from you into heaven, will come in the same way as you saw him go into heaven"), Ignatius points out:

> But if they saw that He will come at the end of the world without a body, how shall those 'see Him that pierced Him' [Revelation 1:7], and when they recognize Him, 'mourn for themselves?' [Zechariah 12:10]. For incorporeal beings have neither form nor figure, nor the aspect

[mark] of an animal possessed of shape, because their nature is in itself simple.[10]

While Spong imagined the Bible needs to be "rescued," John Stott correctly noted we must do our homework and understand it. Speaking of the mode of Jesus' Ascension Stott wrote:

> There is no need to doubt the literal nature of Christ's Ascension, so long as we realize its purpose. It was not necessary as a mode of departure for "going to the Father" did not involve a journey in space and presumably he could simply have vanished as on previous occasions. The reason he ascended before their eyes was rather to show them that this departure was final. He had now gone for good, or at least until his coming in glory. So they returned to Jerusalem with great joy and waited—not for Jesus to make another resurrection appearance, but for the Holy Spirit to come in power, as had been promised.[11]

Jesus made it clear He was going into the nearer presence and the glory of God the Father by entering a cloud. He needed to disappear dramatically and not just simply vanish or walk over the next hill; otherwise His followers would spend time looking for Him. ("Where did He go?" "Will He be back next week?") He needed to leave in a way that made it clear He was leaving Earth permanently until His second coming.

C. S. Lewis argued for the necessity of the Ascension from the fact that the risen Christ was not a ghost or hallucination.

> For a phantom can just fade away; but an objective entity must go somewhere – something must happen to it.... If [the risen Christ] were a vision then it was the most systematically deceptive and lying vision on record. But if it [Christ's body] were real, then something happened

to it after it ceased to appear. You cannot take away the
Ascension without putting something else in its place.[12]

There was further symbolism in His entering a cloud. As
Jews, these first-century Christians would likely make the connection to the pillar of cloud—the Shekinah glory of God—that
descended upon the tabernacle in the wilderness and filled the
new temple built by Solomon (Exod. 13:21; 40:34; 1 Kings 8:10–11).
Arthur Michael Ramsey (1904–1988), sometime Archbishop of
Canterbury, tying these previous manifestations of the cloud
to the cloud of the Ascension, noted how those beholding the
Lord's Ascension were granted "a theophany: Jesus is enveloped
in the cloud of the divine presence."[13]

No doubt the onlookers had heard of the cloud overshad-
owing Peter, John, and James on the Mount of Transfiguration
when Jesus met with Moses and Elijah (Luke 9:28–36). At the
Transfiguration the cloud dissolved, and the Old Testament figures of Moses and Elijah disappeared, leaving Jesus. Maybe this
present cloud would also dissolve, leaving Jesus. But no. Though
the details change, a major point of the story is exactly the
same. On the Mount of Transfiguration, Moses and Elijah were
pointing to Jesus, their fulfillment. When the cloud dissolved
they were gone because it's now about Jesus. At the Ascension
Jesus was gone because it's now about the church, Christ's body
on Earth, filled with the Spirit who was about to be poured out
on Pentecost.

The Ascension as it is described in the Book of Acts is also
how we are reminded who He was and is: God made man. I
appreciate the wisdom of Daniel Eddy for pointing out to me
how similar the Ascension is to the Incarnation in this regard.[14]
The Incarnation tells us that God, the Second Person of the
eternal Trinity, God who is Spirit and without body, parts, or
passion, became flesh and dwelt among us (John 1:14). He did
not merely appear to have a human body, but He had one and

is every way like us, except without sin (Heb. 4:15). The Jesus of the pages of Scripture, therefore, was fully God and fully human. The Ascension underscores this point. His earthly body was not an illusion or a mask to hide his true identity, which was Spirit. His earthly body was part of His true identity. Therefore, the Ascension is not a merely *spiritual* leaving, a sloughing off the useless or pretend physical body. The Ascension is the whole Jesus, body included, going to the Father. It must be done—*and seen to be done*—physically.

The event is loving. Jesus gathered His friends, those whom He especially loved, as a man gathers his friends around him before he goes on a long journey to tell them he is going away. A loving person does not simply disappear.

Acts 1 briefly gives us the picture of Jesus' Ascension from the ground up. The Old Testament Book of Daniel saw the Ascension from heaven's side (Dan. 7). Revelation 4 gives us a glimpse of the beauty and majesty of heaven with the heavenly work of Jesus added in chapter 5. What are these events and pictures trying to tell us about the heaven to which Jesus ascended?

C. B. Moss notes that Jesus did not leave "soaring through tracts unknown to some astronomically remote place. The Ascension is much more wonderful and mysterious than that. He passed out of time and space altogether.... He is not 'in the bright place far away' for he is 'not far from each one of us'" (Acts 18:27).[15]

Richard Zepernick reminds us that astrophysicists tell us 95 percent of the energy and matter in the universe is invisible, its existence merely implied. Since we know so little, how dare we presume to correct God on what He tells us? With many coexisting dimensions, *of course* Jesus could be both beyond time and space, yet also with us.[16]

N. T. Wright comments, "Heaven is not a place thousands of miles up, or for that matter down, in our space, nor would it help us if it were. It is God's dimension of ordinary reality, the dimension which is normally hidden but which we penetrate mysteriously, or rather which penetrates us mysteriously, in prayer, in the scriptures, in the breaking of the bread."[17]

Roy Lawrence asks where Jesus is in these post-Ascension days when he writes, "For him the Ascension was a de-restriction, a reunion with the infinite. Miraculously, at the incarnation he had become small in order to reach out to small beings like ourselves. But the message of the Ascension is that he is small no longer."[18]

Our real skepticism should not be addressed to belief in the Ascension but to the facile way in which some dismiss it with shallow and outdated thinking.[19]

LET'S RESCUE THE CELEBRATION
OF THE ASCENSION

Whether it's because of a lingering Protestant suspicion of holy days (although try removing the observance of such holy days as Mother's Day, Boy Scout Sunday, or Children's Sunday from the calendars of some churches); or whether it's because there's nothing in pop culture or in the shopping malls to hold the Ascension before us; or whether it's because of an overemphasis on the Cross to the virtual exclusion of the Ascension; or whether it's because of an avoidance of a relationship with the Holy Spirit; or whether it's because too many Christians want Christianity to center in "meeting my needs"; or whether it's because we've been influenced too much by the skeptics, the fact is, too many churches make little or nothing of the Ascension.

But some Christian leaders over the centuries have suggested otherwise. Augustine of Hippo (354–430) noted how the Ascension was an important festival of the church in his time. He writes, "This is that festival which confirms the grace of all the festivals together, without which the profitableness of every festival would have perished."[20]

Leo the Great (400–461, Pope from 440) wrote, "With all due

solemnity we are commemorating that day on which our poor human nature was carried up in Christ above all the hosts of heaven, above all the ranks of angels, beyond the highest heavenly powers to the very throne of God the Father."[21]

The Protestant Reformer John Calvin (1509–1564) said, "The Ascension of Christ...is one of the chief points of our faith."[22]

The Lutheran theologian Dietrich Bonhoeffer (1906–1945) wrote from a Nazi prison that he was celebrating Ascension Day as a great festival because he knew what it was about.

Knowing few church members will come out for an Ascension Thursday service, a growing number of churches transfer the celebration to the following Sunday so the importance of the event can be grasped by most worshipers. Though this is an accommodation, at least it is an attempt to reclaim the importance of the observance.

Some contemporary teachers of worship are encouraging pastors to work hard on their Ascension services (whether on Thursday or on Sunday). Harry Boonstra comments:

> Reformed Christians should celebrate the Ascension with verve, with glory, and with full pews. The Ascension, after all, is not marked by an isolated Thursday service in which the church tries to come to terms with a gravity-defying miracle. The Ascension is rather linked to the sunburst expression of the victory and power of the risen Lord that we celebrate on Easter Sunday.... Plan and pray for a King-honoring Ascension service. As Calvin says, the Ascension is 'one of the chiefest points of our faith; such a chief event demands a gala worship service.[23]

Let us now address the reasons why Jesus ascended back to heaven and what this means for us today.

Discussion Questions

1. What do you find most valuable about the celebration of religious anniversaries in the liturgical calendar?

2. As we observe special periods of time such as Lent, ordinary days, Advent, and Christmastide, how significant is the "tarrying time" which runs between the Ascension and Pentecost?

CHAPTER 11

WHY JESUS ASCENDED BACK TO HEAVEN AND WHAT THIS MEANS FOR HIM AND FOR US TODAY

Luke 24:50–53; Acts 1:9–11

I WONDER IF MANY of my fellow baby boomers reading here about the Ascension, are, with me, quietly humming the tune popularized by the Fifth Dimension, "Up, Up and Away."[1] Perhaps even some of us are also humming the Fifth Dimension song in which a woman asks why her man left.

So, why *did* Jesus leave?

Jesus ascended back to heaven because it was and is His home, and from His home He reigns.

From all eternity God is Father, Son and Holy Spirit. Two thousand years ago God the Son was incarnated as a human being named Jesus (John 1:1–14; Luke 1:31). Earth is not His permanent home. In coming to Earth Jesus "emptied Himself," humbling Himself for a season for our sakes (Phil. 2:5–8). When He cried from the cross, "It is finished" (which also translates as "It is accomplished"), He was signifying His work was now

thought about what He was experiencing those three years

171

complete. Those words were a triumphant man's shout of victory, not a defeated man's lament of failure (John 19:30). Then it became time for Him to go home to present to the Father His atoning sacrifice—Himself being both the priest and victim—and to reassume the glory He always had by right but voluntarily laid aside when He came to Earth (Phil. 2:9–11).

While Jesus was on Earth that glory was allowed to burst through only at the Transfiguration (Mark 9:2–13). The Transfiguration illustrated the transfer from the good of the Old Testament to the best of the New. It also gave Peter, James, and John enough advance notice of the victory Jesus would eventually experience that while Peter and James would run during the gut-wrenching events of the last few days of Holy Week, they would not run far. As Peter would later write, "We were eyewitnesses of His majesty....on the holy mountain" (2 Pet. 1:16–18). John, too, would say, "We beheld his glory" (John 1:14, KJV). (This is one of many reasons why conservative scholars insist that the fourth Gospel was written by John, the son of Zebedee, and not some later "redactor," or a "Johannine Community" of followers.)

Everett L. ("Terry") Fullam notes that at Christmas Jesus laid aside His glory; at the Transfiguration it was momentarily allowed to shine through; on the cross His glory was masked; but now in heaven it is visible for all to see. The crown of thorns has been turned to a crown of gold.[2] The Ascension is sometimes given the diminished understanding of merely getting the Son back to where He once was. But now there is much more for Jesus to do than what He did before He left heaven to be incarnate. He ascends as the victorious one who has defeated Satan and inaugurated the kingdom. Compare this to C. S. Lewis' King and Queen of Perelandra and the glory they came to have after winning the victory over evil.[3]

God the Father "disarmed the principalities and powers and made a public example of them, triumphing over them in [Christ]" (Col. 2:15, NRSV; see also Eph. 1:20–22). The comparison is to earthly conquerors returning home from victory with the leaders of the nations they conquered being marched in chains down the main street of their capital.

To celebrate what the ascended Christ now enjoys, Pope Pius XI instituted the Feast of Christ the King in 1925. In 1969, Pope Paul VI renamed it Our Lord Jesus Christ King of the Universe and assigned it the date of the last Sunday in the liturgical year, the Sunday before Advent, to dramatize how the story of Jesus is fulfilled. Churches using the Revised Common Lectionary (chiefly Anglican and Main Line Protestant) call this day either Christ the King Sunday or Reign of Christ Sunday and also observe it as the end of the liturgical year.

Jesus is Christ the King, and yet there is some business unfinished until He returns. We do not know why sometimes God intervenes dramatically and powerfully in the affairs of earth while at other times He gives us the grace to triumph in the midst of our problems, and still other times why He allows an individual to suffer and to die young. It would be easy, as many have done, to discourage people from praying for blessings ("lest you get your hopes up, be disappointed, and lose your faith"). It would also be easy to encourage people to a false triumphalism ("just claim your blessing, believe it will come, and it always will"), blind to the reality that sometimes God does not send that desired blessing. We must live in the tension of what theologians call "partially realized eschatology," or in a more popular phraseology, the "now-but-not-yet" nature of our experiencing the kingdom of God on Earth.

It is true that Satan is a defeated foe, and as such we can and should laugh at him, but he is still a prowling lion "seeking someone to devour" (1 Pet. 5:8). He is dying, but he's not dead yet.

Jesus is not turning His back on Earth. Because of the Ascension the way Christ relates to Earth has changed. Jesus is leaving so the Spirit can come and do Jesus' ministry on Earth (John 16:7–14) while Jesus continues to minister from heaven.

Douglas Farrow reminds us that "Paul's pivotal confrontation with the risen and ascended Jesus was remarkably unlike the pre-Ascension encounters of the disciples. On the way to Damascus Paul did not sit down to eat and drink with the risen Christ. He met up with the Lord of Glory, whom mortal eyes cannot behold without dramatic consequence."[4]

Christian life is best lived in the balance between God's transcendence and God's immanence, that is, between Christ in glory, seated at the right hand of the Majesty on high, and Christ right here on Earth, in our hearts, wherever two or three are gathered in His name, and in the Eucharist. Some people opt mostly for the transcendent Christ of glory expressed in stately hymns, solemn processions, formal liturgies, triumphal art, and soaring church buildings. Other people focus in large part on the immanent Christ right here, the dear, sweet Jesus who "walks with me and talks with me and tells me I am His own" expressed in informal services, rendered in paintings of a smiling Jesus with His arm around a person, and in churches that are designed to look like television talk show sets.

We need both.

We need both because both are true. Jesus is both there and here. He is sovereign Lord and also my friend.

We need both because of what happens to Christianity whenever the transcendent or the immanent triumphs over the other. If the transcendence of the ascended Christ becomes dominant, then Christ disappears into the sky and becomes a Christ principle or an energy force and not a Person of the Trinity. Some of New England Puritanism, so focused on the authoritative, sovereign, transcendent Christ, morphed into Unitarianism. Jesus, then, becomes just another good teacher, and spirituality becomes solely New Age.

On the other hand, if the ascended Christ is chiefly known by how He relates to us here and now, then we have diminished His power and authority. He becomes a friend, but how powerful is that friend? If He's mostly seen as "right here, right now," then where is heaven-sized power? Jesus' role has been reduced to inspiring us to be better and try harder. The sacraments, uncoupled from their heavenly power source, then have to be seen as mere visual aids, only historical reminders and powerless symbols. Moreover, Jesus, my friend, quickly becomes "my pal"—the one who helps my family work together better but not the one who rightly demands my surrender and obedience. Bishop Dan Herzog wisely notes, "Jesus my buddy is under my control."[5]

What should we do? We need to embrace both the transcendence and the immanence of the ascended Christ, our personal preferences for one over the other notwithstanding. We need to worship in grand cathedrals at glorious liturgies illustrating His majesty and in intimate gatherings where we sense our friend Jesus is right here with us. We need to sing the "objective" hymns of the church (where the words are all about God) as well as the "subjective" praise songs (where the word "I" is frequently used). We need this for ourselves as individuals, and we need to get our churches to reflect this. Over and over we need to remind ourselves and our brothers and sisters in Christ, "The Lord of the universe is my friend, *and* my Friend is the Lord of the universe." But we need to avoid the attitude that so places Him above all that He does not relate to me personally, the sentimental "Jesus is my boyfriend" tone of some contemporary Christian songs, and that disrespectful "Jesus is my pal" practice of people who want Him as their waiter but not their Lord.

If we do not actively, intentionally embrace both the transcendence and the immanence of the ascended Christ, sooner or later either we or our children could flee from one imbalance to the other. In the 1970s I watched as many people left the sacramental/liturgical churches to "find Jesus" in Charismatic fellowships. Even some who stayed in their denominations so embraced the charismatic as to devalue the sacramental, even though it is part of basic Christian faith. They swapped one partial experience of Christianity for another partial one. In finding good things they abandoned what was equally good, though now considered devalued.

Nowadays I am watching a number of evangelicals and charismatics leave to an equally imbalanced Eastern Orthodoxy. True, some have kept the richness of the evangelical and Charismatic expressions of the faith while adding to it a newly discovered historic sacramental, liturgical, and theological life. However, while coming into a richness, fullness, and balance for themselves, many do not share this new, integrated fullness with their children or the churches of which they are now a part. They teach and share what's new to them—sacraments, liturgy, hierarchy, the church fathers—but not the other parts of the faith on which they had once focused.

Several former evangelicals and Charismatics who have become Eastern Orthodox have asked me, given the richness they now possess, what I think their children and grandchildren will be like as Christians. My response was not what they expected or wanted to hear: "Some will probably be worshiping in independent Charismatic fellowships, if they're part of the church at all."

The Ascension was not escapism for Jesus. He did not ascend to leave us behind but to give us the Holy Spirit and to work from heaven on our behalf.

Jesus ascended back to heaven in His resurrection body to demonstrate that the same God who created the material world redeemed and redeems it.

The earliest philosophical and theological opponent of the Christian gospel was a movement called Gnosticism. While there was a considerable variety of Gnostic groups, all had in common the belief that the material world was evil. They did not merely believe that matter (physical things) could be used for evil. Gnostics believed that *matter itself* was evil. When countered with the scripture that said everything God made was "good"

(Genesis 1:12, 18, 21, 25, 31), a Gnostic would answer that the God of the Old Testament was not the true God over all but an evil emanation, the result of a cosmic disturbance, a much lesser God. For such a God to call created things good only proves that this God was not good. What is good to a Gnostic is pure spirit only. At death a person gets rid of his or her physical body, and his or her spirit is what lives on in "the immortality of the soul."[6]

We earlier saw that Christianity is not the escapism of Jesus turning His back on Earth. We now need to note that Christianity is not escapism for us either. We are to pray God's will be done on *Earth* as in heaven (Matt. 6:10). While we are not *of* the world, we are still *in* it (John 17:11, 15), and we are to make a difference right here. The Ascension is not Jesus' escape from physicality. If this were so He would be encouraging us to look forward to the day when we, too, will one day leave physicality behind, and, while we wait for that day, to ignore the things of the world. Rather, because Jesus' *body* ascended, physical things and thus the physical things of this world are important.

Because a human body has ascended, our human bodies are important right now. Jesus' miracles were often practical ones, belonging to this life on Earth—changing water into wine, healing bodies, feeding the hungry. His teachings were about practical things of life. Though we have one eye on heaven, we have the other eye on Earth. Because of who we are in Christ and where we're heading for all eternity, our work for justice and our giving cups of cold water are not done from a naive, utopian optimism but with true gospel realism. This world is passing away, but we and others with us are living here now.

Years ago I brought Holy Communion to a dear saint, housebound and unable to get to church. We chatted before receiving Communion together, and during that time she told me how her knees gave her constant discomfort. After we received Communion I asked her how I could pray for her, asking specifically if I could pray for her knees. "No," she said. "Pray that

I become more like Jesus." I told her that if prayer were like Aladdin's lamp where a person got but a few wishes it would be correct, like she was doing, to focus on those few things that were most important. "But," I assured her, "we can pray both for your spiritual growth *and your knees.*" God cared not just about her soul. He cared *for her in her totality, body, soul, and spirit.*

Having said that, we are not citizens of Earth. "Our citizenship is in heaven," Paul told the Philippians (Phil. 3:20). We are seated with Christ in the heavenly places (Eph. 2:6).

> Here [on earth] have we no continuing place, but we seek one [yet] to come.
>
> —Hebrews 13:14, kjv

This is why Christians sometimes do not feel entirely happy or fulfilled despite our salvation and our relationship with the Lord. While sometimes our malaise is seasonal adjustment disorder, a mild case of the blues, our allowing Satan to rub our noses in sins God has already forgiven, lingering hurt over emotional wounds we've suffered, or the Holy Spirit's work of bringing us under conviction of our sin, sometimes it's none of these. Sometimes we are simply homesick for heaven. God is putting that yearning in us for the place where we will spend all eternity. Jesus went home at His Ascension, and one day we, too, will go home. While we await our eventual translation to heaven, we are to be about our Father's business here on Earth. We have one of our eyes on the task before us, while the other one is on our future home, where Jesus has gone on ahead of us.

Jesus ascended back to heaven so He could prepare a place for us (John 14:2–3).

Jesus, first, ascended to heaven because it's His home. Then, second, Jesus ascended back to heaven in His resurrection body to demonstrate the God who created the material world redeemed and redeems it, not destroys it. Now, third, He's preparing a place for us so when we die we would be with Him in heaven.

I deliberately place this point third. Many of us grew up in churches that so emphasized the centrality of the worship of and obedience to God that there was little taught about our personally receiving blessings. In fact, we were often taught that other than salvation and the occasional answered prayer, the real blessings were mostly deferred until heaven. Whether we were taught this or not, what we often heard was *God first, others second, me hardly at all.*

In overreaction to this in some circles there has been too great an emphasis lately on what God will do for us now. In fact, if we don't receive such things as immediate healing, financial prosperity, inner peace and joy, and better families, we're clearly not doing something right. Too often do we hear the phrase, "Claim your blessing," in the context of "It's all about us, not God." We even see newspaper ads for churches stating, "It's all about you."

Jesus' teaching, of course, is right. First focus on God—the worship and praise of God, obedience to God, service in God's name—and *then* God will bless you in ways He knows best.

> But seek first his kingdom and his righteousness, and all these things will be yours as well.
> —MATTHEW 6:33, NIV

We do not know the details of what heaven is like. We *do* know it will be wonderful, perfect, and eternal because Jesus is its builder. We will be reunited with those who have died in the faith of Christ, all our problems will be taken away, we will have resurrection bodies, and we will see God face to face. We do not know the details, but we know enough to say with Julian of Norwich (ca. 1342–1416), "All will be well indeed."

I remember that when I was five years old for several weeks I was not allowed to go down into the cellar to see what my grandfather, whom we called Bumpy, was doing. He was preparing something for me. It was a layout of a Lionel train set. What a present! Bumpy knew all the crafts like carpentry, wiring, painting, so the train layout was glorious. What was he doing those weeks before Christmas when I was not allowed into the basement? He was preparing something for me. I didn't know what the surprise was, but I knew it would be great because he loved me and was good at what he did. We can only begin to imagine what Christ, who loves us completely and is perfect at what He does, has prepared for us.

How does Jesus prepare that place? While Jesus' atoning death on the cross paid the penalty price our sins deserved, Jesus had to present that sacrifice to the Father in person. When He ascended, Christ entered into the true sanctuary—heaven—to offer Himself once for all to the Father (Heb. 9:24–26). Now the sacrifice is complete—offered and accepted—and so our future home in heaven has been erected. By offering His once-for-all sacrifice of Himself for our sins made on Calvary, the ascended Jesus has now prepared that place for us.

Jesus ascended to sit at the right hand of His Father, there to intercede for us.

After 9-11, rock star Bruce Springsteen issued an album titled *The Rising* that included the song "You're Missing." In the refrain, the author suggests that God is drifting. We may wonder, Now that Jesus is no longer around in our midst, does He have a clue or a care about what's going on here on Earth?

We have already noted that the Ascension was neither escapism for Jesus nor for us. The exalted, glorified Jesus is the same Jesus Who, when on Earth, befriended sinners, worked supernatural signs and wonders, and died in our place—the innocent One for the guilty ones—so we could be saved. He has not changed. He is "the same yesterday and today and forever" (Heb. 13:8). John Calvin put it, "Christ was taken up into heaven, not to enjoy blessed rest at a distance from us, but to govern the world for the salvation of all believers."[7] Restricted by geography while on Earth, the ascended Christ now fills all things (Eph. 4:10), making His power universal. The image of Jesus sitting rather than standing means His work is complete and He is enthroned in glory.[8] *Ask for explanation,*

Professor Edith M. Humphrey writes, "His Ascension is not only a celebratory exercise, not simply a victory parade. The One who is utter love has no jealousy, no desire to keep the glory to himself. And so in his Ascension he grants glory to us, whom he calls brothers and sisters."[9]

His work on our behalf continues. In one of the churches I once served was a member named Nelson Parent. One day I preached what I thought was a rather eloquent sermon on how Jesus, Who loved us while we were yet sinners, all the more loves us now that we have been reconciled to the Father through Jesus' atoning death. Nelson, who had a way of reducing complexities to simple statements, caught me after the service and said, "Hey, Canon, what you was tryin' to say was, 'If Jesus died for His enemies, He ain't gonna stiff His friends,' right?" Right!

We have a friend in high places, the One Who sits at God's right hand (Eph. 1:20). He is speaking to the Father on our behalf, interceding for us (Rom. 8:34; Heb. 7:25). In Christ we have obtained access to the Father and His grace (Rom. 5:2; Eph. 2:18). Because of what Jesus did on the cross for those who receive Him as Lord and Savior, when we come to God in prayer we do not have to wonder if we are intruding, soon to be ordered to leave. We've been invited! When we come we can come boldly. Moreover, we are not blessed according to what we deserve. God's throne is the throne of *grace* where we can obtain help and grace in time of need (Heb. 4:16).

Jesus reconciled us to the Father (Col. 1:21–22) and perpetually makes intercession to the Father on our behalf (Rom. 8:34; Heb. 7:25). This is why it is so sad some Christian disciples are afraid of Jesus. Was Jesus used as a threat to such people when they were growing up, a celestial version of a mother's threat of, "You just wait until your father gets home"? Nonbelievers *should* be afraid because Jesus will come again to be their judge. But believers have Jesus as a powerful friend who pleads for us. We can never say about Jesus, "But He wouldn't understand." Jesus can sympathize with us, because he "has been tempted as we are, yet without sin" (Heb. 4:15).

Jesus ascended so He could raise us with Him.

The Epistle reading used on Easter Sunday in liturgical churches is Colossians 3:1–4. In this passage we are told that our "life is hidden with Christ in God." Though we are physically here on Earth, we are also right now in the heavenlies with Christ. We "sit with him in the heavenly places" (Eph. 2:6). This is as much the truth as is our present state on Earth. Therefore, while we are about our Father's business here on Earth, our true citizenship is in heaven (Phil. 3:20). Remember this when things are going badly for you: we are tucked away with Christ in the heavenlies.

Matthew the Poor encourages us:

> To live in the presence of God, conscious of the union with Christ that He freely accomplished in us and for us, is the secret of happiness provided by Christ for us amid the sorrows of the world and despite the helplessness of humanity and its tragic failure. This consciousness should give us an inner peace that transcends the mind with all its troubles and weaknesses.[10]

When we go to heaven we will not lose our identity. The Christian faith does not teach that the risen Christ was absorbed into God the Father, losing His identity, much as a drop of water is no longer distinguishable when it is added into a saucepan of water. Jesus did not take on, nor did He abandon being a distinct person of the Trinity when He came to Earth. He does not abandon it when He returns to the Father. Moreover, He does not abandon either His human nature or His physicality, although it has now changed into a resurrection body. Similarly, when the Christian believer dies, he or she loses neither individuality nor physicality (although we, too, will have resurrection bodies).

Note how heavenly worship includes, in part, twenty-four white-clad, crowned elders sitting on thrones (Rev. 4:4). They are individuals and they are physical.

Jesus ascended so He could send the Holy Spirit to empower believers to multiply Jesus' ministry.

Though we are with Christ in the heavenlies, He is with us on Earth by the Holy Spirit. Though in one sense we are already in heaven, in another sense—something we know only too well— we are here on Earth, and there's work to be done.

Jesus said that if He did not go back to heaven the Holy Spirit would not come upon the believers (John 16:7). Scripture does not explain why Jesus could not remain on Earth for the Spirit to come; it simply states it. Might it be that if Jesus were still here on Earth we would always defer to Him when ministry needed to happen? Why would anyone dare preach when the Master could be heard? Why go to a healing ministry team if one could stand in front of Jesus? Having said this, though, the lines—and the wait—would be incredibly long. Would-be assassins would be everywhere waiting to strike Him. And, since His body was a true human body, what would He be like as a two-thousand-year-old man?

Reine Bethany makes this observation about a carpentry crew.

> Once the builders get the house up, they leave, and the people come to live in the house. As long as the builders are around, the people can't move in. Jesus had built the church. It consisted of his disciples. Time for him

to ascend and allow the church to minister universally instead of being physically centered on the earthly him.[11]

Bishop Dan Herzog comments that "the earthly Jesus limited Himself to one place at one time. By the Spirit's outpouring, the risen Lord is operative wherever there is the 'new quorum' of two or three gathered in His name."[12]

This is why the angel had to tell them to stop gazing into the sky. Jesus will come back at some time in the future at a time we are not to know in advance. Meantime (once they have been empowered with the Holy Spirit on the day of Pentecost) they are to get on with the Great Commission (Acts 1:6–11).

John Stott commented that the apostles made two errors concerning what they were to do now that Jesus had risen from the dead.

> First, they thought the inauguration of the Kingdom of God would be political, like that under the Maccabees. They asked Him, 'Lord, will you at this time restore the kingdom to Israel?' (Acts 1:6). Yet, secondly, they were overly spiritualizing, gazing into heaven, thinking the work of the Church is just to be pietistic, that it's only about worship and prayer and not at all involved in the events of life. The first is too earthy, the second too heavenly, and they managed to err in both directions at once.[13]

Stott calls these two "a false activism and a false pietism."

Today, whether it is out of a false humility, laziness, or ignorance, many Christians settle for innocuous "church work" thinking ministry is only about such tasks as tidying the hymnal racks after a worship service, maintaining the church building and grounds, and making sure supplies are ordered and bills paid. While these things are *not wrong*—every organization needs these sorts of things to be done—the purpose of the Holy

Spirit indwelling and empowering believers is so we can do the works Jesus did (John 14:12). This means teaching so minds are changed, preaching so actions are altered, and ministering so lives are transformed.

In far too many churches great attention is paid to the great events of Bible days and to the great events that will happen when Jesus returns, but little attention is paid to what can happen now. Other than an annual evangelistic outreach, there's not much beyond organizational busywork expected of the members. When challenged to undertake a ministry that would actually change lives and exhibit real, supernatural empowering, too many parishioners respond, "But that's what we hired the minister to do." No wonder few from the outside are attracted to these congregations. No wonder many church members are bored and apathetic and resort to little power struggles or attempts, yet again, to fire the pastor.

The apostle Paul describes what many call the Ascension gifts of Christ in Ephesians 4:11–14. Picking up the image of the conquering hero parading his defeated enemy through the streets, gifts are bestowed on the conqueror's people. (See Genesis 14; Judges 5:30; 1 Samuel 30:26–31; Psalm 68:12; and Isaiah 53:12 for some Old Testament examples.) There are many such supernatural endowments and equippings listed in the New Testament. In Romans 12 they are called gifts of God the Father, here in Ephesians 4 they are gifts of Christ, and in 1 Corinthians 12 and 14, they are gifts of the Holy Spirit. We are not to infer that a different member of the Trinity is, in turn, responsible for certain gifts; rather, knowing how parallelisms are frequently used in Scripture, we are to see each gift as coming from the triune God.

When one realizes the amazing power behind the gifts God bestows, when we realize that our work for the Lord is never in vain (1 Cor. 15:58), a sincere Christian will want to do more than (but not neglect) church organizational work and will want to work for the building-up of God's kingdom.[14] Christian disciples are not to be mere spectators but are to be active partners and participants in God's work on Earth. Jaroslav Pelikan cites John Chrysostom as follows: "In the Resurrection they saw the end, but not the beginning, and in the Ascension they saw the beginning, but not the end."[15]

Jesus taught us to pray (and expect) that the Father's will is to be done on Earth as it is in heaven (Matt. 6:10). After all God has done for me, I want to thank Him by helping to strengthen the church and by helping to extend the kingdom. Don't you? St. Teresa of Ávila expressed it this way: "He has no hands but our hands." While this is not exactly true—God occasionally does things without human agency—her comment is mostly true: God *usually* does His work on the world through His disciples. To be sure, only He can give the increase, that is, only God can take our efforts and turn them into something lasting, but we have to do our part (1 Cor. 3:5–9).

Luke starts the Acts of the Apostles with the phrase, "All that Jesus *began* to do and teach" (1:1, emphasis mine). Jesus was not finished when He ascended. He is working now, through us, empowered by the Holy Spirit.

Thirty years ago I taught a church history course at Barrington College. Many of the students were freshmen, attending college for the first time, armed with their new, leather-bound, onion-skin paper award Bibles given to them for graduating from high school Sunday school in their respective churches. I opened the first class by saying, "Please turn to Acts 29." Most students reached for their Bibles. As good Christian young men and women they had no trouble immediately finding Acts of the Apostles. They tried to locate Acts 29, and, of course, couldn't because the New Testament Book of Acts has only twenty-eight chapters. While they were diligently searching and eventually looking up with puzzlement, one student, the one I knew would be my *A* student, quietly reached for the church history text we were going to use in that course.

Jesus had said that if He did not leave, the Holy Spirit would not come upon believers (John 16:7). His followers would now have to grow into spiritual maturity by working as His instruments in the world. Jesus needed to ascend so the Holy Spirit could descend, and we, confident of what awaits us one day in heaven, buoyed up by both the knowledge Jesus is interceding for us and by the results of that intercession, and aided by the Holy Spirit's power within us, can do the work of kingdom-building on our Lord's behalf.

> ...Father, send us out to do the work You have given us to do.
> —BOOK OF COMMON PRAYER, page 366.

We are instructed to work in the Spirit's power, neither to give up because of the discouragement borne when we do not see fruit immediately borne, nor to try to press on, trying harder and harder, but in our own strength. We can bring comfort to burned-out idealists that there is a better way to work hard for others, one that will truly make a difference and one that will keep them in service for years.

After Jesus ascended, His followers could have gone in a number of directions in terms of what they would do next.

First, they could continue to hang around, aimlessly waiting for something to happen. This seems to be what they did at first. Jesus ascended, and they kept watching the sky. It took two angels dressed as men in white robes to tell them to stop doing this (Acts 1:6–11). John Stott reminds us:

> Their calling was to be witnesses not stargazers. The vision they were to cultivate was not upwards in nostalgia to the heaven which had received Jesus, but outwards in compassion to a lost world which needed him. It is the same for us. Curiosity about heaven and its occupants, speculation about prophecy and its fulfillment,

> an obsession with 'times and seasons'—these are aber-
> rations which detract us from our God-given mission.
> Christ will come personally, visibly, gloriously. Of that
> we have been assured. Other details can wait.[16]

Many Christians today hyperspiritualize things, believing that if God wants something done, He's the One Who will do it, because we cannot nor should not attempt to do it. However, while we cannot build the city of God on Earth, we must be about our Father's business, led by His direction and empowered by the Spirit.

Or, second, they could do something—anything—because they don't want to stand around idle when there's work to be done. I believe the election of Matthias to replace Judas was work of this type. The apostles rightly discerned that Jesus selected twelve apostles because they represented the twelve tribes of Israel. Judas had disqualified himself; was a replacement needed? Two candidates are proposed and Matthias is elected (Acts 1:15–6). It is interesting that we never hear about Matthias again in the history of the church. I wonder if the election of Matthias was a fleshly attempt to "do something" but not a Spirit-led activity. Peter, who proposed this election, like the rest of them, was pre-Pentecost, pre-filled with the Holy Spirit (Acts 1:15ff). Whether this understanding of the election of Matthias is correct or not (and there are certainly many Bible commentators who disagree with my assessment), there are too many people who so want to do something good they attempt just anything. "Doing something good" is, of course, better than doing something bad, but better yet is the discerning of the will of the Lord so we can be in (or be close to being in) the center of His will. Bishop Dan Herzog notes that this method of discerning God's will—the drawing of lots—was not repeated after Pentecost because Spirit-empowered discernment was a better means of decision making.[17]

Third, they could do what they had been instructed to

do—nothing less and nothing more. They had been given the Great Commission (Matt. 28:19–20), but they were told to a wait for the coming of the Spirit (Luke 24:49; Acts 1:4). This waiting was not to be a passive hanging around hoping something might soon occur. Their waiting was a more active waiting, like the activity of the wait-staff of a restaurant which actively, busily waits upon the customers. Nor was it a vague waiting around for "something or other." They were waiting to be clothed with power. They had work to do with each other. Some had to ask forgiveness of others. They needed to worship together. Those who had been privileged to meet the risen Christ needed to share their experiences with those who had not thus met Him. They had to become of one mind and one heart. We will examine all of this in much greater depth in our next chapter.

Then, when they were ready, God would pour out the Spirit, and the next phase of sacred history, the Age of the Church, the Age of the Spirit, could begin. Just look at what plain, ordinary Christians have accomplished throughout the centuries. God calls people like us because it's the only kind of people He made.

Jesus ascended so He could come back at the end of time at His second coming to make the new heavens and the new earth.

There's a lot of nonsense taught and believed on the subject of the second coming. Despite the fact Jesus said *He does not know when He will return* (Matt. 24:36), and despite the fact that those who insist on setting dates for His second coming have been proven wrong again and again, there are people today who insist on stating with cocky arrogance they know exactly the date He will be returning. Too many people have been told to sell everything (what will they do with the money?) and quit their jobs and go up a mountain on a certain date to wait for the Lord's return at midnight (according to our time zone, of course), only to slink back down in embarrassment when He didn't return.

Too many zealous young Christians have failed to plan for the future because they were convinced, "It's unnecessary. Jesus is coming back next year."

In some church circles it is deemed crucial you have precisely the right theology of the second coming. People have asked me, "Are you pre-millennialist [and sometimes, "*What kind* of pre-millennialist?"], a-millennialist, or post-millennialist?" I respond with a quip not original with me: "I'm a *pan*-millennialist. The second coming and the meaning and timing of a possible millennial kingdom on Earth will pan out the way God wants it to."

Wise were the fathers of the church councils of Nicaea and Constantinople in the fourth century when they delineated what we need to believe about the second coming with a simple, brief phrase: "He will come again in glory to judge the living and the dead, and His kingdom shall have no end." Know these truths for a fact and do not be concerned with the details. What is far more important—and far less likely to lead us into strange beliefs and actions—is to ask the question, What difference does the fact of His second coming make on my life? Peter challenges us, since the fact of Jesus' return is certain, "What sort of persons ought you to be in lives of holiness and godliness?" (2 Pet. 3:11). What should we do?

First, wait patiently. James exhorts his readers to "be patient...until the coming of the Lord" (James 5:7). It is easy to be stressed because of our troubles, but we know how things will turn out. We have read "the last page of the novel"! We know God wins decisively in the end and will right all wrongs. Yes, we have to be about our Father's business, abounding in the work of the Lord (1 Cor. 15:58). Yes, there is suffering here on Earth. Yes, we have responsibilities. The key here is patience.

We do not have to be anxious, and we do not have to be constantly active. While we must be about our Father's business, there is not a frenzy about it.

Second, prepare diligently. When Jesus comes back, or when a person dies (whichever is first), there will be no further chance for him or her to be saved. Therefore, if any of you reading this are not trusting Jesus Christ as Lord and Savior, make your profession of faith in Him while you have time. Also, we must cooperate with God's grace for growth in holiness as "all who have this hope in him purify themselves, just as he is pure" (1 John 3:3, NRSV).

Third, work eagerly. Because Jesus is coming back and because we love Him, we want to present Him with the best work we as stewards can do. We know our work will never be in vain. (That verse, 1 Corinthians 15:58, was given me in 1961 by my then pastor as what some would call my "life's verse.") We prepare the way for the Lord's second coming as John the Baptist prepared the way for His first coming. We do this by witnessing to people about the Lord, by helping other Christians grow as disciples (Matt. 28:19), by abounding in good works and specific deeds of charity, and by working for justice in the world.

Fourth, worship ardently. Luke tells us that as Christ ascended they worshiped Him (Luke 24:50–52). Though belief in truth, growth in holiness, and ministry to others are all vital parts of Christian discipleship, worship is the greatest action of which we are capable. As several contemporary Christian praise songs so aptly puts it, the very reason we are alive is to worship God. This worship, while certainly done individually, finds its best expression in the Christian community, the church. Believers have been admonished from New Testament days not to neglect to meet together (Heb. 10:25). The Greek word for "meet together" is *synagoge*, from which we get our word *synagogue*. The exhortation is not merely to avoid being aloof to other believers but to avoid solo Christianity, one that discounts the centrality of the visible, gathered church.

There are, as we have said, very different beliefs concerning the details of the Lord's return. Whatever our views on the millennial kingdom, whatever our take on the symbol system of the Book of Revelation, we must be about our Father's business, doing His work in His way with His power.

WHAT'S NEXT?

Had it not been for Jesus' resurrection and Ascension, present-day followers of Christ would be followers of coffee table book spirituality, akin to those who love to leaf through thick tomes on the Gothic cathedrals of France. They would be celebrating the life of Jesus like many celebrate the life of George Washington—a wonderful person, long dead, who inspires us. However, the church from the beginning has been told not to be "memorializers of a dear departed Friend. They were [and we are] told to be followers of a living Lord."[18]

The earliest Christians had been given the Great Commission to be followers of a living Lord. But first, they needed to wait for the coming of the Holy Spirit. It is to that period of waiting we must now turn.

Each of the post-Resurrection appearances of Jesus teaches us something about what the church would be like after Jesus' Ascension and what the church should be like today. What do Luke 24:50–53 and Acts 1:9–11 teach us? Why did Jesus ascend?

First, Jesus ascended back to heaven because it was and is His home, and from His home He reigns. As much as we would selfishly want Him here right now, those who love the Lord want Him where He truly belongs.

Second, Jesus ascended back to heaven in His resurrection body to demonstrate that the same God who created the material world redeemed and redeems it. He does not devalue the physical world. Some of the blessings God bestows are physical ones. Some of the means God uses to bless are physical ones. We are to make a difference in this world, not just encourage people to plan for the next one.

Third, Jesus ascended back to heaven so He could prepare a place for us. While we do not know what this exactly means, we do know that believers in Christ will have an eternal, heavenly home because of what Jesus did for us.

Fourth, Jesus ascended to sit at the right hand of His Father there to intercede for us. We know He will not do us harm. He is our friend in high places.

Fifth, Jesus ascended so He could raise us with Him.

Sixth, Jesus ascended so He could send the Holy Spirit to empower believers to multiply Jesus' ministry. It is both exhilarating and terrifying to know that, as St. Teresa once put it, with only slight exaggeration, "He has no hands but our hands."

Discussion Questions

1. How would you explain Ascension to a new convert?

2. What does it mean for us to be "joint heirs" with Jesus? (Romans 8:17)

3. The Reverend Tommy Tyson used to proclaim with great enthusiasm, "There's a man on the throne of the universe."[19] What are the implications of this?

CHAPTER 12

WAIT IN JERUSALEM

Acts 1:12–26

THE CLOSEST FOLLOWERS of Jesus had walked with their Lord for three years. They had listened to His teaching and watched Him perform miracles. Although they had received some beginner-level training in ministry and occasionally had ministered in His name, for the most part they had depended entirely on Him. But now He has gone, ascended to the Father. What next?

Perhaps they thought, "He'll quickly return. Obviously He had to do something or other in heaven, and once that was done He'd return, won't He? In the meantime, let's just wait right here where He ascended." But this option was rebuked by angels, the "two men...in white robes" (Acts 1:10–11). The followers of Jesus were not to keep staring up into the sky.

What else might they do? The more energetic and active among them most likely remembered Jesus' Great Commission: "Go therefore and make disciples of all nations, baptizing them in the name of the Father and of the Son and of the Holy Spirit, teaching them to observe ["obey," NRSV] everything that I have commanded you" (Matt. 28:19–20). So if they were not to wait around until Jesus returned, mustn't they then get on with the work? But Jesus had told them to "stay here in the city until you have been clothed with power from on high" (Luke 24:49, NRSV; see also Acts 1:4). The followers of Jesus were not to press on with the work just yet.

If they were not to stand idly by and if they were not to get on with the work as best they could, what then were they to do until they received that power? They were to get ready.

Yes, the emerging leaders of the church had known the Lord in personal way. Yes, they were eager to expand the kingdom of God. But they were not yet ready, nor were they empowered. Those of us who are eager for God's kingdom to advance, for lost sinners to be saved, for believers to mature in the faith, for wrongs to be righted, and for society to be transformed will want to get on with the work right away. This is a noble desire, but until we are matured, taught, trained, equipped, and empowered *we are not yet ready.*

Over the years I've met several people called to ordained ministry who were upset that they had to spend three years in a theological seminary prior to ordination. Some others, called to a lay ministry, resent a period of instruction and supervision before they are allowed to get on with the task. Yet, didn't Jesus' closest followers spend three years with Him before they were ready to lead the church?

R. T. Kendall points out that even Jesus had to undergo a maturation process.

> A man or woman with a secret anointing [a call from God and a clear gifting from God to bear fruit in ministry] always needs further preparation. We do not get the necessary refinement by merely praying for more of the Holy Spirit. Jesus had all the Holy Spirit that there was—the Spirit without limit (John 3:34). Yet, "although

he was a son, he learned obedience from what he suffered" (Hebrews 5:8).[1]

EMPOWERMENT

I first started leading teaching conferences and healing missions in churches around the United States in the mid 1980s. One of the first places I went to was Bartlesville, Oklahoma, the home of Phillips Petroleum Company. One afternoon I had a tour of the Phillips Petroleum Company Museum, a fascinating place to learn about the early days of the oil industry in the United States.

One of the people accompanying me on the tour showed me a photograph and asked, "What do you see?"

I responded, "Tepees, oil derricks, and several large automobiles. And there are people standing around who look from their skin tone and with those tepees in the background like they might be Indians'"

"Yes," was the response. "Do you want to know the background of this?"

"Sure," I replied. I had long been a fan of Paul Harvey's radio program *The Rest of the Story*, so here was a chance to get some background on this interesting photo.

The story was this: After oil had been discovered in that corner of Oklahoma, agents for the oil company wanted to secure rights to what was under the ground owned by people in the area. They visited families, including Native American families, to negotiate agreements. All of a sudden many who had been quite poor now had more money than they could have ever dreamed of. And who should show up next but Cadillac salesmen?

So the heads of the families bought Cadillacs. They agreed with what the salesman had told them: in your Cadillac the ride to town is so much more pleasant, and one does not get wet when it rains. Then something went wrong. The cars no longer worked. "Not to worry," the salesman reassured the buyers. "You're not familiar with driving a car. You've broken it. But that's OK. You have lots of money. You can just buy another one. But be more careful this time."

Some Indian families were on their third automobile before honest people intervened. The problem was not that the men had broken the cars. The problem was simply that they were out of gas, a problem easily remedied once one had figured out the need.

There's a lesson here for us. No matter how luxurious the automobile is, no matter how elegant it looks, no matter how comfortable it rides, it's not going to go anywhere if it's out of gas. We will not bear fruit for Christ and His church if we're trying to minister in our own power.

Jesus informed His disciples and He informs us that He wants us to bear fruit:

> I am the vine, you are the branches. Those who abide in
> me and I in them bear much fruit, because apart from
> me you can do nothing.... My Father is glorified by this,
> that you bear much fruit and become my disciples.
> —JOHN 15:5, 8, NRSV

Those of us who are activists—who are psychologically attuned to being busy trying to accomplish things and who are spiritually attuned to wanting God's kingdom to advance, His people blessed, and His name glorified—are tempted to roll up our sleeves and plow into the task without adequate infilling. I know that I, looking at everything that has to get done in the days ahead, am tempted to diminish my time of prayer and devotion. "Every minute spent in prayer and devotional reading is a minute taken from working to get those things done," I sometimes conclude. The fact is, if we have a lot of work to do for God's kingdom, we need *more* time spent in prayer and devotion, not less. Otherwise, we may work hard but we will produce foliage, not fruit.

For several years I led a Friday night service of prayer and praise with healing ministry at St. Paul's Church in Malden, Massachusetts. Team members would arrive right after work, do the necessary set-up tasks, and then spend ten minutes before the service for prayer, knowing that we could bear fruit only if we were yielded to God and filled with the Holy Spirit. We knew that the "fruit of the Spirit" (Gal. 5:22–23) is exactly that, fruit *of the Holy Spirit*, and if we were trying to minister in our own strength nothing meaningful would happen.

After a few years, however, it occurred to us that perhaps we needed to spend more time in prayer. Ten minutes was better than nothing, but was it enough? The sense grew: spend more time with the Lord. But how?

We found a few others and asked them to do some of the set-up tasks. We started praying for thirty minutes, not ten, and the difference was immediately obvious. More people understood, took to heart, and applied to their lives the sermons that were preached; more people were convicted of their sin and repented of it; more people realized and gratefully received the incredible love God has for His children; and more people were physically healed, immediately and lastingly, than on previous weeks.

It's axiomatic in mathematics and science that if one introduces a single change into an equation or formula and there's a different outcome, unless there is clear evidence to the contrary, our working hypothesis is it was the introduction of the change that *caused* the difference in outcome. We concluded things had suddenly become more fruitful in the service because we were now spending more time in prayer asking for God's grace and the empowerment of the Holy Spirit.

Jonathan Edwards (1703–1758) was one of the principal leaders of the First Great Awakening (1730s–1740s), the first major revival America experienced. He once said that if he knew he was going to have a busy day with lots of people to minister to he'd pray for an hour for wisdom and strength. If he knew he was going to have a *very busy* day he'd pray for *two hours*. Many people, including some devout Christians, to whom I tell this story, immediately suggest this was foolish. Typical of the comments is, "But he's got so much to do. He needs every moment he can get to get on with the job."

But consider this analogy. You're going on a long trip and your car needs some gas. You stop at the gas station, and you're pumping gas. You look at your watch. You've got a long trip ahead of you, and yet you're not progressing toward your destination because you've stopped at a gas station. So you stop pumping part way through filling your tank so you can more quickly get on with your driving. Isn't this foolish? The longer trip you take, the more gas your tank needs to get you there. It takes longer to fill up the tank—taking up minutes during which you could be driving—but there's no other way to complete your journey successfully than to have as much gas in the tank as it will hold.

So, the closest followers of Jesus were told, "Stay here in the city until you have been clothed with power from on high." They were to wait.

TWO KINDS OF WAITING

There are two kinds of waiting, passive and active.

Passive waiting is a bored, lazy mere hanging out. In Samuel Beckett's play *Waiting for Godot*, two men, Vladimir and Estragon, sit on a park bench waiting for their friend Godot. The whole play is the dialogue between these two men as to whether their friend would ever show up. Some have suggested that Beckett, known to be a vocal skeptic of the Christian faith, was making a statement: people wait for God (how similar to the name Godot) to show up but He never does. (Though he was often asked the meaning of the play, Beckett never gave a definitive answer.)

The other kind of waiting is an *active waiting*. Think of waiting on tables. Look at the wait-staff at a busy restaurant. They're the antithesis of passive as they scurry about to wait on the customers. It is this active kind of waiting Jesus called His followers to undertake. He saying to them, "Do not just hang around aimlessly, passively, hoping that this promised power of the Holy Spirit might someday appear. Instead, be active in your waiting. Do the things you need to be doing so when the Spirit comes, you'll be ready to receive."

Years ago I heard about a particular football team. Most football teams carry three quarterbacks. If the team's number one quarterback is exceptionally good there's little for the other two quarterbacks to do. The number two quarterback might play a few minutes toward the end of games with lopsided scores. Often he holds the ball for the field goal kicker in case there's a bad snap and suddenly he has to run or pass. Other than that, he doesn't do much.

One day something happened to the number one quarterback of this team. Someone landed on his leg and broke it. He was out for the rest of the season. Naturally, the coach turned to the number two quarterback, but it immediately became clear he wasn't ready. Instead of using the time he was sitting on the bench to learn the plays and study how his teammates ran and caught, he was just hanging out, chatting with other benchwarmers about cars and girlfriends.

The coach turned to the number three quarterback. If there's not normally much for the number two quarterback to do, what occupies the time of the number three quarterback? A friend of mine suggests the only task of the number three quarterback is to guard the Gatorade™ bucket. But this number three quarterback used his bench time wisely. He studied the plays, he noted how his teammates would run and catch. So when the coach, in desperation, turned to his number three quarterback, he was ready. He certainly wasn't the best athlete on the team, but he had made the most the time he was sitting with nothing to do. For him, waiting wasn't a bored, lazy hanging around. It was an attentive, active waiting.

Jesus, in exhorting people to be watchful for that unknown hour of His second coming, said, "Therefore...be ready" (Matt. 24:44). If God has promised you something in the future are you just hanging around, or are you actively preparing for it so when it comes you'll be ready? Think of Simeon. Luke tells us he was "waiting for the consolation of Israel" (Luke 2:25, NKJV). He waited by becoming "righteous and devout" (NRSV), by listening to the Holy Spirit so that he would hear the Spirit's promise (he would not die before seeing the Messiah), by following the Spirit's direction (going to the temple at the moment the Holy Family would appear), by uttering the Spirit's words (the hymn called the "*Nunc Dimittis*," or "The Song of Simeon"), and by announcing the Spirit's prophecy (Luke 2:25–35).

The apostles were to wait before they got on with the task of ministry, but not by standing around gazing into heaven after Jesus ascended (Acts 1:11).

PRESENT IN THE UPPER ROOM

Acts 1:12–14 tells us that those closest to Jesus—the remaining apostles, women followers, Mary, and Jesus' brothers—gathered together in the Upper Room. Verse 15 tells us the total number was about one hundred and twenty.

We note the presence of some women. Women had been included in Jesus' inner circle (see, for example, Luke 8:2–3; 23:49; 23:55–24:10), and they followed Jesus during His earthly ministry, even to the cross.

Who were "His brothers"? We would assume they were the same as those who had previously thought Jesus was out of His mind or even demon possessed for teaching as He did (Mark 3:21–35). We would assume they were the same who at one point in His ministry simply did not believe in Him (John 7:2–10). Who were they? The most likely explanation is the obvious one. After Jesus was born, Mary and Joseph married and had children.

Roman Catholics insist that the term *brothers* means "cousins" because Mary was "ever virgin." There is no Scriptural warrant for the perpetual virginity of Mary, and there is no theological need for it. The point of Mary being a virgin is not that sexual relations between a man and a woman married to each other are sin. God kept Mary a virgin *when Jesus was conceived* so that Jesus would be perfect human *and perfect God*, not just a particularly spiritually attuned human. After Jesus' conception, Mary remaining a virgin was irrelevant. Some in the early church gravitated toward a belief in the perpetual virginity of Mary because of the influence of both Gnostic and Greek philosophical ideas that sex is inherently evil and abstinence from it was spiritually superior, and even that the physical—and not just its misuse—was sinful.

This period in this Upper Room is the last mention of Mary in Scripture. Like with so many things in Christian life, Protestants and Roman Catholics have much to learn from each other. If some Protestants have a pathological aversion to Mary despite the tremendous role model she is as an ideal Christian disciple, some Roman Catholics make her to be things she is not (such as a co-mediatrix or co-redemptix with her Son).[2]

The best answer is to assume that the Greek word here, *adelphois*, means "brothers," as it is usually translated, and that those named brothers here in this upper room were Jesus' half-brothers, the natural offspring of Mary and Joseph.

What we find is that there is a diversity of people here. There are men and women. There are those who have been called to be apostles (the first bishops, or leaders, of the early church), and there are people who are not. There are people who are named and people left unnamed.

The church tends to swing between two extremes on such matters as this. Either it gets unbiblically clerical, with its clergy—particularly its lead clergy—being the only ones who can think, decide, and lead; or it gets unbiblically anticlerical, turning its clergy into mere hired hands or even questioning the need to have clergy at all. However, in the New Testament, we find a body of believers with both servant-leaders in charge and laity bearing fruit in ministry.

Acts 1:15 speaks of one hundred and twenty persons. John Stott quotes Howard Marshall as to why this number was important. According to Marshall, "In Jewish law a minimum of 120 Jewish men were required to establish a community with its own council," so the believers were numerous enough "to form a new community."[3] Indeed, the church is the New Israel.

Some upper rooms were large enough to accommodate such a number not just for daytime events but also for evening sleeping. In many of the larger homes the downstairs was divided into smaller rooms, the walls of which supported a large upstairs room encompassing the entire floor (see also Acts 20:8–9). These upper rooms were above the noise of street level. They were above easy interruptions.

But which upper room was this one? Was it *the* Upper Room where Jesus celebrated the Passover and inaugurated the sacrament of Holy Communion (Mark 14:12–16)? Might the Scriptural use of the definite article *the* indicate that this particular upper room had significance to those first reading the Book of Acts?[4] Or, was it another upper room, the one in which He appeared after He rose (Luke 24:33–43; John 20:19, 26)? Or, was it the upper room of John Mark's mother, Mary, where the church later met (Acts 12:12)? We don't know for certain.

WHAT WERE THEY ACTIVELY DOING WHILE WAITING FOR THE COMING OF THE HOLY SPIRIT?

Some people are immediately bored with waiting because either they do not know what they are waiting for, or, if they do know, they do not know how to prepare for it. Might this group, like most groups of Christians, be at the intersection of self-directed activity and God-led preparation?

As was previously noted, the selection of Matthias to replace Judas (Acts 1:15–26) is believed by some to have been a God-led activity and by others to have been self-directed. Kenyan scholar Paul Mumo Kisau is a good representative of the former group. He asserts, "The procedure followed in the election of Judas' replacement sheds light on the state of spirituality of the believers after the departure of their Lord. They clearly relied on Scripture to guide their actions. Peter cited Psalms 69:25 and 109:8.... The disciples were, therefore, acting in direct obedience to the Word of God in seeking to replace Judas."[5]

Or, was the election of Matthias really Peter's need to "just do something"? Just because there are Bible verses that *could possibly apply* to a particular situation doesn't mean they *must apply* and that God is directing their application in a particular case. Michael Gemignani is of this opinion. He writes, "Peter did not seek guidance about whether there should have been an election in the first place. He simply concluded that there had to be a twelfth apostle and that was that."[6] The only prayer was that God would pick the right candidate of the two put forward.

I agree with those who believe Peter's actions were fleshly. We never hear about Matthias again in church history. Saul of Tarsus, it seems, was God's choice to be the replacement apostle. When James was martyred a few years later, there was no move to replace him in the circle of the twelve.

Whether this understanding of the selection of a replacement apostle is correct or not, we must be on our guard not to push things along because we cannot stand waiting. If God says to do something we should, but if not, then we should not.

What were our Lord's disciples actively doing during that period between the Ascension and Pentecost? We will address this question in our next chapter.

Discussion Questions

1. "They that wait upon the LORD shall renew their strength" (Isa. 40:31, KJV). What does it mean to wait upon the Lord?

2. The instruction was to tarry in Jerusalem until they were endowed with power from on high, *i.e.* Pentecost. Since we live after Pentecost, is there occasion for us to tarry in this manner?

3. What do we learn from the conduct of the apostles between the Ascension and Pentecost?

4. Have you ever felt commanded, *"Don't just do something—sit there"*?

CHAPTER 13

WHILE THEY WERE WAITING

Acts 1:12–26

Wнат wеrе оur Lord's disciples actively doing during that period between the Ascension and Pentecost?

First, they were meeting together "with one accord" (Acts 1:14). Many commentators have noted that when Acts 2:1 says, "They were all together in one place," the seeming redundancy of the words *together* and *in one place* is intentional. To highlight this redundancy, several Bible teachers have rendered the phrase as, "They were *together together*." The biblical text is trying to emphasize that these people were not just a crowd; they were becoming a fellowship. They were together in both senses of the word. The Greek word used here for "together," *homothymadon*, is the one used in Acts 4:24 for *united* prayer and in Acts 15:25 for a *united* decision.

I doubt this unity is just something in which they found themselves. Rather, I believe it was the result of hard work, aided by God's grace. What would they have to overcome in order to have this fellowship, this accord?

There had previously been some acrimony in the apostolic band; there had been vying for position as to who is greatest (Mark 9:33–34). Perhaps some, previously annoyed at Peter for his boastfulness, were now angry at him for his denying Jesus at the very time Jesus needed him most (John 18:15–18). Perhaps John might have been disturbed at the other apostles because he was the only one of them remaining at the cross after all the rest had fled (John 19:25–27). Some, although they saw the heightened honor Jesus gave to women, might still have been struggling with centuries of ingrained attitudes and were at best condescending to the women in their midst. Certainly everyone had to struggle with the same baser thoughts with which believers throughout the centuries have had to contend.

Whatever it was they were struggling against to overcome, they knew that if the Christian mission was to succeed they had to do their part in seeking and granting forgiveness.

Coming together as one is an oft-repeated Scriptural theme. The psalmist celebrates "how good and pleasant it is when brothers dwell in unity" (Ps. 133:1). Paul exhorted the Ephesian Christians to be "eager to maintain the unity of the Spirit in the bond of peace" (Eph. 4:3). He entreated Euodia and Syntyche to come to agree in the Lord (Ph. 4:2).

But in striving for unity we must be careful to avoid two pit-falls. The first is the mistaken notion that to have unity we must have uniformity. In the 1980s I was asked to intervene in divisions that had sprung up in a number of congregations in New England over both musical style and musical instrumentation in church services. This dispute was sometimes called "The Music Wars," and it was raging all over the English-speaking world. One issue was between the pipe organ and guitars or praise band. Another issue was between classical hymns and contemporary praise songs. A third dispute was about whether music should be spread throughout the service or whether music should be sung in a block of several pieces in a row at the beginning. Many churches fought over all of these points of dispute. But these are not issues of good versus evil. The choices are options, and there can be a legitimate diversity on these points.

The real issues in Christian music are, first, that our music, in whatever style we choose, is to honor and glorify the Lord. Second, we are to give God our best as we sing and play instruments. And third, the words of the hymns and songs are always to be congruent with basic doctrinal truth. Get those points right, and there can be a rich diversity of style.

One of my favorite quotes is from the Preface to the *Book of Common Prayer*. It starts, "It is a most invaluable part of that blessed 'liberty wherewith Christ hath made us free,' that in his worship different forms and usages may without offence be allowed, provided the substance of the Faith be kept entire."[1] In sum, the first pitfall to avoid in striving for unity is the mistaken notion that to have unity we must be alike in everything.

The second pitfall is that unity is more important than truth. There are certain basics to which all must agree to be in unity. God asked and asks through the prophet Amos, "Can two walk together, except they be agreed?" (Amos 3:3, NIV). Paul continues his unity theme in Ephesians 4 by telling us the kind of unity he meant: "unity of the faith" (Eph. 4:13). Note that quote from the *Book of Common Prayer*. It ends, "provided the substance of the Faith be kept entire."[2] The Anglican expression of the faith is full and rich when it adheres to this principle. When one departs from basic Christian orthodoxy of doctrine and morality, he or she is not being inclusive or tolerant but rather aberrant and hurtful. *departing from an accepted standard*

One of the ways Satan seeks to wreak havoc in God's church is by confusing our minds about the truth. He has managed to convince us that not only is questing for the truth an impossible task, but the very concept of truth is mean-spirited. A woman was telling me about some behavior in which her son was engaging. When I responded with a gentle expression of

"I'll join you in prayer that he repents," she got angry and barked at me, "Why do you hate my son?" She fell into that trap far too common today that to disagree with someone is to judge and hate them, and that merely to point out that a belief or an action that is in nonconformity to the clear teaching Scripture is mean-spirited instead of wise.

It was the cynical Pontius Pilate who asked, "What is truth?" (John 18:38). It was Jesus of Nazareth who told us, "The truth will make you free" (John 8:32, NRSV). It was Jesus that contradicted the errors of both the Pharisees and Sadducees. To this latter group that denied the Resurrection, Jesus did not say, "You have an interesting opinion, and, for what it's worth, here's mine." He said, straightforwardly, objectively, "You are wrong" (Matt. 22:29). Objectively wrong. There is objective truth and the Sadducees, said Jesus, did not possess it. To belong to Jesus demands that we both accept the idea of objective truth and accept what He says it is. If you do not do this, then Jesus is merely a religious advisor to you and, if you're honest, an advisor you do not really trust since He so insists on adherence to specific doctrinal beliefs and moral practices.

Of course, so many of us have been hurt and angered when someone's quest for the truth was a power grab, an ego trip, or something not based on the clear teaching of Scripture as understood by the consensus of God's faithful throughout the centuries. Such a misguided quest for the truth is off-putting and often harmful.

And yet, the opposite error, a denial of the necessity of truth, also hurts. We know this in most things in life. Several years ago I watched a television exposé of a hospital cited for sloppy procedures. Wrong medicines were administered, and in one surgical case the wrong leg was amputated. Would we settle for mere sincerity on the part of hospital workers when clear errors had occurred? Would we not want the truth—objective, factual truth—to prevail?

Or, what of the financial scandals of the last several years? Would we want some financial planner to make horrible, perhaps even criminal mistakes, or would we want all accounts to be handled according to the standards set by the industry?

Of course we demand truth in most areas of our life. Might it be our egotism or our rebellion against God that says any opinion about religion, especially our own, is valid? We no longer fashion golden calves as false gods, but might we not be fashioning false beliefs about God as the twenty-first century's equivalent?

It is sad that the church is fragmented into thousands of denominations. The quest to ascertain which one is the true one is a fool's errand. But are there not basics of the faith around which orthodox Christians, whatever their differences on secondary matters, can unite? It seems so. Most orthodox Christians subscribe to the Apostles' Creed and the Nicene Creed. Many interdenominational Protestant parachurch ministries such as Gordon-Conwell Theological Seminary and the Billy Graham Evangelistic Association have statements of faith one must adhere to in order to work for them. In these statements of faith ministry leaders are saying that these doctrinal statements are necessary not because of arrogance on their part but because over the centuries God's people have come to a consensus that these statements express reality, give life, and deny falsehood that harms. Far from being narrow-minded and mean-spirited in insisting on these things, not to insist on them would be unloving. Ideas have consequences and bad ideas have bad consequences. Sometime seminary professor, church rector, and diocesan bishop C. FitzSimons Allison wrote a most helpful book on this very subject entitled *The Cruelty of Heresy*.[3]

In this upper room the proto-early church was forging unity, a unity based on forgiveness and love, a unity that recognized diversity, but a unity that insisted on mutual adherence to the basic doctrines of the faith that Jesus had taught. This gathering anticipated the first appearance of this wise aphorism: "In essentials unity, in nonessentials diversity, in all things charity."[4]

So what was going on in the Upper Room? First, they were meeting together with one accord. What else did they do?

Second, they worshipped collectively "in church." Luke describes this post-Ascension, pre-Pentecost period of waiting at the end of Luke 24 and in Acts 1. In his Gospel he notes that when they returned to Jerusalem they were "continually in the temple blessing God" (Luke 24:53). They weren't always in that upper room. They ventured out, and, as a group, they joined the corporate worship of Israel in the temple.

While we can and should worship God individually at various times and in various places during the week, we must be intentionally devoted to the corporate worship of the church. American Christianity, Protestantism in particular, is imbalanced toward an excessive individualism. This does not come from Scripture. This excessive individualism comes, in part, from the legacy of the Puritans, whose attitude of "no king, no bishop" quickly extended to one of "nobody's going to tell *me* what to think or do." This excessive individualism in America also comes from our love of the rugged individualist. Present-day attitudes of "me and Jesus" and "just me and my Bible" all evidence this excessively individualistic mentality.

Scripture, by contrast, gives a much more corporate picture of one's spiritual life. While, of course, a person has to make an individual commitment to Christ as one's personal Lord and Savior, Scripture speaks much about the community.

When the question was being decided as to what was necessary for those Gentile converts to Christianity, there was no mention of the possibility that individual congregations—much less individual Christians—could decide this question for themselves. Instead, a council of church leaders met to decide the matter, which was then binding on everyone (Acts 15).

God has rigged the game against soloist Christianity. Because we see through a glass darkly and know only in part (1 Cor. 13:12) no one possesses all wisdom about God. We need the collective wisdom of believing church people throughout the centuries to help us understand. Paul does not envision individuals knowing the truth simply by reading the New Testament by themselves. He tells Timothy that it is *the church* that is "the pillar and bulwark of the truth" (1 Tim. 3:15, NRSV). "Just me and my Bible" is as foolish as it is egotistical.

Wise are the words of the British John Stott, considered one of the top evangelical Christians of the twentieth century:

> ...the church has a place in God's plan to give his people a right understanding of his Word. The individual Christian's humble, prayerful, diligent and obedient study of Scripture is not the only way the Holy Spirit makes clear what he has revealed. It would hardly be humble to ignore what the Spirit may have shown to others. The Holy Spirit is indeed our teacher, but he teaches us indirectly through others as well as directly to our own minds. It was not to one man that he revealed the truths now enshrined in Scripture, but to a multiplicity of prophets and apostles; his work of illumination is given to many also. It is not as individuals merely, but "with all the saints" that we are given "power...to grasp how wide and long and high and deep is the love of Christ...that surpasses knowledge" (Eph. 3:18–19).[5]

In addition, since no one possesses all the gifts of the Spirit, we need others in the body for the fullness of ministry to take place (1 Cor. 12:14–26).

We also need ordained leaders. Like it or not, three (*three!*) books of the New Testament are devoted to the qualifications and job descriptions of the clergy (1 Timothy, 2 Timothy and Titus). When the church in Crete needed leadership there were not congregational meetings during which pastors were elected by the people who paid their salaries as hired hands. Instead, Paul chose Titus to be the overseer (bishop), who was then to select presbyters (elders) for each congregation (Titus 1:5).

Jesus did not say, "I will build a collection of individual believers relating individually to me," but "I will build my church" (Matt. 16:18). Paul did not refer to Christ as the one to whom people relate only as individuals but to Him as "the head of the body, the church" (Col. 1:18). Christ does not have a disembodied collection of body parts but the "church, which is his body" (Eph. 1:22–23). Building on the teaching that these and other New Testament passages reflect, Cyprian of Carthage, a church leader in the middle of the third century could write, "He can no longer have God for his Father who has not the Church for his mother."[6]

It is too self-serving to point out the faults of the leaders in the church so we can excuse our absence from the church. We don't walk away from professional medical care because of the occasional incompetence or gross negligence by a small percentage of medical providers. As we look through Scripture we clearly see the faults of those whom God appointed—and kept—in leadership, their faults notwithstanding. Spend some time reading 2 Samuel 1:1 to 1 Kings 2:46 to see the many faults of King David, yet he was a man after God's own heart (1 Sam. 13:14; Acts 13:22). While there are times when God's leaders need to be set straight (and note how God raised up the prophet Nathan to do just that with David in 2 Samuel 12:1–15), to leave the corporate structure of the church is to give in to the egotism of the self.

One of the best known definitions of evangelism comes from a committee formed a century ago by the Archbishops of Canterbury and York, England: "To evangelize is so to present Christ Jesus in the power of the Holy Spirit, that men shall come to put their trust in God through him, to accept him as their Saviour, and serve him as their King in the fellowship of his Church."[7] Note that last phrase, "in the fellowship of his

Church." That phrase is as important as all the other ones. To come to Christ means to come to His church. To be a Christian means more than weekly corporate attendance for study and worship in a local fellowship, but *it never means less.*

These Christians in this upper room were prepared to receive the Holy Spirit in part because they worshiped corporately in church. The author of the Epistle to the Hebrews warned his readers against skipping church (Heb. 10:25). We must do nothing less.

So what was going on in the Upper Room? Those gathered were in one accord, and they worshiped collectively in church. What else?

Third, they were *devoted* to prayer. As Luke lists those present in this upper room, he adds, "All these were constantly devoting themselves to prayer" (Acts 1:14, NRSV).

Before we look at the subject of prayer, let's first look at the word devoted. The word for "devoted" in the Greek is *proskartereo*, which means "persistent, dedicated activity with expectation that something good will happen as a result." So often Christians wonder why Christianity "doesn't work" for them. I tell them that it is for the same reason my golf game doesn't work for me. I tried it a few times. I remained a lousy player, so I gave up. Nearly every golfer to whom I tell this quickly shoots back, "You've got to be devoted to golf to get good at it." So it is with the Christian faith. Prayer, worship, and Bible study, done occasionally without much fervor, will do nothing for us when we need it.

I once heard someone negatively describe the devotional practice of a friend this way: "Christianity is merely a hobby for him." The more I thought about this remark the more I became convinced that our faith *should* be a hobby for us! What does a hobbyist do? I know someone who is a model train enthusiast. He knows exactly when his model train magazines come in the mail each month and is excited all day anticipating going home to read the latest issue. He spends the evening devouring the issue from cover to cover. Nothing—telephone calls from friends, favorite television programs, invitations to go out—will interrupt the evenings of the days the magazines arrive. He sets aside money to buy something for his hobby, even neglecting to replace worn-out clothing. He spends time learning from those wiser in the subject than he is, and he spends time teaching those new to model railroading. He often mentions model trains in his conversation. While, yes, he can talk about other things, and while, no, he doesn't ram the subject of trains down people's throats, a stranger doesn't need long to know this man loves model trains. Why does he do all of these things about model trains? Because it is his hobby. Would to God more Christians were devoted at this level. Christianity as one's *hobby*? Please, God, may it be so for more of us.

Part of the definition of *proskartereo* is "persistence." This means doing our spiritual duty "in season and out of season" (2 Tim. 4:2), whether we are in the mood or not. Sometimes great spiritual fruit is birthed in those times of prayer and study while we are rushed or not emotionally disposed. Additionally, sometimes the best spiritual lessons we learn come not from a marathon session of prayer and Bible reading but from half an hour of spiritual activity done day-in and day-out.

Part of the definition of *proskatereo* is "expectancy." In other words, they were not just persistent and devoted; they expected that something good would happen as a result.

So what was going on in this upper room? Those gathered were in one accord, they worshipped collectively in church, and they had expectancy. What else was going on?

Fourth, they were devoted to prayer. Prayer involves several elements. Asking for things for ourselves and for others, thanksgiving, praise, and confession are among the most common. One much neglected part of prayer is a humble listening to God to discern His will as we celebrate His presence and enjoy

His company. No doubt those present in the Upper Room were engaged in all of these kinds of prayer. → *Obvious*

It has become (axiomatic) that no great revival has ever happened without a period of intense prayer preceding it. Those present in the Upper Room were expectant of the promised outpouring of the Holy Spirit to empower them to set the world on fire for Jesus. They knew that no great work for God would ever happen if God's children did not bathe themselves in prayer.

They had been promised something special, something devout Jews had been waiting for since the prophecies of Joel: the outpouring of the Holy Spirit upon all flesh (Joel 2:28–29). The Holy Spirit, as the third member of the Godhead, had been present for all eternity. The Holy Spirit was at work in the Old Testament. But now there would be a big change.

- In Old Testament times the Holy Spirit came upon individuals *for a period of time*. Now the Holy Spirit would be *a permanent presence*.

- In Old Testament times the Holy Spirit worked *through* individuals. Now the Holy Spirit would also dwell *within them*.

- In Old Testament times the Holy Spirit would come upon and work through *only a few individuals* in the community of believers. Now the Holy Spirit would be poured out on *all believers*.

While we can never merit the blessings of God, we can make ourselves more ready to receive them when they are graciously bestowed. I have a friend, a retired professor at Duke University, who likes what he calls "Old Mountain Pennycostal [*sic*] Music," meaning the songs of Pentecostal churches in the mountains of Appalachia of a few generations ago. One of his favorite songs is "Under the Spout Where the Glory Comes Out." The point of the song is to remind us that God blesses in certain ways, and if we wish to receive those blessings we will be in conformity with what He directs. In other words, we intentionally place ourselves not where we wish but "under the spout where the glory comes out." We do not deserve the blessings in any case, but if we are rebellious, if we are self-directed rather than God-directed, we will be in the wrong place and miss what He has in store for us.

These believers needed to know that the prophecy of Joel, declaring that God would pour out His Spirit in abundance, would soon be fulfilled. These believers also needed to humble themselves before the Lord so that they might receive that out-pouring and be used to grow the church.

Those gathered in this upper room had walked with and worked for the Lord. Now Jesus had ascended. One part of their walk and work was concluded as another part was about to begin. These devout believers were praying that God would bless and use them for His purpose. They knew what we must know, that we are ever and always mere "unprofitable servants" who have simply done our duty (Luke 17:10, KJV). We have the trea-sure in earthen vessels (2 Cor. 4:7). Any merit we possess is by the imputed righteousness of Christ. But if our discipleship is not about our own merit, it is about availability, yieldedness, and humility expressed in asking to be blessed and to be a blessing to Him and to others. They were humble, knowing they couldn't do it in their own strength but that they needed the promise of the Spirit. But they were also confident and eager to serve, knowing that they had walked with Jesus, had heard His gra-cious words, and had seen His mighty deeds. They had been told to teach what He had taught (Matt. 28:20) and do what He had done (John 14:12).

Humility is yet another place where we can go into unbib-lical extremes. One extreme is to confuse humility with humili-ation. Humility says, "I cannot bear fruit for God in myself, but I can with God's help" (as said Paul in Phil. 4:13); humiliation says, "I cannot bear fruit, period." Humility says, "I do not know everything, but what I know from Scripture is true because God said it"; humiliation says, "I don't know anything, so I should say nothing." Humility says that "God, working through me can accomplish great things" (see 1 Cor. 15:58); humiliation says, "God would never use anyone like me." Humility says, "I sometimes *do* wrong, but can be forgiven in Christ"; humiliation says, "I *am* wrong, and that's the end of it."

Do not let Satan humiliate you, but do let God humble you and you humble yourself (James 4:10). Regularly go to God directly and with representatives of His church present (James 5:16), confess your inadequacies, ignorance, and sin, and receive empowerment, wisdom, and forgiveness. Then serve with humility and with great expectation of what God can do through a yielded vessel.

If humiliation is one false extreme of humility, the other is such an inflated confidence in oneself that God's grace and the help and correction of others are not needed. In the early 1980s when my ministry changed from that of a full-time parish priest to that of an itinerant leader of teaching conferences and healing missions, I wanted to make sure that I wouldn't crash and burn. I had seen too many itinerant speakers disgrace themselves and bring discredit to the Lord they were serving. I knew there were risks in being an itinerant and in the ego-stroking of being the one flown in from a great distance to teach and minister to a group of people who had been working for months toward this very day.

I was helped by reading John Pollock's biography of Billy Graham. In the 1960s and 1970s Church of England priest Pollock's book was considered *the* biography of this great evangelist. I had read this book at least thirty times when I was in college and graduate school and wanted to read it again, slowly and carefully, to see how Dr. Graham made the transition to full-time evangelist. The book tells the story that Dr. Graham got together his closest friends and asked them why people so hated itinerant evangelists. They answered that it was not that those people despised evangelism. They knew that evangelism was needed to help people come to Christ. The problem was with many of the evangelists. They too often took an obscene amount of money for themselves and were accountable to no one. Graham, by contrast, vowed to turn all the offerings over to a ministry organization and take a reasonable salary. Additionally, Graham opted for a board of directors, people who were not "yes men" but were people who loved him and believed in his ministry enough to stand up to him when they thought he needed it. Over the years I have followed Graham's example in both cases.[8]

I have seen so many churches harmed by out-of-control, rebellious individuals—clergy and laity both—people who are legends in their own minds, who are submitted to no one, who think that the fruit borne in their ministries comes from their innate spiritual superiority and not from the grace of God.

While I travel the world speaking, while I write books, while I am a guest lecturer at Christian colleges and seminaries, I am the part-time pastor of a small congregation in New Hampshire. These people love me, and I them, and they keep me earthbound, grounded, and, I hope, humbled. Thank you, God, and thank you, Trinity Church!

I believe those gathered in that upper room were praying humbly before the Lord that He would give them what they needed so they could fulfill the call on their lives. They were humble but not humiliated. They were confident but not arrogant. They knew, by the grace of God and as they had fellow believers to hold them accountable, that they could set the world on fire once the fire of the Holy Spirit came. Please, Jesus, may this be ever so in us.

So what was going on in that upper room? Those gathered were in one accord, they worshiped collectively in church, they were expectant, and they were devoted to prayer. What else was going on?

Fifth, they searched Scripture. Of course, at this juncture, Scripture meant the Old Testament, although Jesus was making provision for there to be New Testament Scripture as well. Jews, especially after the sixth-century BC exile in Babylon, were "people of the Book." Jesus had recently "interpreted to [the Emmaus travelers] in all the Scriptures the things concerning himself" (Luke 24:27). No doubt, as godly Jews, as followers of Jesus who constantly quoted the Old Testament, these people in that upper room were searching Scripture to discover how it applied to the incredible developments of the past several weeks.

Those gathered were in one accord, they worshiped collectively in church, they were expectant, they were devoted to prayer, and they searched Scripture. We know they were doing these things from the New Testament record. What else might be going on?

Sixth, they might have been reviewing what Jesus had taught. This is only natural. It's what we do with someone we idolize. When I was an undergraduate student at Williams College (class of 1971), one of the most beloved professors was Robert Gaudino (1925–1974). I never took a course from him, but those who did idolized him then and continue to idolize him all these years after his untimely death. There are Gaudino blogs. There have been Gaudino lectures and reunions at Williams, and many of the students who had had him as a professor return for these. I've been told by a few who attend that much of the conversation is taken up by students reminiscing about Professor Gaudino, sharing anecdotes about him, quotes of class lectures, and private conversations. Occasionally a former student will bring up something others did not hear or else had forgotten. Occasionally a former student will be corrected by others whose remembrance of what he had said is more accurate. This is what people do with someone they admire.

As the New Testament was later being written down, witnesses abounded to the events thus recorded. Many had heard Jesus teach. Any factual errors would have been roundly challenged. I think it is reasonable to speculate that this is part of what was happening in this upper room. If the truth is important (and Jesus said that it's the truth that will make people free [John 8:32] and that He is the truth [John 14:6]), we want to get it right. If words came from someone we adore, we want to have as best a recollection as possible. If we were not present some of those times when He taught, we want to know all the rest of what He said from those who were present.

Some time in the future some of the close followers of Jesus would be embarking on a life of full-time ministry. Others would be witnessing while holding down other responsibilities. In this upper room they were rehearsing the words and deeds of Jesus so they would be accurate in what they later said and wrote.

It has been fashionable during the past century and a half for skeptical theologians to impugn the accuracy of the Gospel accounts, suggesting that the Gospel writers either wrote down things as best they could remember years after the events or else made up quotations and events to serve an agenda. But is this how life actually works? If Professor Gaudino's students take pains to remember all of what their idol said and remember it as accurately as possible, why wouldn't Jesus' "students" have done the same? We simply need to know that this is what people do with someone they admire. Even apart from any doctrine of Scriptural inerrancy, this alone should make us trust, not distrust, the Gospel record.[9]

But we trust the Gospel record for another reason: Jesus had a high view of the authority and reliability of Scripture. Jesus showed in three different ways His acceptance of the Old Testament as God's authoritative Word:

1. By doing things that the Scriptures might be fulfilled (Mark 14:49; Luke 24:44–45; John 17:12; 19:28).

2. By repeatedly using such phrases as "Have you not read?" and "It is written..." (better translated as "It stands written forever") (Matt. 19:4; 21:13; Mark 2:25; 9:12).

3. By challenging the Pharisees who added to Scripture their personal customs and traditions, which had the effect of nullifying what the Old Testament taught (Matt. 23:23; 15:3).

Jesus also prepared for a New Testament with similar authority:

1. In saying that the Holy Spirit would jog the minds of the Gospel writers so that they would be accurate in what they wrote (John 14:26).

2. In saying that those writing the Epistles would be transmitting God's revelation, not their own opinions (John 16:12–13).

3. In commanding them to teach those who would come to faith through the witness of the church "all that I have commanded you" (Matt. 28:19–20). I think we can reasonably infer our Lord wanted His teachings and commandments written down, remembered, and taken to heart until He should return at His second coming.

Just as each of the post-Resurrection appearances of Jesus teaches us something about what the church would be like after Jesus' Ascension and what the church should be like today, Acts 1:12–26 teaches us some things about what this week and a half waiting period was about, things we individually and as the church must be about today. First, they needed to come into one accord. There was unfinished business between some of them. They needed to come into unity, which is a sense of brother/

sisterhood, not a uniformity of ideas. Second, they worshiped together. Third, they were expectant. Fourth, they were devoted to prayer. We saw how the word *devoted* means "to do something thoroughly and with the expectation that God will do something wonderful in response." Fifth, they searched Scripture together. And, perhaps, sixth, they reviewed what Jesus had taught them.

They were now ready. It was Pentecost, and devout Jews "from every nation under heaven" (Acts 2:5, NRSV) were in Jerusalem for the festival. Their desire was to worship and serve God. Just around the corner were these one hundred twenty Jewish followers of Jesus, also with the desire to worship and serve God. Then the Holy Spirit fell upon this latter group.[10] Many from the former group were attracted, and Peter preached to them that Jesus was "both Lord and Christ" (Acts 2:36). Three thousand were converted (Acts 2:41).

They all then "devoted themselves to the apostles' teaching and fellowship, to the breaking of bread and the prayers" (Acts 2:42)—that is, to authoritative teaching about Jesus' actions and reminder of Jesus' words, active participation in the corporate church under the leadership of the apostles, reception of Holy Communion at least weekly, and prayer. Add to it the various supernatural signs and wonders (miracles) recorded in Acts 3 and following, and what do we have? The various things our Lord Jesus did during His forty-day post-Resurrection period, both demonstrating He was the risen Christ and modeling for the church what church life should ever be like.

Discussion Questions

1. Of the various things in which the one hundred twenty gathered in this upper room were engaged, which comes easiest to you?

2. Which is most difficult?

3. How could we observe and celebrate this short "tarrying time" in our churches and as individuals?

CHAPTER 14

CONCLUSION

I N HIS RESURRECTION appearances, in His Ascension, and in His telling His core disciples to wait for the coming of the Spirit, what was Jesus trying to do? What was He teaching His people then and throughout the centuries? And what was He telling us to keep central in our individual and corporate discipleship today? Let's answer those questions by summing up in one place what we've seen throughout this book.

CHRISTIANITY IS PERSONAL

In Jesus' appearance to Mary Magdalene (Matt. 28:1–10; Mark 16:1–10; Luke 24:1–11; and John 20:1–18,) God is telling us that Christianity is personal. It is not just doctrines on what to believe about foundational things, although it involves that. It is not just imperatives on how to be and do good, although it involves that, too. Though it is always in the context of the church, our faith is about a personal relationship with God, Who chose to be incarnate as a person, Jesus of Nazareth. In His personal ministry to Peter (John 21:15–19), Jesus' tender love to a man who denied Him shouts across the centuries that God forgives. Though Jesus

227

called His followers to reach the nations, His concern never is at the expense of the individual soul.

CHRISTIANITY IS SCRIPTURAL

In Jesus' appearance on the road to Emmaus (Luke 24:13–27, 32) and in His appearance to the ten in Jerusalem (Luke 24:36–47), God is telling us that Scripture is central to Christianity and that it all points to Jesus, the unifying theme of both Old and New Testaments.

CHRISTIANITY IS EUCHARISTIC

In Jesus' being revealed during the breaking of the bread in Emmaus (Luke 24:28–31), God is telling us that Holy Communion is to be front and center in the life of the church. To contemporary Protestants I believe Jesus is saying that Holy Communion is to be celebrated at least weekly and to be seen as His body and blood, not just as an occasional memorial meal to a past event. To contemporary Roman Catholics, picking up on how Jesus unfolded Scripture, I believe Jesus is saying that Sunday worship should not just be a mass, or a mass with a brief homily, but mass with Scripture taught in depth and at length.

CHRISTIANITY IS BOTH SUPERNATURAL AND PHYSICAL

In Jesus' sudden appearance to the ten behind a locked door in Jerusalem on the night of the first Easter (Luke 24:36–43; John 20:19–25) and in Jesus' knowing where a mighty catch of fish was to be had (John 21:6), God is telling us that the Christianity is both supernatural and physical. Jesus can quickly relocate from one place to another, He can pass through doors, and He can know where a large number of fish are to be found from a hundred yards away with dim light. Soon after these events the Holy Spirit would fall on believers at the day of Pentecost, and the church would manifest signs and wonders—supernatural workings of the Spirit. Such things are to be a central part of the life of the corporate church and of individual believers today.

And yet, Jesus still had a body, He could speak and He could eat. Until He returns, the church will still be in the world, and Christians will still accomplish great things for God, not always by watching Him perform something supernatural through them but sometimes by rolling up their sleeves and going to work. Sometimes people will be healed miraculously, and sometimes, like Timothy, who was instructed to take wine for his stomach ailments (1 Tim. 5:23), we will have to take our medicine. Because God called creation good, God cares for the entire person—body, soul, and spirit.

Christianity Is an Honest Search for the Truth, Not Playing Games, nor Forbidding Questioning

In Jesus' appearance one week later with the ten as on the previous Sunday (but now with "Doubting Thomas" also present; John 20:26–29), God is telling us that doubt is not wrong as long as we are honest doubters, not playing games but searching diligently for the truth.

Christianity Centers in Christ, Who Is Lord and God

Thomas, once convinced that Jesus had truly risen from the dead, committed himself to Jesus as both Lord to be obeyed and God to be worshiped (John 20:28).

CHRISTIANITY, WHILE IT DOES INCLUDE MOUNTAIN-TOP EXPERIENCES, IS ALSO ABOUT THE NORMAL EVENTS OF LIFE

In Jesus having breakfast with the seven by the Sea of Galilee (John 21:9–13), God is telling us how He wishes to have fellowship with us during the ordinary moments of life.

CHRISTIANITY IS ABOUT RECONCILIATION

In Jesus' sitting down with Peter one on one (John 21:15–19), God is telling us that He desires to reconcile to Himself those who have gone astray.

CHRISTIANITY MINISTERS TO OUR INNER HURTS

When the resurrected Jesus met with Peter by a charcoal fire with roosters crowing in the background (John 21:9, 15–19)—under the same kind of conditions at which Peter denied knowing Jesus (John 18:18)—He shows the church that we can be healed of painful memories.

***

Each one of these lessons our resurrected Lord taught is important, or He would not have stayed forty additional days to teach them. Each one of these points made is to be part of our individual and corporate relationship with God. Each one of these items demonstrated is to be an intentional, well-developed part of the church.

Might I suggest you, the reader, go through the above list and do two things. First, note those areas where you are doing well, where your Christian discipleship includes at some level of maturity this or that particular item. Thank God, and also thank those individual Christians and those churches that have helped you come to the level of discipleship you're at. It's wise to celebrate what God has done and what we've done in response to His call on us so we will know that our work for Lord (including that work done on ourselves to make us better Christians) "is not in vain" (1 Cor. 15:58).

Then, second, note those areas where you still need some improvement. Realize that God wants us to be full-gospel Christians, enjoying and doing everything He asks, not just those things we agree with or that are the distinctives of our particular local congregation or denomination. Ask Him for His help where you are weak. Ask other Christians who might be strong in an area where you are weak to help you. You need to do this for both your walk with and your work for the Lord.

The Resurrection has something to say about the past: Jesus truly rose from the dead as He said He would. George Carey, sometime Archbishop of Canterbury, asserts, "His life was given an authoritative interpretation. People might ask, 'Did He teach the truth? Was He who He said He was?' The Resurrection answered the questions with a resounding, 'yes'."[1]

In addition, the Resurrection has something to say about the present and the future: how life as Christian disciples should be lived and how life in the church should be ordered until He returns. Lord Carey comments that the blessings received by those first Christians from the resurrected Christ are the same blessings available today to us, Christians "who can still walk with Christ on the road to Emmaus, know Him in the breaking of bread, be addressed in their grief (as Mary was), in their doubt (Thomas), or in their remorse (like Peter by the lakeside)."[2]

The resurrected Christ comes to us in the real world doing the things we do every day, like walking or fishing. He comes to us in our disappointments, as He did to the disciples who caught nothing while fishing. He comes to us who love Him as we persevere and watch Him reveal Who He is to us. While He does not have to prove Himself to us—we have to prove ourselves to Him—nevertheless, to those who truly and humbly seek Him, He will do whatever it takes to make Himself known.

All of this flows from Jesus' Resurrection. Then comes the Ascension. Why did Jesus ascend?

First, Jesus ascended back to heaven because it was and is His home, and from His home He reigns. As much as we would selfishly want Him here right now, those who love the Lord want Him where He truly belongs.

Second, Jesus ascended back to heaven in His resurrection body to demonstrate that the same God who created the material world redeemed and redeems it. He does not devalue the physical world. Some of the blessings God bestows are physical ones. Some of the means God uses to bless are physical ones.

Third, Jesus ascended back to heaven so He could prepare a place for us. While we do not know what this exactly means, we do know that believers in Christ will have an eternal, heavenly home because of what Jesus did for us.

Fourth, Jesus ascended to sit at the right hand of His Father, there to pray and intercede for us. We need not believe He will do us harm. He is our friend in high places.

Fifth, Jesus ascended so He could raise us to be with Him. If we are in Christ, we are where He is. Although in one sense we are here on Earth with all of its trials and tribulations, we are also truly with Him in the heavenlies right now.

Sixth, Jesus ascended so He could send the Holy Spirit to empower believers to multiply His ministry. It is both exhilarating and terrifying to know that, as St. Teresa once put it, "He has no hands but our hands."

Jesus' Resurrection. Jesus' Ascension. And then the ten day waiting period. Why? What did they need to do to prepare for the coming of the Holy Spirit on Pentecost?

First, they needed to come into one accord. There was

unfinished business between some of them. They needed to come into unity, which is a brotherhood/sisterhood attitude, not necessarily a uniformity of ideas or practices.

Second, they worshiped together. They went to the temple, and no doubt they worshiped in the Upper Room.

Third, they were *"devoted"* to prayer. Prayer was an essential part of what they did together. We saw how the word devoted means "to do something thoroughly and with the expectation that God will do something wonderful in response."

Fourth, they searched Scripture together.

Fifth, perhaps they recollected with each other what Jesus had said and done. Powerful, incredible things. Things we are called to do. Things we can do, by God's grace, by the help of others, and by our diligent work. Were they ready for the Holy Spirit to fall and the work to commence? While no one is ever ready, there are things they needed to do first, and they did them. When we've done our part we can then confidently trust God to give the increase (1 Cor. 3:6–7). Powerful, incredible things. Things we are called to do. Things we *can* do. Are you willing to do your part?

NOTES

INTRODUCTION

1. Thomas Jefferson, *The Jefferson Bible: The Life and Morals of Jesus of Nazareth Extracted Textually from the Gospels*, ed. Eyler Robert Coates Sr. (Radford, VA: Wilder Publications, 2007), 87.

2. Merrill C. Tenney, *The Expositor's Bible Commentary, vol. 9—John and Acts* (Grand Rapids, MI: Zondervan, 1981), 187.

3. Bonnell Spencer, *They Saw the Lord* (Wilton, CT: Morehouse-Barlow Co., Inc., 1983), 3.

4. Bruce Birdsey, "Celebrating the Resurrection of Jesus," *The Living Church* (April 23, 2000), 11.

5. John Updike, "Seven Stanzas at Easter," *Telephone Poles and Other Poems* (New York: Alfred A. Knopf, Inc., 1963). He wrote this for a religious arts festival held at the Clifton Lutheran Church of Marblehead, Massachusetts, in 1960. It won a one-hundred-dollar prize, which he gave back to the church. It was first published in the religious journal *The Christian Century*.

6. Robert Tuttle (retired professor of World Christianity, Asbury Theological Seminary), e-mail message to author.

7. John Donne, "Holy Sonnet 10," *John Donne: The Complete English Poems* (New York: Penguin Putnam Inc., 1986), 313.

8. N. T. Wright, *Surprised by Hope: Rethinking Heaven, the Resurrection, and the Mission of the Church* (New York: HarperOne, 2008), 236.

9. Rick Founds, "Lord I Lift Your Name on High," Maranatha! Music (Copyright 1989).

10. George W. Briggs, "Come, Risen Lord, and Deign to Be Our Guest," *Enlarged Songs of Praise* (Oxford: Oxford University Press).

CHAPTER 1: JESUS CALLED TO HER BY NAME

1. Wright, *Surprised by Hope*, 53.

2. Wright makes this point for the Resurrection narratives as a whole and not just the one under consideration here: "Even when the writers are telling the same story, they manage to find quite different phraseology." Ibid., 301, footnote 3. N. T.

3. Frederick Buechner, *Whistling in the Dark* (New York: HarperOne, 1993), 42.

4. Lee Strobel, "Reflections," *Christianity Today*, April, 2007, 78.

5. Joe M. Kapolyo, "Matthew," *Africa Bible Commentary* (Tokunboh Adeyemo, Nairobi, Kenya: WordAlive Publishers, 2006), 1169.

6. Jo Kadlecek, *A Desperate Faith: Lessons of Hope from the Resurrection* (Grand Rapids, MI: BakerBooks, 2010), 41.

7. Joseph Fitzmyer, ed., *The Anchor Bible* (Garden City, NY: Doubleday & Co., 1985), Introduction and Commentary.

8. David Kletzing, e-mail message to author.

9. Paul M. Youngdahl, quoted in *Synthesis* (April 19, 1992).

10. Kapolyo, "Matthew," *Africa Bible Commentary*, 1169.

11. Jo Kadlecek, *A Desperate Faith*, 25.

12. *Book of Common Prayer* (1928), 18.

13. Rebecca Hall, e-mail message to author.

14. Elie Wiesel, *Night* (New York, NY: Hill and Wang, 2006).

15. Handley C. G. Moule, *Jesus and the Resurrection: Expository Studies on St. John 20, 21, Third Edition* (London: Seeley, 1898), 48.

16. Rodney A. Whitacre, *John (IVP New Testament Commentary Series)*, (Downers Grove, IL: InterVarsity Press, 1999), 474.

17. Wright, *Surprised by Hope*, 79.

18. J. Lee Grady, "How the Resurrection Brok Eden's Curse," *Fire in My Bones* e-newsletter (March 30, 2010).

19. Angels appear at many of the significant points in God's dealing with the human race. To cite but four examples: in the Old Testament the angel stopping Abraham from sacrificing his son Isaac (Gen. 22:15–18), and the angel shutting the lions' mouths so they would not kill Daniel (Dan. 6:19–24); in the New Testament Gabriel's annunciation to Mary (Luke 1:26–38) and the angelic chorus at the Incarnation (Luke 2:8–20). Their presence indicates "that the powers of heaven have been at work here." G. R. Beasley-Murray, *The Gospel of John* (Waco, TX: Word Biblical Commentary Series, 1988), 374.

20. Norval Gendenhuys, "The Gospel of Luke," *The New International Commentary on the New Testament* (Grand Rapids, MI: Eerdmans, 1951).

21. St. John Chrysostom, *The Homilies on the Gospels of St. John*, 86.1.

22. Harry Griffith, e-mail message to author.

23. I remember many years ago talking with the pastor of an evangelical church that emphasized warm piety towards Jesus and deemphasized theology about the person of Christ. He told me, "We have no creed but Christ." I asked him, "What is Christ? No, really, I mean that. Is this Christ a hero of yours who lived a few centuries ago, died, and left behind some interesting writings? Who is he?" As he started to distinguish the Christ he knew and loved from some "straw man" Christ I could be positing, this pastor recited the tenets of the Apostles and Nicene Creed. It is impossible to have a creedless Christ. Otherwise, Christ becomes a totally empty word.

24. There is an absurd notion floating around in highly speculative theological circles that the pain Jesus suffered was child abuse at the hands of God the Father. Mark Galli addresses this nonsense well in his article, "Proof of a Good God: 'Crucified Under Pontius Pilate,'" Christianity Today, April 4, 2012, accessed October 7, 2013, http://www.christianitytoday.com/ct/2012/april/crucified-under-pilate.html.

25. C. S. Lewis, *Mere Christianity* (London: Geoffrey Bles, 1952), 42.

26. See Philip J. Lee, *Against the Protestant Gnostics* (Oxford University Press, USA, 1993). Further, Robert Tuttle notes that Hassidic Jews "bob and weave

when they pray because the Bible says to worship God with your body, mind and spirit. The bobbing gets the body into the act." Robert Tuttle, e-mail message to the author.

27. Robert Tuttle, e-mail message to author.

28. Harry Griffith, e-mail message to author.

29. Paul John Isaak, "Luke," *Africa Bible Commentary*, 1250.

30. Henry Barclay Swete, *Appearances of Our Lord After the Passion* (Memphis: TN, General Books, 2010, reprint of original, Macmillan, 1915), 10.

31. Edward A. Schroder, "Look Forward to the Future," Sermon, April 8, 2012.

32. Ben Witherington III, in Harold W. Rast, ed., *New Proclamation Year B, 2003* (Minneapolis, MN: Fortress Press, 2003), 7.

33. Martin Luther, *Martin Luther's Easter Book*, ed. Roland Bainton (Minneapolis, MN: Augsburg, 1997), 92–93.

34. Whitacre, *John, op. cit.*, 477.

35. Richard G. Zepernick has written helpful materials and conducts an effective workshop in local churches called "1-2-3 Witness." He may be contacted at rick@123witness.com.

36. David Lyle Jeffrey, *Luke* (Grand Rapids, MI: BrazosPress, 2012), 283.

37. Cited by Joseph Fitzmyer, "Introduction and Commentary to Luke," *The Anchor Bible*.

CHAPTER 2: ON THE ROAD TO EMMAUS

1. See his book *The Emmaus Mystery* (New York: Continuum, 2005).

2. Ibid., 92–93.

3. Luther, *Martin Luther's Easter Book*, 94.

4. William Barclay, *The Gospel of Luke*, (Philadelphia: The Westminster Press, 1975), 294.

5. Alternatively, it has been suggested that Jesus' resurrection body was so different that quick identification would have been difficult. (Paul contrasts earthly bodies with resurrection bodies in 1 Corinthians 15:42–49.) And yet, though Jesus' resurrection body indeed was different, in the Scriptural text there is the clear statement that the lack of recognition was nothing less than a God-designed event.

6. See R. C. Sproul, *The Glory of Christ* (Wheaton, IL: Tyndale House, 1990), 173–174.

7. "Liar, lunatic or Lord" is how C. S. Lewis put it. This statement appears in his book *Mere Christianity*, a collection of short essays which were originally fifteen-minute radio broadcasts given on the BBC Home Service in 1943. The second series of talks was titled "What Christians Believe," and the third in the series was titled "The Shocking Alternative."

8. Jacob Neusner, *A Rabbi Talks with Jesus* (Montreal: McGill-Queens University Press, 1993). Thank you to Professor Rod Whitacre of Trinity School for Ministry, Ambridge, Pennsylvania, for pointing out to me this book and the thought behind it.

9. Josh McDowell, *Evidence That Demands a Verdict* (San Bernadino, CA: Here's Life Publishers, 1986), 144.

10. It is not that the church decided which books were to be in the official New Testament and which were not. Had that been the case, the church in a later century could revise the list of Scriptural books, removing those it no longer liked. While this possibility appeals to some people today—they can get rid of embarrassing prohibitions against this or that behavior—it is a naïve view. Who is to say that the church in a subsequent era could not go in the opposite direction and add various prohibitions or remove Jesus' commands to love and forgive? Instead of the church deciding which books to include, the church, through a long process of testing and weighing, *discerned* which books had divine authorship and should, therefore, be in the New Testament canon. The church did not bestow authority on the Scriptures; it discerned authority in it and bowed before it. The church, and each of those who profess the Christian faith, must do the same today.

11. John D. Witvliet, "The Emmaus Road: The Surprise of the Easter Jesus," a sermon preached at the Eastern Avenue Christian Reformed Church, Grand Rapids, MI on April 3, 2005 (http://cepreaching.org/archive/jwitvliet-luke24).

12. G. D. Arnold, *Risen Indeed: Studies in the Lord's Resurrection* (London: Oxford University Press, 1959), 66.

13. This is our human understanding of what God is doing. God, though entering into space and time, sees all time simultaneously. Therefore, it is not a matter of "how good that God chose to plan far ahead." In the very eternal nature of God there is no other possibility than that God knows and inhabits all times simultaneously.

14. Irenaeus, *Against Heresies*, 4.26.1.

15. Malcolm Muggeridge, *Another King* (Edinburgh: St. Andrew's Press, 1968), 14. This is a printed copy of a sermon he gave at St. Giles Cathedral, Edinburgh, on January 14, 1968.

CHAPTER 3: BE KNOWN TO US IN THE BREAKING OF THE BREAD

1. Perhaps the most famous rendering of this is *The Light of the World* by W. Holman Hunt (1827–1910). The original is now in a side room off the main chapel at Keble College, Oxford. A second version is at St. Paul's Cathedral, London. When asked what the door represented, Hunt said, "The obstinately shut mind."

2. P. M. J. Stavinskas, "The Emmaus Pericope: Its Sources, Theology and Meaning for Today," *Bible Bhashyam* 3 (1977), 115.

3. Liturgical scholars have commented on what is called the "four-action shape" of the liturgy, involving these very four actions central to the prayer of consecration in the Eucharist: take bread, bless it, break it, give it. See, in particular, *The Shape of the Liturgy*, first published in 1945, by English Anglican Benedictine monk Dom Gregory Dix (1901-1952).

4. Fleming Rutledge, e-mail message to author.

5. William Dickson, e-mail message to author.

6. Robert Barron, *Eucharist* (Maryknoll, New York: Orbis Books, 2008), 9.

7. N. T. Wright, "The Resurrection and the Postmodern Dilemma," *STRev 41* (1998), 150–151; *idem.*, *Luke for Everyone* (London: SPCK, 2001), 296; *idem.*, *The*

Resurrection of the Son of God (Christian Origins and the Question of God 3, Minneapolis, MN: Fortress, 2003), 652.

8. Arthur A. Just, Jr., *The Ongoing Feast: Table Fellowship and Eschatology at Emmaus* (Collegeville: Pueblo, 1993), 66–67.

9. Dane C. Ortlund, "And Their Eyes Were Opened, And They Knew: An Inter-canonical Note on Luke 24:31," JETS 53.4 (December 2010): 717. The article is available online at http://www.etsjets.org/files/JETS-PDFs/53/53-4/JETS 53-4 717-728 Ortlund.pdf. Ortlund comments that though many connect this meal with the inauguration of the Lord's Supper on the previous Thursday, "scholars almost universally fail to link Luke 24:30–32 with Genesis." He credits Timothy Johnson, N. T. Wright, and Arthur Just as appropriately seeing the comparison.

10. William Frey, *The Dance of Hope: Finding Ourselves in the Rhythm of God's Great Story* (New York, NY: Random House, 2003).

11. Many scholars date this work around AD 90, but some others as early as just before the destruction of Jerusalem in AD 70. One reason is they note how John speaks of the pool of Bethesda in the present, not past tense.

12. John Marsh, *Saint John* (Baltimore, MD: Penguin Books Inc., 1968), 638.

13. Daniel Eddy, e-mail message to author.

14. Gregory Dix, *The Shape of the Liturgy* (Westminster: Dacre Press, second edition, 1945), 743–774.

15. Daniel Eddy, e-mail message to author.

16. Thomas Howard, *Evangelical Is Not Enough* (San Francisco, CA: Ignatius Press, 1984), 98, 100.

17. Sally Rowan, e-mail message to author.

18. Martin E. Marty, "Baptistification Takes Over," *Christianity Today*, September 2, 1983, 33–36.

19. Mark P. Shea, *By What Authority? An Evangelical Discovers Catholic Tradition* (Huntington, IN: Our Sunday Visitor Publishing Division, 1996), 137.

20. Michael Green, *Man Alive* (Downers Grove, IL: Inter-Varsity Press, 1968), 53.

21. Ignatius of Antioch, *Letter to the Romans*, 7:3.

22. Justin Martyr, *First Apology*, chapter 66.

23. The author (and many others) heard him say this over and over and over at numerous conferences over the years.

24. Philip J. Lee, *Against the Protestant Gnostics* (New York: Oxford University Press, Inc., 1987), 270–271.

25. Of all the various Christian groups, the Eastern Orthodox best understand the future dimension of the sacrament.

26. Henry George Liddell and Robert Scott, *A Greek-English Lexicon*, eds. Sir Henry Stuart Jones and Roderick McKenzie (Oxford: Clarendon Press, 1940).

27. Dix, *The Shape of the Liturgy*, 161.

28. Alexander Schmemann, *The Eucharist—Sacrament of the Kingdom* (Crestwood, NY: St. Vladimir's Seminary Press, 2003), 125.

29. John Cosin. D.D., *The History of Popish Transubstantiation*, revised (London: J. Leslie, 1840), 12–13.

30. T. S. Eliot, "The Waste Land," accessed October 8, 2013, at *Bartleby.com*, http://www.bartleby.com/201/1.html.

31. William Dickson, e-mail message to author.

32. Francis J. Moloney, SDB, *A Body Broken for a Broken People* (Peabody, MA: Hendrickson Publishers, Inc., 1997), 108–110.

33. Barron, *Eucharist*, 138.

34. Moloney, A Body Broken for a Broken People, 108–110.

35. Barron, *Eucharist*, 139.

36. B. W. "Pete" Wait III, e-mail message to author.

37. Barron, *Eucharist*, 140–141.

38. Until recently Harding was a professor at Trinity School of Ministry, Ambridge, Pennsylvania. See Harding's book *In the Breaking of the Bread* (Eugene, OR: Wipf and Stock Publishers, 2011).

CHAPTER 4: BEHIND A LOCKED DOOR

1. N. T. Wright, Lecture, November 18, 2008, Gordon-Conwell Theological College, S. Hamilton, MA.

2. Ignatius lived from around AD 35 to AD 108. He took to himself the nickname Theophorus, or "God-bearer." He was most likely a disciple of John the Apostle and was Bishop of Antioch after, first, Peter the Apostle, and then Evodius.

3. See J. B. Phillips, *Your God Is Too Small* (New York: Macmillan, 1961).

4. Sally Rowan, email message to author.

5. Harry Camp, e-mail message to author.

6. Ted Schroder, *SOUL FOOD: Daily Devotions for the Hungry*, vol. 1 (Amelia Island, FL: Amelia Pulpit, 2013), 273.

7. Bonnell Spencer, *They Saw the Lord* (Wilton, CT: Morehouse-Barlow Co., Inc., 1983), 88.

8. Darrell L. Bock points out that angels, also supernatural beings, took food (Gen. 18:8 and 19:3). Darrell L. Bock, *Exegetical Commentary on the New Testament* (Grand Rapids, MI: Baker Books, 1996).

9. Hans Holzer, author of a 761-page book on the subject of ghosts, writes, "Ghosts...are the surviving emotional memories of people who have not been able to make the transition from their physical state into the world of the spirit." Hans Holzer, *Ghosts* (New York: Black Dog & Leventhal Publishers, Inc., 1997), 45.

10. Frederick Denison Maurice, *The Gospel of the Kingdom of Heaven: A Course of Lectures on the Gospel of St. Luke* (New York: Macmillan and Co., 1893), 365–366.

11. C. K. Barrett eloquently speaks of "the mysterious power of the risen Jesus, who was at once sufficiently corporeal to show his wounds and sufficiently immaterial to pass through closed doors." C. K. Barrett, *The Gospel According to St. John, Second Edition* (Philadelphia, PA: Westminster Press, 1978), 568.

12. Ignatius of Antioch, *Smyrnaeans*, 3:20.

13. Maurice, *The Gospel of the Kingdom of Heaven*, 365–366.

14. Patrick Henry Reardon, "The Son Risen With Healing," *Touchstone*, April, 2007, 21.

15. Edgar Gardner Murphy, *The Larger Life: Sermons and an Essay* (New York: Longmans, Green, & Co., 1897), 183.

16. Thanks to Sally Rowan for this insight.

17. Anonymous quotation in *The Clergy Journal* (2006): 110.

18. Bonaventure, *Tree of Life*, public domain.

19. Harry Camp, e-mail message to author.

20. C. S. Lewis, *Miracles* (New York: The Macmillan Company, 1944), 137.

21. Whitacre, *op. cit.*, 479.

22. G. R. Beasley-Murray, *Gospel of Life: Theology in the Fourth Gospel* (Peabody, MA: Hendrickson Publishers, 1991), 54. For further insight into the richness of this peace see John 14:27 and 16:33; Romans 5:1; and Philippians 4:7.

23. Ben Witherington III, *New Proclamation Year B, 2003*, ed. Harold W. Rast (Minneapolis, MN: Fortress Press, 2003), 20.

24. Matta el Meskin (Matthew the Poor), *The Communion of Love* (Crestwood, NY: St. Vladimir's Seminary Press, 1984), 154–155.

25. B. F. Westcott, *The Gospel According to St. John* (London: John Murray, 1882), 294.

26. John Marsh, *Saint John* (Baltimore, MD: Penguin Books Inc., 1968), 644.

CHAPTER 5: THE APOSTLES' COMMISSION RESTATED

1. A modern rendition of the service is found in Hoyt L. Hickman, Don E. Saliers, Laurence Hull Stookey and James F. White, eds., *The New Handbook of the Christian Year* (Nashville, TN: Abingdon Press, 1992), 78ff.

2. For more information, please see my book *Christian Healing: A Practical & Comprehensive Guide* (Lake Mary, FL: Charisma House, 2004).

3. Everett F. Harrison, *John: The Gospel of Faith* (Chicago, IL: Moody Press, 1962), 120.

4. Raymond E. Brown, "The Gospel According to John XIII-XXI," *The Anchor Bible*.

5. Rowan Williams, *Resurrection* (London: DLT, 1982), 34.

6. Found in "Reconciliation," *The Westminster Collection of Christian Quotations*, Martin H. Manser, ed. (Westminster John Knox Press, 2001), 311.

7. Lester Durst, e-mail message to author.

CHAPTER 6: "DOUBTING THOMAS"

1. Paul Vitz, *Faith of the Fatherless, the Psychology of Atheism* (Dallas, TX: Spence Publishing Company, 2000).

2. David Baumann, e-mail message to author.

3. This quote comes from Tertullian's *Apology*, 39.7, written in approximately AD 200. The actual quote is, "'Look,' they [the non-believers] say, 'how they [Christians] love one another' (for they themselves hate one another); 'and how they are ready to die for each other' (for they themselves are readier to kill each other)."

4. This idea comes to me from Brother David Vryhof, SSJE.

5. James Cirillo, Sermon, March 30, 2008.

6. Craig Kallio, "Doubting Thomas," *The Living Church* (Easter 2002): 19–20.

7. Russ Parker, e-mail message to author.

8. David Baumann, e-mail message to author.

9. Frederick Buechner, *Wishful Thinking* (New York, NY: HarperOne, 1993).

10. Kevin Martin, e-mail message to author.

11. Fyodor Dostoevsky, *The Brothers Karamozov* (New York, NY: Bantam Classics, 1984).

12. Ted Schroder, *Buried Treasure* (Amelia Island, FL: Amelia Island Publishing, Inc., 2005), 28.

13. Pope Benedict XVI, quoted in "Archive of April 8, 2007," *Catholic News Agency*, April 8, 2007, accessed October 9, 2010, at http://www.catholicnewsagency.com/archive/2007/04/08/.

14. Allen Quain, e-mail message to author.

15. William H. Willimon, *Pulpit Source* 34, no. 2 (April–June 2006), Inver Grove Heights, MN: Logos Productions, Inc., 24.

16. Ibid., 25.

17. Thank you to Karen Towsley for her insights in this section.

18. Harry Emerson Fosdick, *Dear Mr. Brown* (New York City, NY: Harper & Brothers, 1961), 26, quoted in *Synthesis* (Chattanooga, Tennessee: The Synthesis Company, 1995), 3.

19. Ted Schroder, "Doubting Thomas," *VirtueOnline.org*, April 3, 2005, accessed October 9, 2013, at http://www.virtueonline.org/portal/modules/news/print.php?storyid=2300.

20. Helmut Thielicke, "How Can I Be Sure of the Risen Christ?" *Christianity Today*, March 18, 1983, 14.

CHAPTER 7: THOMAS' FAITH: "MY LORD AND MY GOD!"

1. Russ Parker, e-mail message to author.

2. Ibid.

3. R. V. G. Tasker, *The Gospel According to St. John* (London: Tyndale Press, 1960), 227.

4. Samuel M. Ngewa, "John," *Africa Bible Commentary*, ed. Tokunboh Adeyemo (Nairobi, Kenya: WordAlive Publishers, 2006).

5. Philip Yancey, "Where Is God When It Hurts?" *Christianity Today*, June 2007, 55–59.

6. Sir Edwyn Hoskyns, *The Fourth Gospel* (London: Faber and Faber, 1940), Chapter 6.

7. Kevin Martin, e-mail message to author.

8. C. K. Barrett, *The Gospel According to St. John*, 573.

9. John 13:13, Romans 10:9, 1 Corinthians 12:3, Philippians 2:11.

10. R. C. Sproul, *The Glory of Christ* (Phillipsburg, NJ: P & R Publishing Company, 1990), 179–180.

11. See N. T. Wright, *The Resurrection of the Son of God* (Minneapolis, MN: Fortress Press, 2003), 575–576.

12. Reginald Fuller, *The Formation of the Resurrection Narratives* (Philadelphia, PA: Fortress Press, 1988), 143.

13. John Marsh, *Saint John*, 647–648.

14. Raymond E. Brown, *The Gospel According to John XIII-XXI* (Garden City, NY: Doubleday & Company, Inc., 1970), John 20:29.

15. R. William Dickson, Sermon, April 3, 2005.

CHAPTER 8: JESUS AND THE SEVEN BY THE SEA OF GALILEE

1. John Marsh writes that John "makes it quite plain that the call to Christian discipleship is not really fulfilled until the Lord is crucified and glorified; and that when the call proceeds from this point, it is finally and completely effective in the world." John Marsh, *Saint John*, 663.

2. Harry Griffth, e-mail message to author.

3. I cover this point more extensively using the Myers-Briggs Type Indicator categories of personality type in my book *Why Can't I Be Me?* (Grand Rapids, MI: Chosen Books, 1992), later published in a mass market edition as *Free to Be Me!* (Grand Rapids, MI: Fleming H. Revell, 2001). Both are out of print but available from Institute for Christian Renewal, 80 Route 125, Kingston, NH 03848. Msgr. Chester P. Michael and Marie C. Norrisey demonstrate how different prayer forms work for different personality types according to the Myers-Briggs categories in their book *Prayer and Temperament* (Charlottesville, VA: The Open Door, Inc., 1991). Tim LaHaye makes the same point using the personality categories of sanguine, choleric, melancholy, and phlegmatic in his book *Transformed Temperaments* (Wheaton, IL, Tyndale House Publishers, Inc., 1971).

4. D. A. Carson, *The Gospel According to John* (Grand Rapids, MI: William B. Eerdmans Publishing Company, 1991), 669.

5. R. V. G. Tasker, *The Gospel According to St. John* (London: The Tyndale Press, 1960), 229.

6. Peter, responding to Jesus' request for some fish, turned around to drag the net ashore. Again, this is so typical of Peter. First he abandons the others to the work so he could get to Jesus first. Then he drags the net ashore as if he had caught the fish all by himself.

7. Merrill C. Tenney, *The Expositor's Bible Commentary Vol. 9*, "John and Acts" (Grand Rapids, MI: Zondervan, 1981), 200.

8. Michael Brecht, e-mail message to author.

9. See more in Sir Edwyn Hoskyns, *The Fourth Gospel* (London: Faber and Faber, 1940); R. M. Grant, "One Hundred Fifty-Three Large Fish," Harvard Theological Review 42 (1949): 273.

10. Robert Atkinson, *Mystic Journey: Getting to the Heart of Your Soul's Story* (New York: Cosimo, 2012), 14–15.

CHAPTER 9: JESUS RESTORES AND HEALS PETER

1. The first is cited in 1 Corinthians 15:5, paralleled in Luke 24:34. The other two times Jesus was with Peter are the ones explored in previous chapters, Luke 24:36–43; John 20:19–25; and John 20:26–29.

2. Gordon Bridger, *The Man from Outside* (London: Inter-Varsity Press, 1969), 187–188.

3. Gregory the Great, *Forty Gospel Homilies*, trans. Dom David Hurst (Kalamazoo, MI: Cistercian Publications, 1990), Homily 21:160, cited in Christopher A. Hall, *Reading Scripture with the Church Fathers* (Downers Grove, IL: InterVarsity Press, 1998), 128–129.

4. Sir Edwyn Hoskyns, *The Fourth Gospel* (London: Faber and Faber, 1940).

5. N. T. Wright, Surprised by Hope, 241.

6. For a further discussion see J. Harold Greenlee, "More Than These?" *Journal of Translation* vol. 1, no. 2 (2005): 19. Dr. Greenlee's article also supports this third possible meaning.

7. Rowan Williams, *Resurrection*, 34.

8. Everett L. Worthington, Jr., *A Just Forgiveness: Responsible Healing without Excusing Injustice* (Downers Grove, IL: Intervarsity Press, 2009), 14–15.

9. Many have noted that such a minor detail speaks to the accuracy of the account. Note C. S. Lewis's comments in his essay "Modern Theology and Biblical Criticism," *Christian Reflections*, ed. Walter Hooper (Grand Rapids, MI: Wm. B. Eerdmans Publishing Co., 1994), 152ff.

10. For more information on inner healing, also called emotional healing and healing for damaged emotions, see chapter 6 of my *Christian Healing: A Practical & Comprehensive Guide, 3rd edition* (Lake Mary, FL: Charisma House, 2004). See other books on the subject, such as Charles Kraft, *Deep Wounds, Deep Healing* (Ann Arbor, MI: Vine Books, 2004); Brad Long and Cindy Strickler, *Let Jesus Heal Your Hidden Wounds* (Grand Rapids, MI: Chosen Books, 2001); Terry Wardle, *Healing Care, Healing Prayer* (Orange, CA: New Leaf Books, 2001); Linda H. Hollies, *Inner Healing for Broken Vessels* (Nashville, TN: Upper Room Books, 1992); David A. Seamands, *Healing for Damaged Emotions* (Wheaton, IL: Victor Books, 1981); Flora S. Wuellner, *Prayer, Stress, and Our Inner Wounds* (Nashville,TN: Upper Room Books, 1992).

11. Scholars disagree about the significance of the use of the two terms for "love" used here. Some agree with the explanation outlined above, while others note occasions when the two words for love were used interchangeably. Raymond E. Brown points out that except for Origen, the great Greek commentators John Chrysostom and Cyril of Alexandria, and Reformation-era scholars such as Erasmus and Grotius did not see much if any significance in the different words used. (Raymond E. Brown, "The Gospel According to John XIII-XXI," *The Anchor Bible*.) R. V. G. Tasker (*The Gospel According to St. John*, 233) notes that both verbs are used "to denote the Father's love for the Son, and to describe the love of Jesus for Lazarus and for 'the beloved disciple.'" Sir Edwyn Hoskyns believes the two words are used synonymously (*The Fourth Gospel*). However, several nineteenth-century British commentators like Trench, Westcott, and Plummer do find important shades of meaning in the change of words. See B. F. Westcott, *The Gospel According to St. John*, 302–303.

12. Father Raniero Cantalamessa, "Fishers of Men," February 2, 2007, accessed October 9, 2013, at *Zenit.com*, http://www.zenit.org/en/articles/father-cantalamessa-on-fish-and-sheep.

13. I acknowledge that there is fluidity in the apostolic era between the terms bishop and elder.

14. Gregory the Great, *Forty Gospel Homilies*, cited in Hall, *Reading Scripture with the Church Fathers*, 128–129.

CHAPTER 10: RESCUING AND DEFENDING THE CELEBRATION OF THE ASCENSION

1. J. G. Davis, *He Ascended into Heaven* (London: Lutterworth, 1958), 9.

2. Sproul, *The Glory of Christ*, 184.

3. Adolf Harnack, *The Acts of the Apostles*, trans. J. R. Wilkinson (London: Williams & Norgate, 1909), 157ff.

4. These are those books that claimed to be worthy of inclusion in the canon of the New Testament but were rejected by the early Christian community as containing details of Jesus' life and citations of Jesus' teaching that did not square with what was handed down from those who knew Christ.

5. John R. W. Stott, *The Message of Acts* (Downers Grove, IL: Intervaristy Press, 1994).

6. Douglas Farrow, *Ascension and Ecclesia* (Grand Rapids, MI: Wm. B. Eedrmans Publishing Co., 1999), 19, footnote 17.

7. Richard Zepernick, e-mail message to author.

8. John Spong, *Rescuing the Bible from Fundamentalism* (New York: Harper-Collins Publishers, 1992), 3.

9. N. T. Wright, *The Resurrection of the Son of God*, 655.

10. Ignatius, "Christ Was Possessed of a Body After His Resurrection," *The Epistle of Ignatius of Antioch to the Smyrnaeans*, accessed October 9, 2013, at *Christian Classics Ethereal Library*, http://www.ccel.org/ccel/schaff/anf01.v.vii.iii.html.

11. John R. W. Stott, *Understanding the Bible, Revised Edition* (Grand Rapids, MI: Zondervan, 1980), 103.

12. C. S. Lewis, *Miracles* (New York: The MacMillan Company, 1947), 154.

13. A. M. Ramsey, "What Was the Ascension?" *Studiorum Novi Testamenti Societas, Bulletin II* (Oxford, 1951), 49, as cited in F. F. Bruce, *The Book of Acts* (London: Marshall, Morgan & Scott,1954), 41.

14. Daniel Eddy, e-mail message to author.

15. C. B. Moss, *The Christian Faith: An Introduction to Dogmatic Theology* (London: SPCK; New York: Morehouse-Gorham, 1957), 124. The full text of The Christian Faith can be found at http://orthodoxanglican.net/downloads/faith.pdf. Full citation: "'While they beheld, He was taken up; and a cloud received Him out of their sight.' The traditional site of the Ascension is a spot on the road from Jerusalem to Bethany now occupied by a small mosque. It is on the brow of the hill just beyond the place where the city ceases to be visible. Our Lord appears to have risen up off the earth and passed into a cloud as a sign that He would be seen on earth no more. We are not to think of Him disappearing into the blue sky like a skylark, still less as "soaring through tracts unknown" to some astronomically remote place. The Ascension is much more wonderful and mysterious than that. He passed out of time and space altogether. He did not go

up as one ascends in an airplane. He went up as an heir to the throne becomes king, as a boy goes up from the fourth form into the fifth form [or, in American terms, from being a high school sophomore to being a high school junior], as a soldier rises when he becomes a general. He is not 'in the bright place far away,' for He is 'not far from each one of us' (Acts 18:27); but He is too glorious to be seen by human eye, except in vision as St. Paul saw Him at his conversion and was blind for three days (Acts 9:9), and as St. John in Patmos saw Him and fell at His feet as one dead (Rev. 1:17)."

16. Richard Zepernick, e-mail message to author.

17. N. T. Wright, *For All God's Worth* (Grand Rapids, MI: Wm. B. Eedrmans Publishing Co., 1997), 85.

18. Roy C. Lawrence, *The King Is Among Us: Why Jesus' Ascension Matters* (Bletchley, England: Scripture Union, 2004), 18.

19. For further reading on the Ascension please see Tim Perry and Aaron Perry, *He Ascended into Heaven* (Brewster, MA: Paraclete Press, 2010; William Milligan, *The Ascension and the Heavenly Priesthood of Our Lord* (New York: Macmillan and Co., 1892), since reprinted by a variety of publishing houses).

20. Augustine, "Sermones 53.4," *Collectio Selecta SS Ecclesiae Patrum*, ed. D. A. B. Caillau, quoted in Roy C. Lawrence, *The King Is Among Us*, 10.

21. Leo the Great, quoted in "Commentary: Leo the Great," *Thoughts from the Early Church*, New City Press, 1993, accessed October 9, 2013, http://liturgy .slu.edu/7EasterB052012/theword_journeya.html.

22. John Calvin, *Commentary on Acts*, Acts 1:9, quoted in Lawrence, *The King Is Among Us*, 10.

23. Robert De Moor authored the helpful article, "The Descent of Ascension Day: Meeting the Crowning Event of the Church Year with More than a Yawn" published in *Worship: Resources for Planning and Leading Worship*, March 1997, http://reformedworship.org/article/march-1997/descent-Ascension-day -meeting-crowning-event-church-year-more-yawn, accessed November 12, 2013.

CHAPTER 11: WHY JESUS ASCENDED BACK TO HEAVEN AND WHAT THIS MEANS FOR HIM AND FOR US TODAY

1. Lyrics by Jimmy Webb.

2. E-mail to the author. Harry Boonstra is Theological Librarian and Editor emeritus of *Reformed Worship*; Calvin College and Seminary, Grand Rapids, MI. John Calvin's quote comes from his commentary on the Book of Acts, 1:9. Lest people think that interest in liturgy and the church seasons are the province of Roman Catholics and High Church Anglicans, take note of the excellent work done by Faith Alive Christian Resources and the Calvin Institute of Christian Worship. They are from the Dutch Calvinist tradition and offer such resources as *Reformed Worship*, a periodical, and *The Worship Sourcebook*. Contact them at www.faithaliveresources.org and at www.calvin.edu/worship.

3. C. S. Lewis, *Perelandra* (New York: Scribner, 2003).

4. Farrow, *Ascension and Ecclesia*, 21.

5. Daniel Herzog, e-mail message to the author.

6. The church's chief theological opponent of Gnosticism was Irenaeus (c. 130–202), bishop of Lugdunum, what is now called Lyons, France. Irenaeus' best-known book is *Adversus Haereses* or *Against Heresies* (c. 180). Gnosticism has recently reasserted itself in various New Age groups.

7. John Calvin, "Commentary on Mark 16," *Calvin's Commentary on the Bible*, accessed October 9, 2013, *StudyLight.org*, http://www.studylight.org/com/cal/view.cgi?bk=mr&ch=16#bibliography.

8. Stephen, the church's first martyr, saw Jesus standing. In a court room the judge, then and now, remains seated, but the prosecuting and defense attorneys stay standing. Jesus is standing with Stephen in defense. Additionally, Jesus stands so He can receive Stephen upon his martyrdom. See Acts 7:56.

9. Edith M. Humphrey, "Wearing the Robe of Human Frame," Sermon, Pittsburgh Theological Seminary, Ascension Day, May 5, 2005.

10. Matta el Meskin (Matthew the Poor), *The Communion of Love*, 162.

11. Reine Bethany, e-mail message to author.

12. Dan Herzog, e-mail message to author.

13. John R. W. Stott, *The Message of Acts* (Downers Grove, IL: Intervaristy Press, 1994).

14. I am a particular fan of the recent hymn "Lord, You Give the Great Commission" by Bishop Jeffrey Rowthorn. The refrain asks the Holy Spirit to bestow upon us spiritual gifts so we can abound in ministry. Although composer Alec Wyton wrote a hymn tune specifically for these words and even named it "Rowthorn," Jeffrey Rowthorn thought the words should be sung to the tune "Austria" ("Glorious Things of Thee Are Spoken") by Franz Joseph Haydn (1732–1809). The words can also be effectively sung to the tune "Abbot's Leigh," or, indeed, any tune with an 87.87. D meter.

15. Chrysostom, "Homilies on Acts 2," *A Select Library of the Nicene and Post-Nicene Fathers of the Christian Church*, first series (Grand Rapids, MI: Eerdmans, 1956), 11:13, cited in Jaroslav Pelikan, *Acts* (Grand Rapids, MiI, Brazos Press, 2005), 41.

16. John R. W. Stott, *The Message of Acts*.

17. Dan Herzog, e-mail message to author.

18. Frank E. Wilson, *Faith and Practice* (Nashville, TN: Morehouse Publishers, 1989).

19. Harry Camp, Esq., wrote me that he personally heard the late Tommy Tyson exclaim these precise words as the climax of a sermon preached at his Aqueduct Conference Center.

CHAPTER 12: WAIT IN JERUSALEM

1. R. T. Kendall, *The Anointing: Yesterday, Today, Tomorrow* (Lake Mary, FL: Charisma House), 2003.

2. See my article "The Blessed Virgin Mary" in *Boot Camp for Christians* (Kingston, NH: Institute for Christian Renewal, 2000). This article first appeared in the December 1996 issue of *Charisma* magazine and simultaneously in volume XVII, number 4 of the December 1996 issue of my own Institute for Christian Renewal Newsletter. This article, as submitted by *Charisma* Magazine,

won first place in the Biblical Exposition category in the Evangelical Press Association's annual competition for 1996.

3. John R. W. Stott, *The Message of Acts*, 52.

4. Th. Zahn, *Die Apostelgeschichte des Lucas* (Erlangen, 1922), 44, cited in F. F. Bruce, *The Book of Acts* (London: Marshall, Morgan & Scott, 1954), 42.

5. Paul Mumo Kisau, "Acts," *Africa Bible Commentary*, 1301.

6. Michael Gemignani, Commentary on the Scripture reading for the seventh Sunday of Easter, *The Clergy Journal* (May/June 2005), Inver Grove Heights, MN: Logos Productions, Inc.: 117.

CHAPTER 13: WHILE THEY WERE WAITING

1. *Book of Common Prayer*, 9.

2. Ibid.

3. C. FitzSimons Allison, *The Cruelty of Heresy: An Affirmation of Christian Orthodoxy* (Harrisburg, PA: Morehouse Publishing, 1992).

4. See http://www9.georgetown.edu/faculty/jod/augustine/quote.html

5. John Stott, *Understanding the Bible, Revised Edition* (London: Scripture Union, 1984), 162.

6. Cyprian of Carthage, *De unitate ecclesiae*, vi. Thascius Caecilius Cyprianus was born some time in the early third century and died a martyr on September 14, 258.

7. "Archbishops' Committee of Enquiry on the Evangelistic Work of the Church," 1918, p. 25, cited in David Watson, *I Believe in Evangelism* (Grand Rapids, MI: Wm. B. Eerdmans Publishing Co. 1976), 25. The 1918 definition was repeated in the report "Towards the Conversion of England, being the Report of a Commission on Evangelism Appointed by the Archbishops of Canterbury and York Pursuant to a Resolution of the Church Assembly Passed at the Summer Session, 1943." Westminster, England: Press and Publications Board of the Church Assembly, 1945.

8. John Pollock, *Billy Graham, The Authorized Biography* (Pana, IL: World-Wide Publications, 1966).

9. Readers may wish to consult the book *The Theology of Facts vs. The Theology of Rhetoric* (Fort Wayne, IN: Lutheran Legacy, 2008) by August Vilmar (1800–1868). Vilmar had embraced a theology of skepticism, which he discovered to be lifeless. His transformation from doubt, what he called the theology of rhetoric, to Confessional Lutheran Orthodoxy, what he called the theology of facts, took to task the smugness of those academic theologians who projected their own ideologies onto the Scriptural text instead of letting it speak for itself.

10. Gary Heniser, "#409," *Spiritual Snack* online devotional series, May 31, 2007.

CHAPTER 14: CONCLUSION

1. George Carey, "Raised from Death," *The Anglican Digest*, Easter 1992, 62–63.

2. Ibid.

⚜ABOUT THE AUTHOR⚜

A CLERGYMAN FOR FORTY years, Mark Pearson is cofounder and president of the Institute for Christian Renewal, which seeks to help bring a balanced spiritual renewal to churches and individuals, and is cofounder and chief executive officer of New Creation Healing Center, which combines medicine, biblical counseling, massage, and prayer to minister healing to the whole person, body, soul, and spirit. Both are based in Kingston, New Hampshire. Pearson has long been a leader of teaching, renewal, and healing conferences around the world and has guest taught at numerous Christian colleges and theological seminaries. He earned a masters degree from Oxford University and a doctorate from Boston University. He is married to Dr. Mary Pearson and has three adult children and a Basset Hound. He describes himself as an avid vegetable gardener, a moderately competent pipe organist, and a fanatic Boston Red Sox fan.

Institute for Christian Renewal, led by Mark A. Pearson, was founded in 1980 to assist churches and individuals in growing in a balanced spiritual renewal. The Institute sponsors Pearson in leading teaching, evangelistic, renewal, and healing conferences in churches and for parachurch groups around the world. The

Institute may be reached by mail at 80 Route 125, Kingston, NH 03848; by telephone at (603) 642-3002; and by e-mail at canon-pearson@yahoo.com. Its Web site is www.christianrenewal. wordpress.com.

New Creation Healing Center, co-led by Mark A. Pearson, was founded in 1994 to combine family practice medicine, Christian counseling, massage, and prayer to minister wellness to the whole person, body, soul, and spirit. It has a large outpatient population of patients and clients in its immediate vicinity, attracts people from a wide area for its teaching/healing day conferences and longer retreats, and is building a residential facility for long-term, in residence, whole-person healing ministry. New Creation Healing Center may also be reached by mail at 80 Route 125, Kingston, NH 03848. It may be reached by telephone at (603) 642-6700 and by e-mail at office@newcreationhc.org. Its website is www.newcreationhc.org.

ᴀʟsᴏ ʙʏ ᴍᴀʀᴋ ᴀ. ᴘᴇᴀʀsᴏɴ

Christian Healing: A Practical & Comprehensive Guide (Grand Rapids, MI: Chosen Books, first edition, 1990; second edition, 1995; Lake Mary, FL: Charisma House, third edition, 2004).

Why Can't I Be? Understanding How Personality Type Affects Emotional Healing, Relationships, and Spiritual Growth (Grand Rapids, MI: Chosen Books, 1992). Republished as *Free to Be Me* (Grand Rapids, MI: Spire [Fleming H. Revell], pub. 2001).

Jack Hayford, John Wimber, and Reinhard Bonnke, eds., "Gifts of Healing," *The Gifts of the Spirit* (Lake Mary, FL: Creation House Books, 1992).

The Basics of the Faith (Dallas, TX: Latimer Press, 1994).

Boot Camp for Christians (Kingston, NH: Institute for Christian Renewal Press, 2000).

CONTACT THE AUTHOR

While the author regrets he is not available for spiritual counseling, he may be reached for the purposes of booking him to speak and minister in churches and for other groups at:

Institute for Christian Renewal
80 Route 125
Kingston, NH 03848
(603) 642-3002
canonpearson@yahoo.com

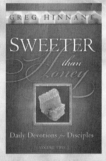

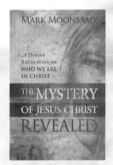